French

lonely planet

phrasebooks
and
Michael Janes

French phrasebook
4th edition – February 2011

Published by Lonely Planet Publications Pty Ltd
ABN 36 005 607 983

Lonely Planet Offices
Australia Locked Bag 1, Footscray, Victoria 3011
USA 150 Linden St, Oakland CA 94607
UK 2nd fl, 186 City Rd, London, EC1V 2NT

Contact
talk2us@lonelyplanet.com.au
lonelyplanet.com/contact

Cover illustration Evi Oetomo

ISBN 978 1 74179 332 1

acknowledgments

This 4th edition of Lonely Planet's *French* phrasebook is based on the previous three editions by the Lonely Planet Language Products team, Michael Janes for the French translations and pronunciation guides, and Jean-Pierre Masclef who translated the Sustainable Travel section. For this edition, new content was added by French translator and author Jean-Bernard Carillet. *Merci bien Jean-Bernard, Michael et Jean-Pierre!*

Thanks also to the others who contributed to the previous editions on which this one is based:

Jane Atkin, Julie Burbidge, Karina Coates, Francesca Coles, Adrienne Costanzo, Ben Handicott, Jim Jenkin, Piers Kelly, Yukiyoshi Kamimura, Emma Koch, Paul Piaia, Fabrice Rocher, Karin Vidstrup Monk, Meg Worby, and last but not least, Daniel New who created the inside illustrations.

Lonely Planet Language Products

Associate Publisher: Tali Budlender
Managing Editor: Annelies Mertens
Editor: Branislava Vladisavljevic
Managing Layout Designer: Celia Wood
Layout Designer: Wibowo Rusli
Cartographer: Wayne Murphy
Production Support: Yvonne Kirk, Glenn van der Knijff

make the most of this phrasebook ...

Anyone can speak another language! It's all about confidence. Don't worry if you can't remember your school language lessons or if you've never learnt a language before. Even if you learn the very basics (on the inside covers of this book), your travel experience will be the better for it. You have nothing to lose and everything to gain when the locals hear you making an effort.

finding things in this book

For easy navigation, this book is in sections. The Tools chapters are the ones you'll thumb through time and again. The Practical section covers basic travel situations like catching transport and finding accommodation. The Social section gives you conversational phrases, pick-up lines, the ability to express opinions – so you can get to know people. Food has a section all of its own: gourmets and vegetarians are covered and local dishes feature. Safe Travel equips you with health and police phrases, just in case. Remember the colours of each section and you'll find everything easily; or use the comprehensive Index. Otherwise, check the two-way traveller's Dictionary for the word you need.

being understood

Throughout this book you'll see coloured phrases on the right-hand side of each page. They're phonetic guides to help you pronounce the language. You don't even need to look at the language itself, but you'll get used to the way we've represented particular sounds. The pronunciation chapter in Tools will explain more, but you can feel confident that if you read the coloured phrase slowly, you'll be understood.

communication tips

Body language, ways of doing things, sense of humour – all have a role to play in every culture. 'Local talk' boxes show you common ways of saying things, or everyday language to drop into conversation. 'Listen for ...' boxes supply the phrases you may hear. They start with the phonetic guide (because you'll hear it before you know what's being said) and then lead in to the language and the English translation.

MAKE THE MOST OF THIS PHRASEBOOK

Throughout

french

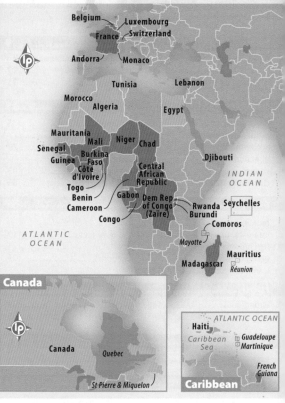

Belgium
Luxembourg
France
Switzerland
Andorra
Monaco

Tunisia
Lebanon
Morocco
Algeria
Egypt

Mauritania
Mali
Niger
Chad
Senegal
Guinea
Burkina
Faso
Côte
d'Ivoire
Central
African
Republic
Djibouti
Togo
Benin
Cameroon
Gabon
Dem Rep
of Congo
(Zaïre)
Rwanda
Burundi
Congo
Comoros

INDIAN
OCEAN

Seychelles

ATLANTIC
OCEAN

Mayotte

Mauritius
Madagascar
Réunion

Canada

Canada
Quebec

St Pierre & Miquelon

ATLANTIC OCEAN
Haiti
Guadeloupe
Caribbean
Sea
Martinique

French
Guiana

Caribbean

▬ official language
▬ co-official
▬ widely understood

For more details, see the **introduction**.

language map

French is one of the most widely taught languages in the world – chances are you already know a few phrases. Thanks to an invasion of England in the 11th century, it's also been a major contributor to the vocabulary of English.

After centuries of contact with English and a shared prehistoric ancestor, French offers English-speakers a relatively smooth path to communicating in another language. The structure of a French sentence won't come as a surprise and the sounds of the language are generally found in English as well or familiar to most through television and film examples of French speakers.

Though distantly related to English, French is more commonly associated with its Romance language siblings, Italian and Spanish. These languages developed from the Latin spoken by the Romans during their conquests of the 1st century BC. French evolved in a different way to Spanish and Italian though – comparing the modern forms of these languages gives an idea of just how distinct French is.

After enjoying some of the practical advantages of speaking French (such as being told of a cosy vineyard way off the tourist track, discovering that there's little merit in the cliched reference to the French being rude), you'll find the reasons to speak

at a glance ...

language name: French

name in language:
français fron·say

language family: Romance

key country: France

approximate number of speakers:
1st language: 80 million
2nd language: 50 million

close relatives: Italian, Spanish, Portuguese

donations to English:
numerous – some estimate three-fifths of everyday English vocabulary arrived via French

French just keep growing. *Regardez* the significant body of literature, film, music ... but perhaps the biggest incentive is that it's spoken all around the world.

Almost 30 countries cite French as an official language. In Canada, the use of French is most common in Quebec; in Belgium, its use is more prevalent in the south. Although some of the language's spread is due to France's colonisation of various countries in Africa, the Pacific and the Caribbean, French remained the language of international diplomacy until the early 20th century. It's still an official language of a number of international organisations, including the Red Cross, the United Nations and the International Olympic Committee.

Need more encouragement? Remember, the contact you make through using French will make your experiences unique. Local knowledge, new relationships and a sense of satisfaction are on the tip of your tongue, so don't just stand there ...

> abbreviations used in this book

f	feminine	sg	singular
inf	informal	pl	plural
m	masculine	pol	polite

South Pacific   ■ official language

PACIFIC
OCEAN

Vanuatu

New
Caledonia

Wallis &
Futuna

French
Polynesia

TOOLS > pronunciation
prononciation

The sounds used in spoken French can almost all be found in English. There are a few exceptions: nasal vowels, the 'funny' u sound and that deep-in-the-throat r, but throwing caution to the wind and mimicking every French accent you've heard can be surprisingly effective.

vowel sounds

Generally, French vowel sounds are short and don't glide into other vowels. As you order another coffee, listen to fellow patrons and note some of the differences in their pronunciation, like the ay in *café*. It's close to the English sound, but it's shorter and sharper.

symbol	english equivalent	french example	transliteration
a	run	*tasse*	tas
ai	aisle	*travail*	tra·vai
air	fair	*faire*	fair
ay	say	*musée*	mew·zay
e	red	*est*	est
ee	bee	*lit*	lee
er	her	*deux*	der
ew	ee with rounded lips	*tu*	tew
o	pot	*pomme*	pom
oo	moon	*chou*	shoo

nasal vowel sounds

Nasal vowels are pronounced as if you're trying to force the sound out of your nose rather than your mouth. It's easier than it sounds! English also has nasal vowels to some extent – when you say 'sing' in English, the 'i' is nasalised by the 'ng'. In French though, nasal vowels cause the nasal consonant sound that follows them to be omitted, but a 'hint' of what the implied consonant is can sometimes be heard. We've used nasal consonant sounds (m, n, ng) with the nasal vowel to help you produce the sound with more confidence.

Although there are four nasal vowels in French, our pronunciation guides use only two: o and u. These approximate the actual sounds. The four nasal sounds can be quite close, so to get you out there speaking, we've simplified it in the following way:

symbol	english equivalent	french example	transliteration
om	like the 'o' in 'pot' + nasal consonant sound	*mouton*	moo·ton
on			
ong			
um	similar to the 'a' in 'bat' + nasal consonant sound	*magasin*	ma·ga·zun
un			
ung			

consonant sounds

Swallow deeply and prepare for just one sticking point when it comes to pronouncing French consonants: the r sound. It's made in the back of the throat, a little like a growl. Using an English 'r' sound will get you by, but it's one of the French sounds that will really help you sound natural – it's well worth working on. The other consonant sounds can all be found in English.

symbol	english equivalent	french example	transliteration
b	**b**ig	*billet*	bee·yay
d	**d**in	*date*	dat
f	**f**un	*femme*	fam
g	**g**o	*grand*	gron
k	**k**ick	*carte*	kart
l	**l**oud	*livre*	leev·rer
m	**m**an	*merci*	mair·see
n	**n**o	*non*	non
ng	sa**ng**	*cinquante*	sung·kont
ny	ca**ny**on	*signe*	see·nyer
p	**p**ig	*parc*	park
r	**r**un	*rue*	rew
s	**s**o	*si*	see
sh	**sh**ow	*changer*	shon·zhay
t	**t**in	*tout*	too
v	**v**an	*verre*	vair
w	**w**in	*oui*	wee
y	**y**es	*payer, billet*	pay·yay, bee·yay
z	i**s**	*vous avez*	voo za·vay
zh	plea**s**ure	*je*	zher

word stress & rhythm

Syllables in French words are, for the most part, equally stressed. English speakers tend to stress the first syllable, which is definitely unusual in French, so try adding a light stress on the final syllable to compensate.

The rhythm of a French sentence is based on breaking the phrase into meaningful sections, then stressing the final syllable pronounced in each section. The stress at these points is characterised by a slight rise in intonation.

French pronunciation, unlike that of English, is quite easy.

La prononciation du   la pro·non·see·a·syon dew
français, à la différence   fron·*say* a la dee·fair·rons
de l'anglais, est assez facile.   der long·*glay* ay ta·*say* fa·*seel*

The 'beat' of the sentence is quite regular because of these stressed syllables (in italics in the example above).

intonation

A rising intonation in French is used when asking a question. There is also a rise in intonation when listing items: your voice goes up after each item until you say the final item in the list, at which point your voice falls.

reading & writing

Writing French is a little more complicated than speaking it. The spelling of verb endings is a great example: sometimes an ending might consist of up to five letters and sound the same as a two-letter ending (eg both -*aient* and -*ai* sound like ay). Take heart though, the French themselves have difficulty with spelling – the annual national spelling competition attests to that.

If you try to compare the written French and the pronunciation guides in this book, you'll start to notice some of the relationships between sound and writing.

french alphabet					
A a	a	*B b*	bay	*C c*	say
D d	day	*E e*	er	*F f*	ef
G g	zhay	*H h*	ash	*I i*	ee
J j	zhee	*K k*	ka	*L l*	el
M m	em	*N n*	en	*O o*	o
P p	pay	*Q q*	kew	*R r*	air
S s	es	*T t*	tay	*U u*	ew
V v	vay	*W w*	doo·bler·vay	*X x*	iks
Y y	ee·grek	*Z z*	zed		

This chapter is designed to explain the main grammatical structures you need in order to make your own sentences. Look under each heading – listed in alphabetical order – for information on functions which these grammatical categories express in a sentence. For example, demonstratives are used for giving instructions, so you'll need them to tell the taxi driver where your hotel is, etc. A glossary of grammatical terms is included at the end of the chapter to help you.

adjectives & adverbs

describing people/things • doing things

As a rule, adjectives come after the noun in French. There are exceptions, however, such as *grand* gron (big) and *petit* per·tee (small), which come before the noun.

an expensive hotel   *un hôtel cher*   un o·tel shair
(lit: a hotel expensive-m-sg)

In French, adjectives agree with the noun in gender (see also **gender**). Generally, for the feminine form of an adjective just add an *-e* to the end. Note though that this ending usually causes the consonant before it to be pronounced, or it may change the final vowel sound or the preceding consonant.

	masculine		feminine	
small	*petit*	per·tee	*petite*	per·teet
next	*prochain*	pro·shun	*prochaine*	pro·shen
white	*blanc*	blong	*blanche*	blonsh

Adjectives whose masculine form ends in *-e* don't change form for gender, eg *jeune* zhern (young) or *riche* reesh (rich).

Other adjectives differ more significantly in their masculine and feminine form, eg *beau/belle* m/f bo/bel (beautiful).

Adjectives also agree with the noun in number. In general, to make an adjective plural, add *-s* to the end (see also **plurals**).

gay venue	*boîte gaie*	bwat gay
gay venues	*boîtes gaies*	bwat gay

To form adverbs in French, you generally add the ending *-ment* ·mon (just like you add '-ly' in English) to the feminine form of the adjective, or to the masculine form if it ends in a vowel. Adverbs are placed after the verb they modify (see also **verbs**).

slow	*lent(e)* m/f	lon(t)
to speak slowly	*parler lentement*	par·lay lon·ter·mon

articles

naming people/things

French has three words for the definite article (ie 'the' in English), depending on the noun's gender and number (see **gender** and **plurals**). Both *le* and *la* become *l'* before a word beginning with a vowel or *h*, eg *l'hôtel* lo·tel (hotel) or *l'eau* lo (water).

definite articles					
m sg	*le*	ler	the steak	*le biftek*	ler beef·tek
f sg	*la*	la	the tart	*la tarte*	la tart
pl	*les*	lay	the snails	*les escargots*	lay zes·kar·go

Similarly, there are three words for the indefinite article (ie 'a' or 'an' in English), to match the gender and number of the noun.

indefinite articles					
m	*un*	un	a ticket	*un ticket*	un tee·kay
f	*une*	ewn	a postcard	*une carte postale*	ewn kart pos·tal
pl	*des*	day	some apples	*des pommes*	day pom

be

describing people/things • making statements

The verb *être* e·trer (be) changes form depending on the subject, just like in English. For information on negative forms, see **negatives**.

ÊTRE (be) – present tense		
I am	*je suis*	zher swee
you are sg inf	*tu es*	tew ay
you are sg pol	*vous êtes*	voo zet
he/she is	*il/elle est*	eel/el ay
we are	*nous sommes*	noo som
you are	*vous êtes*	voo zet
they are	*ils/elles sont* m/f	eel/el son m/f

demonstratives

giving instructions • indicating location • pointing things out

The easiest way to point something out in French is to use the phrase *c'est* say (lit: it-is).

That's the right train.
    C'est le bon train.   say ler bon trun
    (lit: it-is the-m-sg good-m-sg train)

The demonstrative adjectives 'this' and 'that' are translated with the same word in French – *ce* ser for masculine singular nouns and *cette* set for feminine singular nous. The plural form of both words is *ces* say (these/those). See also **gender** and **plurals**.

this/that group	*ce groupe*	se groop
this/that woman	*cette femme*	set fam
these/those people	*ces gens*	say zhon

gender

In French, all nouns (words which denote a thing, person or idea) have either masculine or feminine gender. You can recognise the noun's gender by the article, demonstrative, possessive or any other adjective accompanying the noun, as they change form to agree with the noun's gender (see **adjectives & adverbs**, **articles**, **demonstratives**, **possessives**). The gender of words is also indicated in the dictionary, but here are some general rules:

- a word is masculine/feminine if it refers to a man/woman
- words ending in a consonant, -acle, -age, -ème or -isme are generally masculine
- words ending in -e, -ion or -aison are usually feminine

The masculine and feminine forms of words are indicated with m and f throughout this phrasebook where relevant. See also the box **m before f**, page 117.

have

Possession can be indicated in various ways in French (see also **possessives**). One way is by using the verb *avoir* a·vwar (have). For information on negative forms, see **negatives**.

AVOIR (have) – present tense		
I have	j' ai	zhay
you have sg inf	tu as	tew a
you have sg pol	vous avez	voo za·vay
he/she has	il/elle a	eel/el a
we have	nous avons	noo za·von
you have	vous avez	voo za·vay
they have	ils/elles ont m/f	eel/el zon m/f

negatives

To make a sentence negative, French uses two words – *ne* ner and *pas* pa, both meaning 'not' – around the verb:

I don't know.
   Je ne sais pas.   zher ner say pa
   (lit: I not know not)

If there are two words that make up the verb, the *ne ... pas* goes around the first verb:

I don't want to go.
   Je ne veux pas aller.   zher ner ver pa za·lay
   (lit: I not want not go)

With another negative word in the sentence, *pas* is omitted:

I have nothing to declare.
   Je n'ai rien à déclarer.   zher nay ryun a day·kla·ray
   (lit: I not-have nothing to declare)

The word *pas* pa (not) is used alone when there is no verb:

Not yet.	*Pas encore.*	pa ong·kor
Not bad.	*Pas mal.*	pa mal

personal pronouns

Personal pronouns ('I', 'you' etc) change form in French depending on whether they're the subject or the object in a sentence, just like English has 'I' and 'me' as the subject and object pronouns (eg 'I see her' and 'She sees me'). The subject pronoun *on* on (one) is often used to refer to a non-specific subject:

French is spoken here.
   On parle français ici.   on parl fron·say ee·see
   (lit: one speaks French here)

grammar

subject pronouns

I	*je*	zher	we	*nous*	noo
you sg inf	*tu*	tew	you pl	*vous*	voo
you sg pol	*vous*	voo			
he/it	*il*	eel	they	*ils* m	eel m
she/it	*elle*	el		*elles* f	el f

When talking to someone familiar or younger than you, use the informal form of 'you', *tu* tew, rather than the polite form, *vous* voo. Phrases in this book use the form of 'you' that is appropriate to the situation. Where both forms are used, they are indicated by pol and inf. See also the box **getting friendly**, page 88.

object pronouns

me	*me*	mer	us	*nous*	noo
you sg inf	*te*	ter	you pl	*vous*	voo
you sg pol	*vous*	voo			
him/it	*le/lui*	ler/lwee	them	*les/leur*	lay/ler
her/it	*la/lui*	la/lwee			

*the forms separated by a slash are direct/indirect object pronouns

The direct and indirect object pronouns differ only for the third person ('he', 'she', 'it', 'they').

I see him.
> *Je le vois.*   zher ler vwa
> (lit: I him see)

I gave him the ticket.
> *Je lui ai donné le billet.*   zher lwee ay do·nay ler bee·yay
> (lit: I to-him have given the-m-sg ticket)

The object pronouns are placed before the verb. The direct object pronoun comes before the indirect object pronoun.

I gave it to him.
> *Je le lui ai donné.*   zher ler lwee ay do·nay
> (lit: I it-m-sg to-him have given)

TOOLS

18

plurals

naming people/things

To form the plural form of a noun in French, an -s is added to the noun in writing (though there are exceptions), but it's often not pronounced. In spoken language, the easiest way to indicate plural is to use words like *beaucoup de* bo·koo der (a lot of), numbers or the plural articles *les* lay and *des* day (see **articles**).

I'd like two tickets.
Je voudrais deux billets.   zher voo·dray der bee·yay
(lit: I would-like two tickets)

possessives

possessing

A common way of indicating possession is by using possessive adjectives before the noun they refer to. Like other adjectives, they agree with the noun in number, and sometimes also in gender (see also **gender** and **plurals**).

possessive adjectives					
my	*mon/mes* m	mon/may m	**our**	*notre/*	no·trer/
	ma/mes f	ma/may f		*nos*	no
your sg inf	*ton/tes* m	ton/tay m	**your** pl	*votre/*	vo·trer/
	ta/tes f	ta/tay f		*vos*	vo
your sg pol	*votre/vos*	vo·trer/vo			
his **her** **its**	*son/ses* m	son/say m	**their**	*leur/*	ler/
	sa/ses f	sa/say f		*leurs*	ler

*the forms separated by a slash are used with a singular/plural noun

When a singular noun begins with 'h' or a vowel sound, *mon*, *ton* and *son* are used, regardless of the noun's gender:

my team   *mon équipe*   mon ay·keep
(lit: my team-f-sg)

grammar

19

Another way to indicate possession is by using possessive pronouns, which also agree in number and sometimes gender with the noun. The corresponding definite article is used before the possessive pronoun (see **articles**).

That bag is mine. *Ce sac est le mien.*　　ser sak ay ler myun
(lit: that-m-sg bag is the-m-sg mine-m-sg)

possessive pronouns					
mine	*mien/* *miens* m *mienne/* *miennes* f	myun/ myun m myen/ myen f	ours	*nôtre/* *nôtres*	no·trer/ no·trer
yours sg inf	*tien/* *tiens* m *tienne/* *tiennes* f	tyun/ tyun m tyen/ tyen f	yours pl	*vôtre/* *vôtres*	vo·trer/ vo·trer
yours sg pol	*vôtre/* *vôtres*	vo·trer/ vo·trer			
his hers its	*sien/* *siens* m *sienne/* *siennes* f	syun/ syun m syen/ syen f	theirs	*leur/* *leurs*	ler/ ler

*the forms separated by a slash are used with a singular/plural noun

You can also indicate ownership by using the verb *avoir* a·vwar (see **have**) or with '*de* der (of) + noun', just like in English:

Marie's bag　　*le sac de Marie*　　ler sak der ma·ree
(lit: the-m-sg bag-m-sg of Marie)

prepositions

giving instructions • indicating location • pointing things out

Like English, French uses prepositions to explain where things are in time or space. Common prepositions are listed in the table opposite; for more prepositions, see the **dictionary**.

prepositions					
after	*après*	a·pray	from	*de*	der
at (time)	*à*	a	in (place)	*dans*	don
before	*avant*	a·von	to	*à*	a

questions

asking questions • negating

The easiest way to ask a 'yes/no' question in French is to make
a statement with a rise in intonation. Alternatively, you can use
est-ce que es·ker (lit: is-it that) in front of a statement.

Is this the right train?
Est-ce que c'est le bon train?   es·ker say ler bon trun
(lit: is-it that it-is the-m-sg good-m-sg train)

Another way to ask a yes/no question is to put the verb before
the subject of the sentence, as in English, and link them with a
hyphen.

Do you have a car?
As-tu une voiture?   a·tew ewn vwa·tewr
(lit: have-you-sg-inf a-f-sg car)

Just like in English, there are also question words for more specific questions. These words go at the start of the sentence.

question words					
how	*comment*	ko·mon	where	*où*	oo
what	*qu'est-ce que*	kes·ker	who	*qui*	kee
when	*quand*	kon	why	*pourquoi*	poor·kwa

To answer 'yes' after a question in the affirmative, use *oui* wee,
and to answer 'yes (I do)' after a question in the negative, use *si*
see. The negative answer is *non* non (no).

verbs

There are three verb categories in French – those whose infinitive (dictionary form) ends in -*ir, -er* or -*re*, eg *finir* fee·neer (finish), *parler* par·lay (speak), *vendre* von·drer (sell). Tenses are formed by adding various endings for each person to the verb stem (the part of the verb that remains after removing -*ir, -er* or -*re*), and for most verbs these endings follow regular patterns according to the verb category. The verb endings for the present and future tenses are shown in the following tables. For negative forms of verbs, see **negatives**.

> present tense

present tense		*finir*	*parler*	*vendre*
I	*je*	fin**is**	parl**e**	vend**s**
you sg inf	*tu*	fin**is**	parl**es**	vend**s**
you sg pol	*vous*	fin**issez**	parl**ez**	vend**ez**
he/she	*il/elle*	fin**it**	parl**e**	vend
we	*nous*	fin**issons**	parl**ons**	vend**ons**
you pl	*vous*	fin**issez**	parl**ez**	vend**ez**
they	*ils/elles*	fin**issent**	parl**ent**	vend**ent**

> past tense

The main past tense in French, used for a completed action, is a compound tense, which means it is made up of an auxiliary verb – either *être* e·trer (be) or *avoir* a·vwar (have) – in the present tense, plus a form of the main verb, called 'past participle' (see also **be** and **have**). The past participle is formed by replacing the infinitive endings -*ir, -er* or -*re* with -*i, -é* or -*u* respectively (some past participles are irregular). Past participles of the verbs taking *être* must agree with the subject in gender and number, while past participles of the verbs taking *avoir* don't change form.

| We arrived. | *Nous sommes arrivées.* (lit: we are arrived-f-pl) | noo som za·ree·vay |
| They saw. | *Elles ont vu.* (lit: they-f-pl have seen) | el zon vew |

	infinitive		past participle	
finish	*finir*	fee·neer	*fini*	fee·nee
speak	*parler*	par·lay	*parlé*	par·lay
sell	*vendre*	von·drer	*vendu*	von·dew

> future tense

In the future tense, the endings follow the same pattern for all three verb categories, and they are simply added to the infinitive (dictionary form of the verb), not the verb stem. For verbs ending in -*re* the final *e* is dropped before adding the new endings.

future tense				
		finir	*parler*	*vendre*
I	*je*	fini**rai**	parle**rai**	vend**rai**
you sg inf	*tu*	fini**ras**	parle**ras**	vend**ras**
you sg pol	*vous*	fini**rez**	parle**rez**	vend**rez**
he/she	*il/elle*	fini**ra**	parle**ra**	vend**ra**
we	*nous*	fini**rons**	parle**rons**	vend**rons**
you pl	*vous*	fini**rez**	parle**rez**	vend**rez**
they	*ils/elles*	fini**ront**	parle**ront**	vend**ront**

word order

making statements

The basic word order in French is subject–verb–object, just like in English. See also **negatives** and **questions**.

| I speak French. | *Je parle francais.* (lit: I speak French) | zher parl fron·say |

grammar

grammar glossary

adjective	a word that describes something – 'there are five **basic** types of cheese in France'
adverb	a word that explains how an action is done – 'that are **usually** displayed in cheese shops'
article	the words 'a', 'an' and 'the'
demonstrative	a word that means 'this' or 'that'
direct object	the thing or person in the sentence that has the action directed to it – 'you can sample **them**'
gender	classification of *nouns* into classes (like masculine and feminine), requiring other words (eg *adjectives*) to belong to the same class
indirect object	the person or thing in the sentence that is the recipient of the action – 'and the merchants will often give **you** advice'
infinitive	dictionary form of a *verb* – 'on what to **choose**'
noun	a thing, person or idea – 'it's a **matter** of **taste**'
number	whether a word is singular or plural – 'and the **choices** on offer can be overwhelming'
personal pronoun	a word that means 'I', 'you' etc
possessive adjective	a word that means 'my', 'your' etc
possessive pronoun	a word that means 'mine', 'yours' etc
preposition	a word like 'for' or 'before' in English
subject	the thing or person in the sentence that does the action – '**you** should also consider'
tense	form of a *verb* that tells you whether the action is in the present, past or future – eg 'eat' (present), 'ate' (past), 'will eat' (future)
verb	a word that tells you what action happened – 'which wine **goes** best with each type of cheese'
verb stem	part of a *verb* that doesn't change – eg '**sample**' in '**sampl**ing' and '**sampl**ed'

Do you speak English?
Parlez-vous anglais?   par·lay·voo ong·glay

Does anyone speak English?
Y a-t-il quelqu'un qui   ee·a·teel kel·kung kee
parle anglais?   par long·glay

Do you understand?
Comprenez-vous?   kom·prer·nay·voo

I understand.
Je comprends.   zher kom·pron

I don't understand.
Je ne comprends pas.   zher ner kom·pron pa

false friends

Many French words look like English words but have a different meaning altogether – beware! Here are a few:

car   kar   coach/bus
  not 'car', which is *voiture*, vwa·tewr

information   un·for·ma·syon   news
  not 'information', which is *renseignement*
  ron·sen·yer·mon

introduire   un·tro·dweer   insert
  not 'introduce', which is *présenter* pray·zon·tay

librairie   lee·bray·ree   book shop
  not 'library', which is *bibliothèque* bee·blee·o·tek

menu   me·new   set menu
  not 'menu', which is *carte* kart

prune   prewn   plum
  not 'prune', which is *pruneau* prew·no

vacance   va·kons   holidays
  not 'vacancy', which is *poste vacant* post va·kon

I speak a little.

Je parle un peu.   zher parl um per

I need an interpreter who speaks English.

J'ai besoin d'un interprète   zhay ber·zwun dun nun·tair·pret
de langue anglaise.   der long ong·glay·zer

I'd like to practice French.

Je voudrais parler   zher voo·dray par·lay
en français.   on fron·say

What does *'fesses'* mean?

Que veut dire 'fesses'?   ker ver deer fes

How do you ...?	*Comment ...?*	ko·mon ...
pronounce this	*le prononcez-vous*	ler pro·non·say voo
write *'bonjour'*	*est-ce qu'on*	es kon ay·kree
	écrit 'bonjour'	bon·zhoor

Could you	*Pourriez-vous ...,*	poo·ree·yay voo ...
please ...?	*s'il vous plaît?*	seel voo play
repeat that	*répéter*	ray·pay·tay
speak more	*parler plus*	par·lay plew
slowly	*lentement*	lon·ter·mon
write it down	*l'écrire*	lay·kreer

---

two tips for reading french

> In written French, you'll often see an *l'* in front of a word beginning with a vowel or a silent *h*: this replaces a *le* or a *la* (the) and is pronounced as if the word commenced with an l, eg, *l'orange* lo·ronzh.

> Generally, you don't pronounce a consonant on the end of a word, eg, *faux* fo. There's one exception - final 'c', eg, *sec* sek. Also, you do pronounce a final consonant if the next word starts with a vowel or an *h*, eg, *faux ami* fo zami.

cardinal numbers

		nombres cardinaux
0	*zéro*	zay·ro
1	*un*	un
2	*deux*	der
3	*trois*	trwa
4	*quatre*	ka·trer
5	*cinq*	sungk
6	*six*	sees
7	*sept*	set
8	*huit*	weet
9	*neuf*	nerf
10	*dix*	dees
11	*onze*	onz
12	*douze*	dooz
13	*treize*	trez
14	*quatorze*	ka·torz
15	*quinze*	kunz
16	*seize*	sez
17	*dix-sept*	dee·set
18	*dix-huit*	dee·zweet
19	*dix-neuf*	deez·nerf
20	*vingt*	vung
21	*vingt et un*	vung tay un
22	*vingt-deux*	vung·der
30	*trente*	tront
40	*quarante*	ka·ront
50	*cinquante*	sung·kont
60	*soixante*	swa·sont
70	*soixante-dix*	swa·son·dees
80	*quatre-vingts*	ka·trer·vung
90	*quatre-vingt-dix*	ka·trer·vung·dees
91	*quatre-vingt-onze*	ka·trer·vung·onz
100	*cent*	son
1000	*mille*	meel
1,000,000	*un million*	um meel·yon

ordinal numbers

1st	*premier/*	prer·myay/
	première m/f	prer·myair
2nd	*deuxième*	der·zyem
3rd	*troisième*	trwa·zyem
4th	*quatrième*	ka·tree·yem
5th	*cinquième*	sung·kyem

fractions

fractions

a quarter	*un quart*	ung kar
a third	*un tiers*	un tyair
a half	*un demi*	un der·mee
three-quarters	*trois-quart*	trwa·kart
all	*tout*	too
none	*rien*	ryun

amounts

quantités

How many/much?	*Combien?*	kom·byun
Please give me ...	*Donnez-moi ...,*	do·nay·mwa ...
	s'il vous plaît.	seel voo play
(100) grams	*(cent) grammes*	(son) gram
(half a) dozen	*(demi-)douzaine* f	(der·mee·)doo·zen
a kilo	*un kilo* m	ung kee·lo
a packet	*un paquet* m	um pa·kay
a slice	*une tranche* f	ewn tronsh
a tin	*une boîte* f	ewn bwat
less	*moins*	mwun
(just) a little	*(juste) un peu* m	(zhoost) um per
many/much/a lot	*beaucoup de*	bo·koo der
more	*plus*	plews
some (apples)	*quelques (pommes)*	kel·ker (pom)

For other useful amounts, see **self-catering**, page 146.

telling the time

The 24-hour clock is usually used when telling the time in French. After the half hour, use the next hour minus (*moins*) the minutes until that hour arrives.

What time is it?	*Quelle heure est-il?*	kel er ay·teel
It's one o'clock.	*Il est une heure.*	ee·lay ewn er
It's (10) o'clock.	*Il est (dix) heures.*	ee·lay (deez) er
Quarter past (one).	*Il est (une) heure et quart.*	ee·lay (ewn) er ay kar
Twenty past (one).	*Il est (une) heure vingt.*	ee·lay (ewn) er vung
Half past (one).	*Il est (une) heure et demie.*	ee·lay (ewn) er ay der·mee
Twenty to (one).	*Il est (une) heure moins vingt.*	ee·lay (ewn) er mwun vung
Quarter to (one).	*Il est (une) heure moins le quart.*	ee·lay (ewn) er mwun ler kar
At what time?	*À quelle heure?*	a kel er
At …	*À …*	a …
in the morning	*du matin*	dew ma·tun
in the afternoon	*de l'après-midi*	der la·pray·mee·dee
in the evening	*du soir*	dew swar

days of the week

Monday	*lundi* m	lun·dee
Tuesday	*mardi* m	mar·dee
Wednesday	*mercredi* m	mair·krer·dee
Thursday	*jeudi* m	zher·dee
Friday	*vendredi* m	von·drer·dee
Saturday	*samedi* m	sam·dee
Sunday	*dimanche* m	dee·monsh

the calendar

> months

January	*janvier* m	zhon·vyay
February	*février* m	fayv·ryay
March	*mars* m	mars
April	*avril* m	a·vreel
May	*mai* m	may
June	*juin* m	zhwun
July	*juillet* m	zhwee·yay
August	*août* m	oot
September	*septembre* m	sep·tom·brer
October	*octobre* m	ok·to·brer
November	*novembre* m	no·vom·brer
December	*décembre* m	day·som·brer

> seasons

summer	*été* m	ay·tay
autumn	*automne* m	o·ton
winter	*hiver* m	ee·vair
spring	*printemps* m	prun·tom

dates

What date?
Quelle date?   kel dat

What's today's date?
C'est quel jour aujourd'hui?   say kel zhoor o·zhoor·dwee

It's (18 October).
C'est le (dix-huit octobre).   say ler (dee·zwee tok·to·brer)

TOOLS

30

present

now	*maintenant*	munt·non
right now	*tout de suite*	toot sweet

this ...
afternoon	*cet après-midi*	say ta·pray·mee·dee
month	*ce mois*	ser mwa
morning	*ce matin*	ser ma·tun
week	*cette semaine*	set ser·men
year	*cette année*	set a·nay

today	*aujourd'hui*	o·zhoor·dwee
tonight	*ce soir*	ser swar

past

... ago
(three) days	*il y a (trois) jours*	eel·ya (trwa) zhoor
half an hour	*une demi-heure avant*	ewn de·mee·er a·von
a while	*il y a un moment*	eel·ya um mo·mon
(five) years	*il y a (cinq) ans*	eel·ya (sungk) on

day before yesterday	*avant-hier*	a·von·tyair

last ...
month	*le mois dernier*	ler mwa dair·nyay
night	*hier soir*	ee·yair swar
week	*la semaine dernière*	la ser·men dair·nyair
year	*l'année dernière*	la·nay dair·nyair

since (May)	*depuis (mai)*	der·pwee (may)

yesterday ...
afternoon	*hier ...*	ee·yair ...
	après-midi	a·pray·mee·dee
evening	*soir*	swar
morning	*matin*	ma·tun

future

day after tomorrow	*aprés-demain*	a·pray·der·mun
in ...	*dans ...*	don ...
(six) days	*(six) jours*	(see) zhoor
(five) minutes	*(cinq) minutes*	(sungk) mee·newt
next ...		
week	*la semaine prochaine*	la se·men pro·shen
month	*le mois prochain*	ler mwa pro·shen
year	*l'année prochaine*	la·nay pro·shen
tomorrow ...	*demain ...*	der·mun ...
morning	*matin*	ma·tun
afternoon	*après-midi*	a·pray·mee·dee
evening	*soir*	swar
until (Monday)	*jusqu'à (lundi)*	zhoos·ka (lun·dee)
within an hour	*d'ici une heure*	dee·see ewn er

during the day

afternoon	*après-midi* m	a·pray·mee·dee
dawn	*aube* f	ob
day	*jour* m	zhoor
evening	*soir* m	swar
midday	*midi* m	mee·dee
midnight	*minuit* m	mee·nwee
morning	*matin* m	ma·tun
night	*nuit* f	nwee
sunrise	*lever* m *de soleil*	ler·vay der so·lay
sunset	*coucher* m *de soleil*	koo·shay dew so·lay

How much is it?
Ça fait combien?   sa fay kom·byun

Can you write down the price?
Pouvez-vous   poo·vay·voo
écrire le prix?   ay·kreer ler pree

There's a mistake in the bill.
Il y a une erreur dans la note.   eel ya ewn ay·rer don la not

Do you want to sign or use your PIN?
Vous préférez signer ou   voo pray·fay·ray see·nyay oo
utiliser votre code?   ew·tee·lee·zay vo·trer kod

Do you accept ...?	*Est-ce que je peux payer avec ...?*	es·ker zher per pay·yay a·vek ...
credit cards	*une carte de crédit*	ewn kart der kray·dee
debit cards	*une carte de débit*	ewn kart der day·bee
travellers cheques	*des chèques de voyages*	day shek der vwa·yazh

I'd like to ...	*Je voudrais ...*	zher voo·dray ...
arrange a transfer	*faire un virement*	fair un veer·mon
cash a cheque	*encaisser un chèque*	on·kay·say un shek
change a travellers cheque	*changer des chèques de voyage*	shon·zhay day shek der vwa·yazh
change money	*changer de l'argent*	shon·zhay der lar·zhon
get a cash advance	*une avance de crédit*	ewn a·vons der kray·dee
get change for this note	*faire de la monnaie avec ce billet*	fair der la mo·nay a·vek ser bee·yay
withdraw money	*retirer de l'argent*	rer·tee·ray der lar·zhon

Where's the nearest ...?	*Où est ... le plus proche?*	oo ay ... ler plew prosh
automatic teller machine	*le guichet automatique de banque*	ler gee·shay o·to·ma·teek der bongk
foreign exchange office	*le bureau de change*	ler bew·ro der shonzh
What's the ...?	*Quel est ...?*	kel ay ...
charge	*le tarif*	ler ta·reef
exchange rate	*le taux de change*	ler to der shonzh
It's ...	*C'est ...*	say ...
free	*gratuit*	gra·twee
(12) euros	*(douze) euros*	(dooz) er·ro
I'd like ..., please.	*Je voudrais ..., s'il vous plaît.*	zher voo·dray ... seel voo play
my change	*ma monnaie*	ma mo·nay
a receipt	*un reçu*	un rer·sew
a refund	*un remboursement*	un rom·boors·mon

For more money-related phrases, see **banking**, page 77.

---

makin' wheat

Wheel and deal with these slang terms for 'money' – they're all roughly equivalent to 'dough':

blé m	blé	wheat
flouze m	flooz	from an Arabic translation of 'money'
pèze m	pez	from *peser* (weigh)
pognon m	pong·nyon	from *empoigner* (grab)

Elle a beaucoup de blé.
el a bo·koo der blay   She has plenty of dough.

getting around

voyager

At what time does the ... leave?	À quelle heure part ...?	a kel er par ...
boat	le bateau	ler ba·to
bus	le bus	ler bews
plane	l'avion	la·vyon
train	le train	ler trun
tram	le tramway	ler tram·way
At what time's the ... bus?	Le ... bus passe à quelle heure?	ler ... bews pas a kel e
first	premier	prer·myay
last	dernier	dair·nyay
next	prochain	pro·shun

At what time does it arrive?
À quelle heure est ce qu'il arrive?   a kel er es se keel a·ree·ve

Which platform does it depart from?
Il part de quel quai?   eel par der kel kay

Which bus goes to (Bordeaux)?
Quel bus va à (Bordeaux)?   kel bews va a (bor·do)

Is this seat taken?
Est-ce que cette place est occupée?   es·ker set plas ay o·kew·pay

That's my seat.
C'est ma place.   say ma plas

For bus numbers, see **numbers & amounts**, page 27.

transport

Can I take my car on the boat?
Je peux transporter ma   zher per trons·por·tay ma
voiture sur ce bateau?   vwa·tewr sewr ser ba·to

Can I take my bike?
Je peux amener mon vélo?   zher per am·nay mon vay·lo

Can you tell me when we get to (Nice)?
Pouvez-vous me dire quand   poo·vay·voo mer deer kon
nous arrivons à (Nice)?   noo za·ree·von a (nees)

I want to get off ...	*Je veux*	zher ver
	descendre ...	day·son·drer ...
at (Nantes)	*à (Nantes)*	a (nont)
here	*ici*	ee·see

For phrases on getting through customs and immigration, see **border crossing**, page 47. For phrases on disabled access, see **senior & disabled travellers**, page 83.

For phrases on getting through customs and immigration, see **border crossing**, page 47. For phrases on disabled access, see **senior & disabled travellers**, page 83.

listen for ...

a·new·lay
annulé   **cancelled**

lay vwa·ya·zher dwav shon·zhay der trun
Les voyageurs doivent   **Passengers must**
changer de train.   **change trains.**

new·may·ro der bews ...
numéro du bus ...   **bus number ...**

on rer·tar
en retard   **delayed**

par der ...
part de ...   **leaves from ...**

ser·lwee·see
Celui-ci.   **This one.**

ser·lwee·la
Celui-là.   **That one.**

ler pro·shun a·ray ay ...
Le prochain arrêt est ...   **The next stop is ...**

say la·ray ...
C'est l'arrêt ...   **This stop is ...**

buying tickets

Where can I buy a ticket?
Où peut-on acheter un billet? oo per·ton ash·tay um bee·yay

Do I need to book?
Est-ce qu'il faut es·keel fo
réserver une place? ray·zer·vay ewn plas

I'd like to ... my ticket, please.	*Je voudrais ... mon billet, s'il vous plaît.*	zher voo·dray ... mom bee·yay seel voo play
cancel	*annuler*	a·new·lay
change	*changer*	shon·zhay
collect	*retirer*	re·tee·ray
confirm	*confirmer*	kon·feer·may

How much is it? *C'est combien?* say kom·byun
It's full. *C'est complet.* say kom·play

One ... ticket (to Paris), please.	*Un billet ... (pour Paris), s'il vous plaît.*	um bee·yay ... (poor pa·ree) seel voo play
1st-class	*de première classe*	der prem·yair klas
2nd-class	*de seconde classe*	der sgond klas
child's	*au tarif enfant*	o ta·reef on·fon
one-way	*simple*	sum·pler
return	*aller et retour*	a·lay ay rer·toor
student's	*au tarif étudiant*	o ta·reef nay·tew·dyon

I'd like a/an ... seat.	*Je voudrais une place ...*	zher voo·dray ewn plas ...
aisle	*côté couloir*	ko·tay koo·lwar
non-smoking	*non-fumeur*	non few·mer
smoking	*fumeur*	few·mer
window	*côté fenêtre*	ko·tay fe·ne·trer

Is there air-conditioning?
    Est-qu'il y a la   es·keel ya la
    climatisation?   klee·ma·tee·za·syon

Is there a toilet?
    Est-qu'il y a des toilettes?   es·keel ya day twa·let

How long does the trip take?
    Le trajet dure combien   ler tra·zhay dewr kom·byun
    de temps?   der tom

Is it a direct route?
    Est-ce que c'est direct?   es·ker say dee·rekt

What time do I have to check in?
    Il faut se présenter à   eel fo ser pray·zon·tay a
    l'enregistrement à quelle heure? lon·rer·zhee·strer·mon a kel er

luggage

les bagages

Where's the ...?	*Où est ...?*	oo ay ...
baggage claim	*la livraison*	la lee·vray·zon
	des bagages	day ba·gazh
taxi stand	*la station*	la sta·syon
	de taxis	der tak·see
My luggage	*Mes bagages*	may ba·gazh
has been ...	*ont été ...*	on tay·tay ...
damaged	*endommagés*	on·do·ma·zhay
lost	*perdus*	per·dew
stolen	*volés*	vo·lay

My luggage hasn't arrived.
    Mes bagages ne sont   may ba·gazh ner son
    pas arrivés.   pa za·ree·vay

I'd like a luggage locker.
    Je voudrais une   zher voo·dray ewn
    consigne automatique.   kon·see·nyer o·to·ma·teek

Can I have some coins/tokens?
    Je peux avoir des   zher per a·vwar day
    pièces/jetons?   pyes/zher·ton

train

What station is this?
   C'est quelle gare?   say kel gar

What's the next station?
   Quelle est la prochaine gare?   kel ay la pro·shen gar

Does this train stop at (Amboise)?
   Est-ce que ce train   es·ker se trun
   s'arrête à (Amboise)?   sa·ret a (om·bwaz)

Do I need to change trains?
Est-ce qu'il faut   es·keel fo
changer de train?   shon·zhay der trun

Which carriage is for (Bordeaux)?
C'est quelle voiture pour   say kel vwa·tewr poor
(Bordeaux)?   (bor·do)

Which is the dining car?
Où est le wagon-restaurant?   oo ay ler va·gon·res·to·ron

boat

bateau

Are there life jackets?
Est-ce qu'il y a des gilets   es·keel ya day zhee·lay
de sauvetage?   der sov·tazh

What's the sea like today?
L'état de la mer est bon?   lay·ta der la mair ay bon

I feel seasick.
J'ai le mal de mer.   zhay ler mal der mair

taxi

taxi

I'd like a taxi ...	*Je voudrais un*	zher voo·dray un
	taxi ...	tak·see ...
at (nine o'clock)	*à (neuf heures)*	a (ner ver)
tomorrow	*demain*	der·mun

Where's the taxi stand?
Où est la station de taxis?   oo ay la sta·syon der tak·see

Is this taxi free?
Vous êtes libre?   voo·zet lee·brer

Please put the meter on.
Mettez le compteur,   me·tay ler kon·ter
s'il vous plaît.   seel voo play

How much is the flag fall/hiring charge?
A combien s'élève la   a kom·byun say·laiv la
prise en charge?   pree zan sharzh

How much is it to (the Eiffel Tower)?
C'est combien pour aller à   say kom·byun poor a·lay a
(la Tour Eiffel)?   (la toor ee·fel)

Please take me to (this address).
Conduisez-moi à   kon·dwee·zay mwa a
(cette adresse), s'il vous plaît.   (set a·dres) seel voo play

How much is the final fare?
C'est combien en tout?   say kom·byun on too

Please ...	*..., s'il vous plaît.*	... seel voo play
slow down	*Roulez plus*	roo·lay plew
	lentement	lont·mon
wait here	*Attendez ici*	a·ton·day ee·see

Stop ...	*Arrêtez-vous ...*	a·ray·tay voo ...
at the corner	*au coin de la rue*	o kwun der la rew
here	*ici*	ee·see

For other useful phrases, see **directions**, page 59, and **money**, page 33.

car & motorbike

voiture & moto

> ## car & motorbike hire

I'd like to hire	*Je voudrais*	zher voo·dray
a/an ...	*louer ...*	loo·way ...
4WD	*un quatre-quatre*	ung ka·trer·ka·trer
automatic	*une automatique*	ewn o·to·ma·teek
(small/large)	*une (petite/*	ewn (per·teet/
car	*grosse) voiture*	gros) vwa·tewr
manual	*une manuel*	ewn ma·nwel
motorbike	*une moto*	ewn mo·to

with ...	*avec ...*	a·vek ...
air conditioning	*climatisation*	klee·ma·tee·za·syon
a driver	*un chauffeur*	un sho·fer

How much for ... hire?	Quel est le tarif par ...?	kel ay ler ta·reef par ...
daily	jour	zhoor
hourly	heure	er
weekly	semaine	ser·men

Does that include ...?	Est-ce que ... est compris(e)? m/f	es·ker ... ay kom·pree(z)
mileage	le kilométrage m	ler kee·lo·may·trazh
insurance	l'assurance f	la·sew·rons

Can I return it in another city?

Je peux la rendre dans une autre ville?   zher per la ron·drer don zewn o·trer veel

signs

Cédez la Priorité	say·day la pree·o·ree·tay	Give Way
Entrée	on·tray	Entrance
Péage	pay·azh	Toll
Sens Interdit	sons un·ter·dee	No Entry
Sens Unique	sons ew·neek	One-way
Sortie	sor·tee	Exit
Stop	stop	Stop

> on the road

What's the speed limit?

Quelle est la vitesse maximale permise?   kel ay la vee·tes mak·see·mal per·meez

Is this the road to (Toulouse)?

C'est la route pour (Toulouse)?   say la root poor (too·looz)

(How long) Can I park here?

(Combien de temps) Est-ce que je peux stationner ici?   (kom·byun der tom) es·ker zher per sta·syo·nay ee·see

Where's a petrol station?

Où est-ce qu'il y a une station-service?   oo es·keel ya ewn sta·syon·ser·vees

Please fill it up.
Le plein, s'il vous plaît.   ler plun seel voo play

I'd like (20) litres.
Je voudrais (vingt) litres.   zher voo·dray (vung) lee·trer

Where do I pay?
Où est-ce que je paie?   oo es·ker zher pay

Please check	*Contrôlez ...,*	kon·tro·lay ...
the ...	*s'il vous plaît.*	seel voo play
oil	*l'huile*	lweel
tyre pressure	*la pression*	la pre·syon
	des pneus	day pner
water	*l'eau*	lo

diesel	*diesel* m	dyay·zel
leaded	*au plomb*	o plom
petrol/gas	*essence* f	es·sons
regular	*ordinaire*	or·dee·nair
unleaded	*sans plomb*	son plom

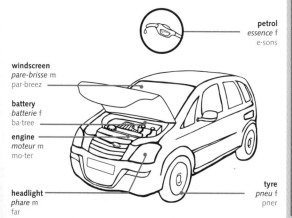

petrol
essence f
e·sons

windscreen
pare-brisse m
par·breez

battery
batterie f
ba·tree

engine
moteur m
mo·ter

headlight
phare m
far

tyre
pneu f
pner

> problems

I need a mechanic.

*J'ai besoin d'un
mécanicien.*

zhay ber·zwun dun
may·ka·nee·syun

The car/motorbike has broken down (at Amboise).

*La voiture/moto est
tombée en panne (à Amboise).*

la vwa·tewr/mo·to ay
tom·bay on pan (a om·bwaz)

I had an accident.

J'ai eu un accident.

zhay ew un ak·see·don

The car/motorbike won't start.

*La voiture/moto
ne veut pas démarrer.*

la vwa·tewr/mo·to
ner ver pa day·ma·ray

Do you have jumper leads/cables?

*Vous avez des câbles de
démarrage?*

voo·za·vay day ka·bler der
day·ma·razh

I need a push start.

J'ai besoin qu'on me pousse.

zhay ber·zwun kom mer poos

I have a flat tyre.

Mon pneu est à plat.

mom pner ay ta pla

I've lost my car keys.

*J'ai perdu les clés de
ma voiture.*

zhay per·dew lay klay der
ma vwa·tewr

I've locked my keys inside.

*J'ai enfermé mes
clés dans la voiture.*

zhay on·fair·may may
klay don la vwa·tewr

I've run out of petrol.

*Je suis en panne
d'essence.*

zher swee zon pan
de·sons

Can you fix my car today?
Vous pouvez réparer   voo poo·vay ray·pa·ray
ma voiture aujourd'hui?   ma vwa·tewr o·zhoor·dwee

How long will it take?
Ça va prendre combien   sa va pron·drer kom·byun
de temps?   der tom

listen for ...

day·po·twar
dépotoir   **junk heap**

set pyes ay tray dee·fee·seel a troo·vay
Cette pièce est très   **Ah, that part's**
difficile à trouver.   **very hard to get.**

say kel mark
C'est quelle marque?   **What make/model is it?**

bicycle

vélo

Where can I ...?	*Où est-ce que je peux ...?*	oo es·ker zher per ...
buy a second-hand bike	*acheter un vélo d'occasion*	ash·tay un vay·lo do·ka·zyon
have my bike repaired	*faire réparer mon vélo*	fair ray·pa·ray mon vay·lo
hire a bicycle	*louer un vélo*	loo·way un vay·lo
leave my bike	*laisser mon vélo*	lay·say mon vay·lo

Are there any bicycle paths?
Est-ce qu'il y a des   es·keel ya day
pistes cyclables?   peest see·kla·bler

Is there a map of bicycle paths?
Est-ce qu'il y a un carte   es·keel ya ung kart
des pistes cyclables?   day peest see·kla·bler

Is there bicycle parking?
Y a-t'il une zone de
stationnement pour
bicyclettes?

ya·teel ewn zon der
sta·syon·mon poor
bee·see·klet

Can I take my bike on the train?
Est-ce que ce train accepte
les vélos à bord?

es·ker ser trun ak·sept
lay vay·lo a bor

Is it within cycling distance?
On peut y aller à vélo?

on per tee a·lay a vay·lo

Do I have to wear a helmet?
Il faut porter un casque?

eel fo por·tay ung kask

bike chain	*chaîne* f *de bicyclette*	shen der bee·see·klet
bike path	*piste* m *cyclable*	peest see·kla·bler
bike pump	*pompe* f *à vélo*	pomp a vay·lo
mountain bike	*vélo* m *tout-terrain (VTT)*	vay·lo too·tay·run (vay tay tay)
racing bike	*vélo* f *de course*	vay·lo der koors

bike bag

Travelling with a bicycle in France can be made a great deal easier if you have *une housse* ewn hoos – a bike bag. In such a bag, your bike can be transported on any train or coach, including the TGV (high-speed train).

passport control

le contrôle des passeports

I'm here ...	Je suis ici pour ...	zher swee zee·see poor ...
on business	le travail	ler tra·vai
on holiday	les vacances	lay va·kons
for study	les études	lay zay·tewd

I'm here for (two) ...	Je suis ici pour (deux) ...	zher swee zee·see poor (der) ...
days	jours	zhoor
months	mois	mwa
weeks	semaines	ser·men

I'm in transit.
Je suis ici de passage. — zher swee zee·see der pa·sazh

We have a joint passport.
Nous avons un passeport commun. — noo za·von un pas·por ko·mun

I'm going to (Paris).
Je vais à (Paris). — zher vay a (pa·ree)

I'm staying at the ...
Je loge à ... — zher lozh a ...

listen for ...

vo·trer ... seel voo play	Votre ..., s'il vous plaît.	Your ..., please.
pas·por	passeport	passport
vee·za	visa	visa
voo vwa·ya·zhay ...	Vous voyagez ...?	Are you travelling ...?
on fa·mee·yer	en famille	with a family
on groop	en groupe	in a group
serl	seul	on your own

at customs

I have nothing to declare.
Je n'ai rien à déclarer.   zher nay ryun a day·kla·ray

I have something to declare.
J'ai quelque chose   zhay kel·ker·shoz
à déclarer.   a day·kla·ray

That's not mine.
Ce n'est pas à moi.   ser nay pa a mwa

I didn't know I had to declare it.
Je ne savais pas que je   zher ner sa·vay pa ker zher
devais déclarer cela.   der·vay day·kla·ray ser·la

I need ...	**J'ai besoin ...**	zhay ber·zwun ...
a lawyer	d'un avocat	dun a·vo·ka
to make a phone call	de téléphoner	der tay·lay·fo·nay

For phrases on payments and receipts, see **money**, page 33.

finding accommodation

trouver un logement

Where's a ...?	*Où est-ce qu'on peut trouver ...?*	oo es·kon per troo·vay ...
bed and breakfast	*une pension*	ewn pon·syon
camping ground	*un terrain de camping*	un tay·run der kom·peeng
guesthouse	*une pension*	ewn pon·see·on
hotel	*un hôtel*	un o·tel
youth hostel	*une auberge de jeunesse*	ewn o·bairzh der zher·nes
Can you recommend somewhere ...?	*Est-ce que vous pouvez recommander un logement ...?*	es·ker voo poo·vay rer·ko·mon·day un lozh·mon ...
cheap	*pas cher*	pa shair
nearby	*près d'ici*	pray dee·see
romantic	*romantique*	ro·mon·teek
mountain hut	*refuge* m	rer·fewzh
ski resort	*station* f *de ski*	sta·syon der skee
wellness centre	*centre* m *de remise en forme*	son·trer der rer·mee zan form

What's the address?
Quelle est l'adresse? kel ay la·dres

For responses, see **directions**, page 59.

booking ahead & checking in

réservation & enregistrement

I'd like to book a room, please.
Je voudrais réserver une chambre, s'il vous plaît. zher voo·dray ray·zair·vay ewn shom·brer seel voo play

I have a reservation.
J'ai une réservation.   zhay ewn ray·zair·va·syon

There are (three) of us.
Nous sommes (trois).   noo som (trwa)

I'd like to stay for (two) nights.
Je voudrais rester   zher voo·dray res·tay
pour (deux) nuits.   poor (der) nwee

From (July 2) to (July 6).
Du (deux juillet)   dew (der zhwee·yay)
au (six juillet).   o (see zhwee·yay)

Do you offer (long-stay) discounts?
Y a-t-il une réduction   ya·teel ewn ray·dewk·syon
(pour les longs séjours)?   (poor lay lon say·zhoor)

Is breakfast included?
Le petit déjeuner   ler per·tee day·zher·nay
est-il inclus?   ay·teel un·klew

Is there parking?
Y a-t-il un parking?   ya·teel ewn par·keeng

Do I need to pay upfront?
Est-ce qu'il faut payer   es·keel fo pay·yay
par avance?   par a·vons

Can I pay by credit card?
Est-ce qu'on peut payer avec   es·kom per pay·yay a·vek
une carte de crédit?   ewn kart der kray·dee

Can I see it?
Est-ce que je peux la voir?   es·ker zher per la vwar

Do you have	*Avez-vous*	a·vay·voo
a ... room?	*une chambre ...?*	ewn shom·brer ...
double	*avec un grand lit*	a·vek ung gron lee
single	*à un lit*	a un lee
twin	*avec des lits*	a·vek day lee
	jumeaux	zhew·mo

How much	*Quel est*	kel ay
is it per ...?	*le prix par ...?*	ler pree par ...
night	*nuit*	nwee
person	*personne*	per·son

For other methods of payment, see **money**, page 33.

day·zo·lay say kom·play
Désolé, c'est complet. I'm sorry, we're full.

kom·byun der nwee
Combien de nuits? For how many nights?

vo·trer pas·por seel voo play
Votre passeport,
s'il vous plaît. Your passport, please.

air-conditioner
climatiseur m
klee·ma·tee·zer

toilet
toilettes f
twa·let

key
clé f
klay

bed
lit m
lee

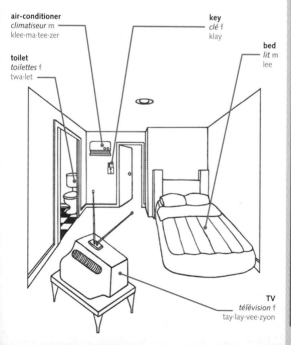

TV
télévision f
tay·lay·vee·zyon

accommodation

51

requests & queries

When/Where is breakfast served?
*Quand/Où le petit
déjeuner est-il servi?*
kon/oo ler per·tee
day·zher·nay ay·teel sair·vee

Please wake me at (seven).
*Réveillez-moi à (sept)
heures, s'il vous plaît.*
ray·vay·yay·mwa a (set)
er seel voo play

Can I use the ...? *Est-ce que je
peux utiliser ...?*
es·ker zher
per ew·tee·lee·zay ...

Internet	*l'Internet*	lun·tair·net
kitchen	*la cuisine*	la kwee·zeen
laundry	*la blanchisserie*	la blon·shees·ree
telephone	*le téléphone*	ler tay·lay·fon

**Do you have
a/an...?** *Avez-vous ...?* a·vay·voo ...

elevator	*un ascenseur*	un a·son·ser
laundry service	*un service de
blanchisserie*	un sair·vees der
blon·shees·ree
message board	*un panneau
d'affichage*	um pa·no
da·fee·shazh
safe	*un coffre-fort*	ung ko·frer·for
swimming pool	*une piscine*	ewn pee·seen

Do you change money here?
Echangez-vous l'argent ici?
ay·shon·zhay·voo lar·zhon ee·see

Do you arrange tours here?
*Organisez-vous des
excursions ici?*
or·ga·nee·zay·voo day
zeks·kewr·syon ee·see

Can I leave a message for someone?
*Je peux laisser un
message pour quelqu'un?*
zher per lay·say um
me·sazh poor kel·kun

Is there a message for me?
*Vous avez un message
pour moi?*
voo za·vay um me·sazh
poor mwa

There's no hot water.
Il n'y a pas d'eau chaude.
eel nya pa do shod

I'm locked out of my room.
Je me suis — zher mer swee
enfermé(e) dehors. m/f — zon·fair·may der·or

The (bathroom) door is locked.
La porte (de la salle de bain) — la port (der la sal der bun)
est verrouillée. — ay ver·roo·yay

It's too ...	C'est trop ...	say tro ...
cold	froid	frwa
dark	sombre	som·brer
expensive	cher	shair
noisy	bruyant	brew·yon
small	petit	per·tee

The ... doesn't work.	... ne fonctionne pas.	... ner fong·syon pa
air-conditioning	La climatisation	klee·ma·tee·za·syon
fan	Le ventilateur	ler von·tee·la·ter
heater	L'appareil de chauffage	la·pa·ray der sho·fazh
toilet	Les toilettes	ler twa·let
window	La fenêtre	la fer·ne·trer

Can I get another ...?	Est-ce que je peux avoir un/une autre ...? m/f	es·ker zher per a·vwar un/ewn o·trer ...
This ... isn't clean.	Ce/Cette ... n'est pas propre. m/f	ser/set ... nay pa pro·prer
blanket	couverture f	koo·vair·tewr
sheet	drap m	drap
towel	serviette f	sair·vee·et

a knock at the door

Who is it?	Qui est-ce?	kee e·ser
Just a moment.	Un instant.	un uns·ton
Come in.	Entrez.	on·tray

Come back later, please.
Veuillez repasser plus tard, — ver·yay rer·pa·say plew tar
s'il vous plaît. — seel voo play

checking out

régler la note

What time is checkout?
Quand faut-il régler? kon fo·teel ray·glay

Can I have a late checkout?
Pourrai-je régler plus tard? poo·rezh ray·glay plew tar

There's a mistake in the bill.
Il y a une erreur dans la note. eel ya ewn ay·rer don la not

I'm leaving now.
Je pars maintenant. zher par mun·ter·non

Can you call a taxi for me (for 11 o'clock)?
Pouvez-vous appeler poo·vay·voo a·play
un taxi pour moi un tak·see poor mwa
(pour onze heures)? (poor on zer)

Can I leave my luggage here until ...?	*Puis-je laisser mes bagages jusqu'à ...?*	pweezh lay·say may ba·gazh zhews·ka ...
next week	*la semaine prochaine*	la ser·men pro·shen
tonight	*ce soir*	ser swar
Wednesday	*mercredi*	mair·krer·dee
Could I have my ..., please?	*Est-ce que je pourrais avoir ..., s'il vous plaît?*	es·ker zher poo·ray a·vwar ... seel voo play
deposit	*ma caution*	ma ko·syon
passport	*mon passeport*	mon pas·por
valuables	*mes biens précieux*	may byun pray·syer

I had a great stay, thank you.

J'ai fait un séjour   zhay fay un say·zhoor
magnifique, merci.   ma·nyee·feek mair·see

You've been terrific.

Vous avez été sensationnel.   voo za·vay ay·tay son·sa·syo·nel

I'll recommend it to my friends.

Je le recommanderai   zher ler rer·ko·mon·dray
à mes amis.   a may za·mee

I'll be back ...	*Je retournerai ...*	zher rer·toor·ner·ray ...
in (three) days	*dans (trois) jours*	on (trwa) zhur
on (Tuesday)	*(mardi)*	(mar·dee)

camping

Where's the	*Où est le ... le*	oo ay ler ... ler
nearest ...?	*plus proche?*	plew prosh
campsite	*terrain*	tay·run
	de camping	der kom·peeng
shop	*magasin*	ma·ga·zun
shower facility	*bloc sanitaire*	blok sa·nee·tair
toilet block	*bloc toilettes*	blok twa·let

How much	*C'est combien*	say kom·bee·un
is it per ...?	*pour chaque ...?*	poor shak ...
caravan	*caravane*	ka·ra·van
person	*personne*	pair·son
tent	*tente*	tont
vehicle	*véhicule*	vay·ee·kewl

Do you have ...?	*Avez-vous ...?*	a·vay·voo ...
electricity	*l'électricité*	lay·lek·tree·see·tay
shower facilities	*un bloc sanitaire*	um blok sa·nee·tair
a site	*un emplacement*	un om·plas·mon
tents for hire	*des tentes*	day tont
	à louer	a loo·ay

accommodation

55

Is it coin-operated?
Est-ce que ça marche es·ker sa marsh
avec des jetons? a·vek day zher·ton

Is the water drinkable?
L'eau est-elle potable? lo ay·tel po·ta·bler

Who do I ask to stay here?
Je m'adresse où zher ma·dres oo
pour rester ici? poor res·tay ee·see

Can I ...?	*Est-ce que je peux ...?*	es·ker zher per ...
camp here	*camper ici*	kom·pay ee·see
park next to	*garer ma*	ga·ray ma
my tent	*voiture à côté*	vwa·tewr a ko·tay
	de ma tente	der ma tont

Could I borrow	*Est-ce que je*	es·ker zher
a ...?	*pourrais*	poo·ray
	emprunter ...?	um·prun·tay ...
mallet	*un maillet*	um ma·yay
spade	*une pelle*	ewn pel
torch/	*une lampe de*	ewn lomp der
flashlight	*poche*	posh

renting

I'm here about the ... for rent.
Je suis ici au sujet zher swee zee·see o sew·zhay
de ... à louer. der ... a loo·ay

Do you have	*Avez-vous un/*	a·vay·voo un/
a/an ... for rent?	*une ... à louer?* m/f	ewn ... a loo·ay
apartment	*appartement* m	a·par·ter·mon
house	*maison* f	may·zon
room	*chambre* f	shom·brer
villa	*villa* f	vee·la

How much is it for ...?	C'est combien pour ...?	say kom·byun poor ...
(one) week	*(une) semaine*	(ewn) ser·men
(two) months	*(deux) mois*	(der) mwa

Is there a bond?
Faut-il verser une caution?   fo·teel vair·say ewn ko·syon

staying with locals

Can I stay at your place?
Est-ce que je peux   es·ker zher per
rester chez vous?   ray·stay shay voo

I have my own sleeping bag.
J'ai un sac de couchage.   zhay un sak der koo·shazh

Is there anything I can do to help?
Y a-t-il quelque chose que   ya·teel kel·ker shoz ker
je peux faire pour aider?   zher per fair poor ay·day

Thanks for your hospitality.
Merci pour votre   mair·see poor vo·trer
hospitalité.   os·pee·ta·lee·tay

Can I ...?	Puis-je ...?	pwee·zher ...
bring anything	*apporter quelque*	a·por·tay kel·ker
for the meal	*chose pour le repas*	shoz poor ler rer·pa
do the dishes	*faire la vaisselle*	fair la vay·sel
set the table	*mettre la table*	me·trer la ta·bler
take out the	*sortir les*	sor·teer lay
rubbish	*poubelles*	poo·bel

To compliment your host's cooking, see **eating out**, page 137.

making a mark

Keeping in touch and thanking people for their hospitality is always appreciated, and if you write in French, it may well be unforgettable. Some of these common letter expressions might help get you started:

> ### beginning a letter

Cher/Chère ... m/f
shair ...   **Dear ...**

Comment allez-vous?/Comment vas-tu? pol/inf
ko·mon ta·lay·voo/   **How are you?**
ko·mon va·tew

Je suis désolé(e) de répondre si tard. m/f
zher swee day·zo·lay   **Sorry for writing so late.**
der ray·pon·drer see tar

Je vous/te remercie de ... pol/inf
zher voo/ter   **Thanks for ...**
rer·mair·syay der ...

> ### ending a letter

informal

Grosses bises	gros bees	**Big kisses**
Je t'embrasse	zher tom·bras	**I kiss you**
Bisous	bee·zoo	**Kisses**

formal

Cordialement	kor·dyal·mon	**Kind regards**
Amicalement	a·mee·kal·mon	**Best wishes**
Amitiés	a·mee·tyay	**Very best wishes**

Where's a ...?	*Où est-ce qu'il y a ...?*	oo es·keel ya ...
I'm looking for a ...	*Je cherche ...*	zher shairsh ...
bank	*une banque*	ewn bongk
hotel	*un hôtel*	un o·tel
police station	*un commissariat de police*	un kom·mee·sar·ya der po·lees

Can you show me (on the map)?
Pouvez-vous m'indiquer (sur la carte)?   poo·vay·voo mun·dee·kay (sewr la kart)

What's the address?
Quelle est l'adresse?   kel ay la·dres

How do I get there?
Comment faire pour y aller?   ko·mon fair poor ee a·lay

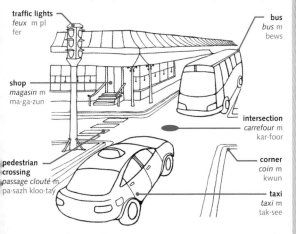

traffic lights
feux m pl
fer

shop
magasin m
ma·ga·zun

pedestrian crossing
passage clouté m
pa·sazh kloo·tay

bus
bus m
bews

intersection
carrefour m
kar·foor

corner
coin m
kwun

taxi
taxi m
tak·see

How far is it?	C'est loin?	say lwun
by bus	en bus	om bews
by taxi	en taxi	on tak·see
by train	en train	on trun
on foot	à pied	a pyay
Turn ...	Tournez ...	toor·nay ...
at the corner	au coin	o kwun
at the traffic lights	aux feux	o fer

listen for ...

say ...	C'est ...	It's ...
a drwat	à droite	right
a gosh	à gauche	left
a ko·tay der ...	à côté de ...	beside ...
a lest	à l'est	east
a lwest	à l'ouest	west
dair·yair ...	derrière ...	behind ...
der·von ...	devant ...	in front of ...
ee·see	ici	here
la	là	there
lwun dee·see	loin d'ici	far away
o kwun	au coin	on the corner
o nor	au nord	north
o sewd	au sud	south
on fas der ...	en face de ...	opposite ...
pray dee·see	près d'ici	near here
too drwa	tout droit	straight ahead
say ta ...	C'est à ...	It's ...
(dee) mee·newt	(dix) minutes	(10) minutes
(son) me·trer	(cent) mètres	(100) metres

looking for ...

Where's a ...?   *Où est-ce qu'il*   oo es·keel
                           y a ...?   ya ...
     bank   *une banque*   ewn bongk
     cake shop   *une pâtisserie*   ewn pa·tees·ree
     supermarket   *un supermarché*   un sew·pair·mar·shay

Where can I buy ...?
   Où puis-je acheter ...?   oo pweezh ash·tay ...

For phrases on getting there see **directions**, page 59, and for
additional shops and services see the **dictionary**.

making a purchase

How much is it?
   C'est combien?   say kom·byun
I'd like to buy ...
   Je voudrais acheter ...   zher voo·dray ash·tay ...
What is this made of?
   C'est fabriqué avec quoi?   say fa·bree·kay a·vek kwa

I'm just looking.
Je regarde.   zher rer·gard

Can you write down the price?
Pouvez-vous écrire le prix?   poo·vay·voo ay·kreer ler pree

Do you have any others?
Vous en avez d'autres?   voo zon a·vay do·trer

Can I look at it?
Est-ce que je peux le voir?   es·ker zher per ler vwar

I don't need a bag, thanks.
Je n'ai pas besoin   zher nay pa ber·zwun
de sac, merci.   der sak mair·see

Do you accept ...?	*Est-ce que je peux*	es·ker zher per
	payer avec ...?	pay·yay a·vek ...
credit cards	*une carte*	ewn kart
	de crédit	der kray·dee
debit cards	*une carte*	ewn kart
	de débit	der day·bee
travellers	*des chèques*	day shek
cheques	*de voyages*	der vwa·yazh

listen for ...

non noo non a·vom pa
Non, nous n'en avons pas.   **No, we don't have any.**

o·trer shoz
Autre chose?   **Anything else?**

voo day·zee·ray
Vous désirez?   **Can I help you?**

voo zon day·zee·ray kom·byun
Vous en désirez   **How much/many**
combien?   **do you want?**

zher voo lom·bal
Je vous l'emballe?   **Would you like it wrapped?**

PRACTICAL

62

Could I have a ..., please?	Puis-je avoir ..., s'il vous plaît?	pweezh a·vwar ... seel voo play
bag	un sac	un sak
receipt	un reçu	un rer·sew

Could I have it wrapped?
Pouvez-vous l'envelopper?   poo·vay·voo lon·vlo·pay

Does it have a guarantee?
Est-ce qu'il y a une garantie?   es keel ya ewn ga·ron·tee

Can I have it sent overseas?
Pouvez-vous me l'envoyer   poo·vay·voo mer lon·vwa·yay
à l'étranger?   a lay·tron·zhay

Can I pick it up later?
Je peux passer le   zher per pa·say ler
prendre plus tard?   pron·drer plew tar

It's faulty/broken.
C'est défectueux/cassé.   say day·fek·twer/ka·say

I'd like ..., please.	Je voudrais ..., s'il vous plaît.	zher voo·dray ... seel voo play
my change	ma monnaie	ma mo·nay
my money back	un remboursement	un rom·boors·mon
to return this	rapporter ceci	ra·por·tay ser·see

shopping

63

bargaining

That's too expensive.
C'est trop cher. — say tro shair

Can you lower the price?
Vous pouvez baisser le prix? — voo poo·vay bay·say ler pree

I'll give you ...
Je vous donnerai ... — zher voo don·ray ...

Do you have something cheaper?
Avez-vous quelque — a·vay·voo kel·ker
chose de moins cher? — shoz der mwun shair

clothes

I'm looking for ... — *Je cherche ...* — zher shairsh ...
  shoes — *des chaussures* — day sho·sewr
  underwear — *des sous-vêtements* — day soo·vet·mon

Can I try it on?
Puis-je l'essayer? — pwee·zher lay·say·yay

My size is (medium).
Je fais du (moyen). — zher fay dew (mwa·yen)

It doesn't fit.
Ce n'est pas la bonne taille. — ser nay pa la bon tai

It's too ... — *C'est trop ...* — say tro ...
  big — *grand* — gron
  small — *petit* — per·tee
  tight — *serré* — say·ray

For clothes items see the **dictionary**, and for sizes see **numbers & amounts**, page 27.

repairs

réparations

Can I have my ...	Puis-je faire	pwee·zher fair
repaired here?	réparer ... ici?	ray·pa·ray ... ee·see
camera	mon appareil	mon a·pa·ray
	photo	fo·to
shoes	mes chaussures	may sho·sewr
(sun)glasses	mes lunettes	may lew·net
	(de soleil)	(der so·lay)

When will it be ready?
   Quand est-ce que ce sera prêt? kon tes·ker ser ser·ra pray

hairdressing

au coiffeur

I'd like (a) ...	Je voudrais ...	zher voo·dray ...
blow wave	un brushing	um brer·sheeng
colour	un shampooing	un shom·pwung
	colorant	ko·lo·ron
haircut	une coupe	ewn koop
my beard	me faire tailler	mer fair tai·yay
trimmed	la barbe	la barb
shave	me faire raser	mer fair ra·zay
trim	une coupe	ewn koop
	d'entretien	don·trer·tyun

I want it cut like this.
   Je voudrais une coupe   zher voo·dray oon koop
   comme cela.   kom ser·la

I want it short.
   Je voudrais une coupe courte.   zher voo·dray ewn koop koort

Don't cut it too short.
   Ne coupez pas trop court.   ner koo·pay pa tro koor

Please use a new blade.
   Utilisez une nouvelle   ew·tee·lee·zay ewn noo·vel
   lame, s'il vous plaît.   lam seel voo play

Shave it all off!
Rasez tout! ra·zay too

For colours, see the **dictionary**.

books & reading

Is there an English-language section?
Y a-t-il un rayon anglais? ya·teel un ray·yon ong·glay

Do you have	*Avez-vous ...*	a·vay·voo ...
... in English?	*en anglais?*	on ong·glay
a book by ...	*un roman de ...*	un ro·mon der ...
an entertainment	*un guide des*	ung geed day
guide	*spectacles*	spek·ta·kler

I'd like a ...	*Je voudrais un ...*	zher voo·dray un ...
dictionary	*dictionnaire*	deek·syo·nair
newspaper	*journal*	zhoor·nal

Can you recommend a book for me?
Pouvez-vous me poo·vay·voo mer
conseiller un roman? kon·say·yay un ro·mon

Do you have Lonely Planet guidebooks?
Avez-vous des guides a·vay·voo day geed
Lonely Planet? lon·lee pla·net

I'm looking for something by (Albert Camus).
Je cherche quelque chose zher shairsh kel·ker shoz
de (Albert Camus). der (al·bair ka·mew)

For more on books and reading, see **interests**, page 100.

music & DVD

I'd like (a) ...	*Je voudrais ...*	zher voo·dray ...
CD	*un CD*	un say·day
DVD	*un DVD*	un day·vay·day
headphones	*un casque*	ung kask

What's his/her best recording?
Quel est son meilleur   kel ay som may·yer
enregistrement?   on·rer·zhees·trer·mon

Will this work on any DVD player?
Est-ce que ça fonctionne   es·ker sa fonk·syon
quel que soit le lecteur   kel ker swa ler lek·ter
de DVD?   der day·vay·day

What region is this DVD for?
Pour quelle région ce   poor kel ray·zhyon ser
DVD est-il codé?   day·vay·day ay·teel ko·day

video & photography

vidéo & photographie

Can you ...?	Pouvez-vous ...?	poo·vay·voo ...
develop	développer	day·vlo·pay
this film	cette pellicule	set pay·lee·kewl
load my	charger ma	shar·zhay ma
film	pellicule	pay·lee·kewl

I need a ...	J'ai besoin d'une	zhay ber·zwun dewn
film for this	pellicule ... pour	pay·lee·kewl ... poor
camera.	cet appareil.	say·ta·pa·ray
B&W	en noir et blanc	on nwar ay·blong
colour	couleur	koo·ler
(200) speed	rapidité	ra·pee·dee·tay
	(deux cent)	(der son)

Can you ...?	Pourriez-vous ...?	poo·ree·yay voo ...
print digital	imprimer des	um·pree·may day
photos	photos numériques	fo·to new·may·reek
recharge the	recharger les	rer·shar·zhay lay
battery for my	piles de mon	peel der mong
digital camera	appareil	na·pa·ray
	numérique	new·may·reek
transfer my	transférer mes	trons·fay·ray may
photos from	photos de la carte	fo·to der la kart
camera to CD	mémoire vers	may·mwar vair
	un CD	ung say·day

Do you have a ...	*Avez-vous ...*	a·vay·voo ...
for this camera?	*pour cet appareil?*	poor set ta·pa·ray
batteries	*des piles*	day peel
flash (bulb)	*un flash*	ung flash
light meter	*un posemètre*	ung poz·may·trer
memory cards	*des cartes mémoire*	day kart may·mwar
zoom (lens)	*un objectif*	ung nop·zhek·teef

digital camera	*appareil* m *photo numérique*	a·pa·ray fo·to new·may·reek
disposable camera	*appareil* m *photo jetable*	a·pa·ray fo·to zhay·ta·bler
underwater camera	*appareil* m *photo sous-marin*	a·pa·ray fo·to soo·ma·run
video camera	*caméra* f *vidéo*	ka·may·ra vee·day·yo

I need a cable to connect my camera to a computer.
J'ai besoin d'un câble pour connecter mon appareil photo à un ordinateur.
zhay ber·zwun dung ka·bler poor ko·nek·tay mong na·pa·ray fo·to a ung nor·dee·na·ter

I need a cable to recharge this battery.
J'ai besoin d'un câble pour recharger cette pile.
zhay ber·zwun dung ka·bler poor rer·shar·zhay set peel

I need a video cassette for this camera.
J'ai besoin d'une cassette vidéo pour cet appareil.
zhay ber·zwun dew ka·set vee·day·yo poor set ta·pa·ray

Do you have one-hour processing?
Vous faites le développement en une heure?
voo fet ler day·vlop·mon on ewn er

How much is it to develop this film?
C'est combien pour développer cette pellicule?
say kom·byun poor day·vlo·pay set pay·lee·kewl

I need a passport photo taken.
J'ai besoin d'une photo d'identité.
zhay ber·zwun dewn fo·to dee·don·tee·tay

I'm not happy with these photos.
Je ne suis pas content de ces photos.
zher ner swee pa kon·ton der say fo·to

communications
les communications

post office

la poste

I want to	Je voudrais	zher voo·dray
send a ...	envoyer ...	on·vwa·yay ...
fax	un fax	un faks
letter	une lettre	ewn le·trer
parcel	un colis	ung ko·lee
I want to	Je voudrais	zher voo·dray
buy a/an...	acheter ...	ash·tay ...
aerogram	un aérogramme	un air·ro·gram
envelope	une enveloppe	ewn on·vlop
stamp	un timbre	un tum·brer
Please send it	Envoyez-le	on·vwa·yay·ler
(to Australia)	(en Australie) ...,	(on os·tra·lee) ...
by ...	s'il vous plaît.	seel voo play
airmail	par avion	par a·vyon
express post	en exprès	on neks·pres
regular post	en courrier	on koor·yay
	normal	nor·mal
surface mail	par voie de terre	par vwa der tair
It contains ...	Cela contient ...	ser·la kon·tyun ...
customs	déclaration f	day·kla·ra·syon
declaration	en douane	on doo·wan
domestic	national(e) m/f	na·syo·nal
fragile	fragile	fra·zheel
international	international(e) m/f	un·tair·na·syo·nal
mail box	boîte f aux lettres	bwat o lay·trer
PO box	boîte f postale	bwat pos·tal
postal address	adresse f postale	a·dres pos·tal
postcode	code m postal	kod pos·tal
(by) registered	en recommandé	on rer·ko·mon·day
mail		
sea mail	voie f maritime	vwa ma·ree·teem

Where's the poste restante section?

Où est le service — oo ay ler sair·vees
de poste restante? — der post res·tont

Is there any mail for me?

Y a-t-il du courrier pour moi? — ya·teel dew koor·yay poor mwa

phone

What's your phone number?

Quel est votre numéro — kel ay vo·trer new·may·ro
de téléphone? — der tay·lay·fon

Where's the nearest public phone?

Où est le téléphone — oo ay ler tay·lay·fon
public le plus proche? — pewb·leek ler plew prosh

I'd like to know the number for ...

Je voudrais connaître le — zher voo·dray ko·nay·trer ler
numéro de ... — new·may·ro der ...

I want to make a local call.

Je veux passer un appel — zher ver pa·say ung na·pel
téléphonique local. — tay·lay·fo·neek lo·kal

I want to make ...	*Je veux téléphoner ...*	zher ver tay·lay·fo·nay ...
a call to (Singapore)	*avec préavis à (Singapour)*	a·vek pray·a·vee a (sung·ga·poor)
an Internet call	*par internet*	par un·tair·net
a reverse-charge/ collect call	*en PCV*	om pay·say·vay

I'd like to ...	*Je voudrais ...*	zher voo·dray ...
buy a phone card	*acheter une carte téléphonique*	ash·tay ewn kart tay·lay·fo·neek
look at a phone book	*consulter un annuaire du téléphone*	kon·sewl·tay un an·wair dew tay·lay·fon
speak for (three) minutes	*parler (trois) minutes*	par·lay (trwa) mee·newt

For telephone numbers, see **numbers & amounts**, page 27.

How much is ...?	*Quel est le prix ...?*	kel ay ler pree ...
a (three)-minute call	*d'une communication de (trois) minutes*	dewn ko·mew·nee·ka·syon der (trwa) mee·newt
each extra minute	*de chaque minute supplémentaire*	der shak mee·newt sew·play·mon·tair

The number is ...
Le numéro est ...   ler new·may·ro ay ...

Do you have international prepaid phone cards?
Avez-vous des cartes   a·vay·voo day kart
téléphoniques prépayées   tay·lay·fo·neek pray·pay·yay
pour les appels à   poor lay za·pel a
l'international?   lun·tair·na·syo·nal

What's the area/country code for ...?
Quel est l'indicatif pour ...?   kel ay lun·dee·ka·teef poor ...

It's busy.
La ligne est occupée.   la lee·nyer ay·to·kew·pay

I've been cut off.
J'ai été coupé(e). m/f   zhay ay·tay koo·pay

The connection is bad.
La ligne est mauvaise.   la lee·nyer ay mo·vayz

Hello. It's ...
Allô. C'est ...   a·lo say ...

---

listen for ...

a kee voo·lay·voo par·lay
À qui voulez-vous parler? — **Who do you want to speak to?**

day·zo·lay voo voo trom·pay der new·may·ro
Désolé, vous vous trompez de numéro. — **Sorry, wrong number.**

kee ay·ser
Qui est-ce? — **Who's calling?**

non eel/el nay pa la
Non, il/elle n'est pas là. — **No, he/she is not here.**

zher per pron·drer um may·sazh
Je peux prendre un message? — **Can I take a message?**

Can I leave a message?
Je peux laisser un message?   zher per lay·say um may·sazh

Tell him/her I called.
Dites-lui que j'ai appelé.   deet·lwee ker zhay a·play

I'll call back later.
Je rappellerai plus tard.   zher ra·pel·ray plew tar

My number is ...
Mon numéro est ...   mon new·may·ro ay ...

mobile/cell phone

téléphone portable

I'd like a/an ...	*Je voudrais ...*	zher voo·dray ...
adaptor plug	*une prise*	ewn preez
	multiple	mewl·tee·pler
charger for	*un chargeur pour*	un shar·zher poor
my phone	*mon portable*	mom por·ta·bler
mobile/cell	*louer un*	loo·ay um
phone for hire	*portable*	por·ta·bler
prepaid mobile/	*un portable*	um por·ta·bler
cell phone	*prépayé*	pray·pay·yay
prepaid	*une carte*	ewn kart
recharge card	*prépayée*	pray·pay·yay
	rechargeable	rer·shar·zha·bler
SIM card for	*une carte SIM*	ewn kart seem
the network	*pour le réseau*	poor ler ray·zo

What are the rates? *Quels sont les tarifs?* kel son lay ta·reef

the internet

l'internet

Where's the local Internet cafe?
Où est le cybercafé   oo ay ler see·bair·ka·fay
du coin?   dew kwun

Do you have public Internet access here?
Avez-vous une connexion   a·vay·voo ewn ko·nek·syon
internet ici?   un·tair·net ee·see

Is there wireless Internet access here?
Avez-vous le wifi ici? — a·vay·voo ler wee·fee ee·see

Can I connect my laptop here?
Est-ce que je peux utiliser — es·ker zher per ew·tee·lee·zay
mon ordinateur — mong or·dee·na·ter
portable ici? — por·ta·bler ee·see

I'd like to buy a card/USB for prepaid mobile Internet.
Je voudrais acheter — zher voo·dray ash·tay
une carte prépayée/ — ewn kart pray·pay·yay/
un modem externe USB — un mo·dem eks·tairn ew·es·bay
pour surfer sur internet. — poor ser·fay sewr un·tair·net

Do you have headphones (with a microphone)?
Avez-vous un casque — a·vay·voo ung kask
(avec un micro)? — (a·vek ung mee·kro)

I'd like to ...	Je voudrais ...	zher voo·dray ...
burn a CD	brûler un CD	brew·lay un se·de
check my email	consulter mon courrier électronique	kon·sewl·tay mong koor·yay ay·lek·tro·neek
download my photos	télécharger mes photos	tay·lay·shar·zhay may fo·to
get Internet access	me connecter à l'internet	mer ko·nek·tay a lun·tair·net
use a printer	utiliser une imprimante	ew·tee·lee·zay ewn um·pree·mont
use a scanner	utiliser un scanner	ew·tee·lee·zay un ska·nair
use Skype	utiliser Skype	ew·tee·lee·zay skaip

How much per ...?	C'est combien ...?	say kom·byun ...
hour	l'heure	ler
page	la page	la pazh

How do I log on?
Comment faire pour me — ko·mon fair poor mer
connecter? — ko·nek·tay

What's the password?
Quel est le mot de passe? — kel ay ler mo der pas

Do you have PCs/Macs?
Avez-vous des PCs/Macs? — a·vay·voo day pay·say/mak

Can you help me change to English-language preference?
*Pouvez-vous m'aider à
choisir l'anglais comme
langue de préférence?*
  poo·vay·voo may·day a
  shwa·zeer long·glay kom
  longk der pray·fay·rons

It's crashed.
C'est tombé en panne. say tom·bay om pan

I've finished.
J'ai terminé. zhay tair·mee·nay

Can I connect my ... to this computer?	*Est-ce que je peux brancher ... sur cet ordinateur?*	es·ker zher per bron·shay ... sewr set tor·dee·na·ter
camera	*mon appareil photo*	mong na·pa·ray fo·to
iPod/iPhone/ iPad	*mon iPod/ iPhone/iPad*	mong nai·pot/ nai·fon/nai·pet
media player (MP3)	*mon lecteur MP3*	mong lek·ter em·pay·trwa
portable hard drive	*mon disque dur portable*	mong disk dewr por·ta·bler
PSP	*ma console portable*	ma kon·sol por·ta·bler
USB flash drive (memory stick)	*ma clé USB*	ma klay ew·es·bay

trawling for new words

bookmark	*signet* m	see·nyay
browser	*logiciel* m *de navigation*	lo·zhee·syel der na·vee·ga·syon
chat	*causette* f	ko·set
email	*mél* m	mel
firewall	*barrière* f *de sécurité*	ba·ree·yair der say·kew·ree·tay
hacker	*fouineur* m	fwee·ner
home page	*page* f *d'accueil*	pazh da·ker·yee
Internet	*Toile* f	twal
smiley	*frimousse* f	free·moos
thread	*fil* m	fee
webmaster	*administrateur* m *de site*	ad·mee·nee·stra·ter der seet

business
les affaires

As you'd expect, doing business in France could be the topic of a whole book. As a starting point though, remember to use polite forms when speaking to clients and colleagues (until invited to use the familiar form – see page 88) and it's probably best to save cheek-kisses for *very* successful meetings ...

I'm attending a ...	*Je participe à un/une ...* m/f	zhe par·tee·seep un/ewn ...
Where's the ...?	*Où est le/la ...?* m/f	oo ay ler/la...
conference	*conférence* f	kon·fay·rons
course	*stage* m	stazh
meeting	*réunion* f	ray·ew·nyon
trade fair	*foire* f *commerciale*	fwar ko·mair·syal
I'm with ...	*Je suis avec ...*	zher swee a·vek ...
the UN	*l'ONU*	lo en oo
my colleague(s)	*mon/mes collègue(s)* sg/pl	mong/may ko·leg
(two) others	*(deux) autres*	(derz) o·trer

I'm alone.
Je suis seul(e). m/f   zher swee serl

I need an interpreter.
J'ai besoin d'un interprète.   zhay ber·zwun dun un·tair·pret

I'm staying at ..., room ...
Je loge à ..., chambre ...   zher lozh a ... shom·brer ...

I'm here for (two) days/weeks.
Je suis ici pour (deux) jours/semaines.   zher swee·zee·see poor (der) zhoor/ser·men

business

Here's my business card.
Voici ma carte. vwa·see ma kart

Can I have your business card?
Pourriez-vous me laisser poo·ree·yay·voo mer lay·say
votre carte de visite? vo·trer kart der vee·zeet

I have an appointment with ...
J'ai rendez-vous avec ... zhay ron·day·voo a·vek ...

That went very well.
Ça c'est très bien passé. sa say tray byun pa·say

Thank you for your interest/time.
Merci pour votre temps/ mair·see poor vo·trer tom/
attention. a·ton·syon

Shall we go for a drink?
On prend un verre? om pron tun vair

Shall we go for a meal?
On va manger? on va mon·zhay

It's on me.
C'est moi qui offre. say mwa kee o·frer

I'm expecting a fax/call.
Je attends un fax/appel. zha·ton un faks/a·pel

I'd like ...	*Je voudrais ...*	zher voo·dray ...
(more) business cards	*(encore) des cartes de visite*	(ong·kor) day kart der vee·zeet
a connection to the internet	*me connecter à l'internet*	mer ko·nek·tay a lun·tair·net
an interpreter	*un interprète*	un un·tair·pret
to use a computer	*utiliser un ordinateur*	ew·tee·lee·zay un or·dee·na·ter
Is there a/an ...?	*Y a-t-il ...?*	ya·teel ...
data projector	*un projecteur data*	um pro·zhek·ter da·ta
laser pointer	*un pointeur laser*	un pwun·ter la·zair
overhead projector	*un rétro-projecteur*	un ray·tro·pro·zhek·ter

banking
les opérations bancaires

at the bank

Where can I ...?	Où est-ce que je peux ...?	oo es·ker zher per ...
I'd like to ...	Je voudrais ...	zher voo·dray ...
arrange a transfer	faire un virement	fair un veer·mon
cash a cheque	encaisser un chèque	ong·kay·say un shek
change a travellers cheque	changer des chèques de voyage	shon·zhay day shek der vwa·yazh
change money	changer de l'argent	shon·zhay der lar·zhon
get a cash advance	une avance de crédit	ewn a·vons der kray·dee
get change for this note	faire de la monnaie avec ce billet	fair der la mo·nay a·vek ser bee·yay
withdraw money	retirer de l'argent	rer·tee·ray der lar·zhon
Where's the nearest ...?	Où est ... le plus proche?	oo ay ... ler plew prosh
automatic teller machine	le guichet automatique	ler gee·shay o·to·ma·teek
foreign exchange office	le bureau de change	ler bew·ro der shonzh

What time does the bank open?
À quelle heure ouvre la banque?
a kel er oo·vrer la bongk

The automatic teller machine took my card.
Le guichet automatique a avalé ma carte de crédit.
ler gee·shay o·to·ma·teek a a·va·lay ma kart der kray·dee

I've forgotten my PIN.
J'ai oublié mon code confidentiel.
zhay oo·blee·yay mong kod kon·fee·don·syel

Can I have smaller notes?
Puis-je avoir des petites coupures?
pweezh a·vwar day per·teet koo·pewr

Has my money arrived yet?
Est-ce que mon argent est arrivé?
es·ker mon ar·zhon ay·ta·ree·vay

What's the ...?	*Quel(le) est ...?* m/f	kel ay ...
exchange rate	*le taux de change* m	ler to der shonzh
charge for that	*le tarif pour cela* m	ler ta·reef poor ser·la
commission	*la commission* f	la ko·mee·syon

For other useful phrases, see **money**, page 33.

For other useful phrases, see **money**, page 33.

---

listen for ...

don ...	*Dans ...*	In ...
ka·trer zhoor	*quatre jours*	four working
oo·vra·bler	*ouvrables*	days
ewn ser·men	*une semaine*	one week

eel ner voo rest plew dar·zhon
Il ne vous reste plus d'argent.
You have no funds left.

eel ya um pro·blem a·vek vo·trer kont
Il y a um problème avec votre compte.
There's a problem with your account.

no·tay·ler
notez-le
Write it down.

pa·pyay dee·don·tee·tay
papiers d'identité
ID

see·nyay ee·see
signez ici
Sign here.

voo pray·fay·ray see·nyay oo ew·tee·lee·zay vo·trer kod
Vous préférez signer ou utiliser votre code?
Do you want to sign or use your PIN?

PRACTICAL

78

sightseeing
tourisme

I'd like a/an ...	Je voudrais ...	zher voo·dray ...
audio set	un écouteur	un ay·koo·ter
catalogue	un catalogue	ung ka·ta·log
city map	un plan de la ville	um plon der la veel
guide	un guide	ung geed
local map	une carte	ewn kart
	de la région	der la ray·zhyon

Do you have information on ... sights?	Avez-vous des renseignements sur les sites ... à visiter?	a·vay·voo day ron·sen·yer·mon sewr lay seet ... a vee·zee·tay
architectural	architecturaux	ar·shee·tek·tew·ro
cultural	culturels	kewl·tew·rel
free	gratuits	gra·tweet
historical	historiques	ees·to·reek
local	locaux	lo·ko
natural	naturels	na·tew·rel
religious	religieux	rer·lee·zhyer
unique	exceptionnels	ek·sep·syo·nel

I'd like to see ...
J'aimerais voir ...   zhem·ray vwar ...

I'd like to hire a local guide.
Je voudrais faire appel aux   zher voo·dray fair a·pel o
services d'un guide.   sair·vees dung geed

What's that?
Qu'est-ce que c'est?   kes·ker say

Who made it?
Qui l'a fait?   kee la fay

How old is it?
Ça date de quand?   sa dat der kon

Can you take a photograph of me?
Pouvez-vous me prendre   poo·vay·voo mer pron·drer
en photo?   on fo·to

sightseeing

Can I take photographs?
Je peux prendre des photos?   zher per pron·drer day fo·to

I'll send you the photograph.
Je vous enverrai la photo.   zher voo zon·vay·ray la fo·to

getting in

What's the admission charge?
Quel est le prix d'admission?   kel ay ler pree dad·mee·syon

What time does it ...?	*Quelle est l'heure ...?*	kel ay ler ...
close	*de fermeture*	der fer·mer·tewr
open	*d'ouverture*	doo·vair·tewr

Is there a discount for ...?	*Il y a une réduction pour les ...?*	eel ya ewn ray·dewk·syon poor lay ...
children	*enfants*	zon·fon
families	*familles*	fa·mee·yer
groups	*groupes*	groop
older people	*seniors*	say·nyor
pensioners	*personnes du troisième âge*	pair·son dew trwa·zyem azh
students	*étudiants*	zay·tew·dyon

galleries & museums

When's the ... open?	*... ouvre à quelle heure?*	... oo·vrer a kel er
gallery	*La galerie*	la gal·ree
museum	*Le musée*	ler mew·zay

What's in the collection?
Qu'est-ce qu'il y a dans la collection?   kes·keel·ya don la ko·lek·syon

It's a/an ... exhibition.
C'est une exposition ...   set ewn ek·spo·zee·syon ...

I like the works of ...
J'aime l'œuvre de ...   zhem ler·vrer der ...

It reminds me of ...
Cela me rappelle ...   ser·la mer ra·pel ...

... art	*l'art ...*	lar ...
contemporary	*contemporain*	kon·tom·po·run
impressionist	*impressionniste*	um·pray·syo·neest
modernist	*moderniste*	mo·dair·neest
Renaissance	*de la Renaissance*	der la rer·nay·sons

tours

Are there (organised) walking tours?
Y a-t'il des visites guidées — ya·teel day vee·zeet gee·day
(organisées) à pied? — (or·ga·nee·zay) a pyay

I'd like to do cooking/language classes.
Je voudrais suivre des — zher voo·dray swee·vrer day
cours de cuisine/langue. — koor der kwee·zeen/long

Can you recommend a ...?	*Pouvez-vous me recommander une ...?*	poo·vay·voo mer rer·ko·mon·day ewn ...
When's the next ...?	*C'est quand la prochaine ...?*	say kon la pro·shen ...
boat-trip	*excursion en bateau*	eks·kewr·syon om ba·to
day trip	*excursion d'une journée*	eks·kewr·syon dewn zhoor·nay
tour	*excursion*	eks·kewr·syon
Is ... included?	*Est-ce que ... est inclus(e)?* m/f	es·ker ... ay tung·klew(z)
accommodation	*le logement* m	ler lozh·mon
food	*la nourriture* f	la noo·ree·tewr
transport	*le transport* m	ler trons·por

Do I need to take ...?
Dois-je prendre ...? — dwa·zher pron·drer ...

The guide will pay.
Le guide va payer. — ler geed va pay·yay

How long is the tour?
L'excursion dure — leks·kewr·syon dewr
combien de temps? — kom·byun der tom

What time should we be back?
On doit rentrer pour — on dwa ron·tray poor
quelle heure? — kel er

I'm with them.
Je suis avec eux. — zher swee za·vek er

I've lost my group.
J'ai perdu mon groupe. — zhay pair·dew mon groop

I'm deaf.
  Je suis sourd(e). m/f   zher swee soor(d)

I'm hard of hearing.
  J'ai des difficultés   zhay day dee·fee·kewl·tay
  d'audition.   do·dee·syon

My companion is blind.
  Mon compagnon   mong kom·pa·nyon ay
  est aveugle. m   ta·ver·gler
  Ma compagne est   ma kom·pa·nyer ay
  aveugle. f   ta·ver·gler

I have a disability.
  Je suis handicapé(e). m/f   zher swee zon·dee·ka·pay

I need assistance.
  J'ai besoin d'aide.   zhay ber·zwun ded

What services do you have for people with a disability?
  Quels services avez-vous   kel sair·vees a·vay·voo
  pour les handicapés?   poor lay zon·dee·ka·pay

Is there wheelchair access?
  Y a-t-il un accès pour   ya·teel un ak·say poor
  fauteuil roulant?   fo·ter·yer roo·lon

How wide is the entrance?
  Quelle est la largeur de la   kel ay la lar·zher der la
  porte d'entrée?   port don·tray

How many steps are there?
  Il y a combien de marches?   eel ya kom·byun der marsh

Is there a lift?
  Est-ce qu'il y a un ascenseur?   es·keel ya un a·son·ser

Are guide dogs permitted?
Est-ce que les chiens es·ker lay shyun
d'aveugle sont permis? da·ver·gler son pair·mee

Is there somewhere I can sit down?
Est-ce qu'il y a un endroit es·keel·ya un on·drwa
où on peut s'asseoir? oo on per sa·swar

Are there any toilets for people with a disability?
Est-ce qu'il y a des toilettes es·keel ya day twa·let
pour handicapés? poor on·dee·ka·pay

Are there rails in the bathroom?
Est-ce qu'il y a des barres es·keel ya day bar
dans la salle de bain? don la sal der bun

Are there parking spaces for people with a disability?
Est-ce qu'il y a des es·keel ya day
emplacements zom·plas·mon
pour handicapés? poor on·dee·ka·pay

Could you call me a taxi for the disabled?
Pouvez-vous appeler poo·vay·voo a·play
un taxi pour personne un tak·see poor pair·son
handicapée? on·dee·ka·pay

Could you help me cross this street?
Pouvez-vous m'aider à poo·vay·voo may·day a
traverser cette rue? tra·vair·say set rew

Braille library	*bibliothèque f*	bee·blee·o·tek
	de braille	der bray·yer
crutches	*béquilles f pl*	bay·kee·yer
guide dog	*chien m d'aveugle*	shyun da·ver·gler
person with a	*handicapé(e) m/f*	on·dee·ka·pay
disability		
ramp	*rampe f*	romp
senior person	*senior m&f*	say·nyor
walking frame	*déambulateur m*	day·om·bew·la·ter
walking stick	*canne f*	kan
wheelchair	*fauteuil m roulant*	fo·ter·yee roo·lon

Is there a/an ...?	Y a-t-il ...?	ya teel ...
baby change room	un endroit pour changer le bébé	un on-drwa poor shon-zhay ler bay-bay
(English-speaking) babysitter	une baby-sitter (qui parle anglais)	ewn ba-bee-see-ter (kee parl ong-glay)
child discount	un tarif réduit pour les enfants	un ta-reef ray-dwee poor lay zon-fon
child-minding service	une garderie	ewn gar-dree
children's menu	un menu pour enfant	un mer-new poor on-fon
creche	une crèche	ewn kresh
family discount	un tarif réduit pour les familles	un ta-reef ray-dwee poor lay fa-mee-yer
highchair	une chaise haute	ewn shay zot
park nearby	un parc près d'ici	um park pray dee-see
I need a ...	J'ai besoin ...	zhay ber-zwun ...
child seat	d'un siège-enfant	dun syezh-on-fon
cot	d'un lit pour bébé	dun lee poor bay-bay
potty	d'un pot de bébé	dum po der bay-bay
stroller	d'une poussette	dewn poo-set
Do you sell ...?	Avez-vous ...?	a-vay-voo ...
baby wipes	des lingettes pour bébé	day lun-zhet poor bay-bay
disposable nappies/ diapers	des couches jetables	day koosh zher-ta-bler
milk formula	du lait maternisé	dew lay ma-tair-nee-say
painkillers for infants	des antalgiques pour enfant	day zon-tal-zheek poor on-fon

Do you mind if I breastfeed here?
Je peux allaiter mon   zher per a·lay·tay mon
bébé ici?   bay·bay ee·see

Are children allowed?
Les enfants sont permis?   lay zon·fon son pair·mee

Is this suitable for (six)-year-old children?
Cela convient-il aux   ser·la kon·vyun·teel o
enfants de (six) ans?   zon·fon der (seez) on

What's your name?
Comment tu t'appelles?   ko·mon tew ta·pel

How old are you?
Quel âge as-tu?   kel azh a·tew

If your child is sick, see **health**, page 175.

local talk

Chatting to children you meet can be a lot of fun – they're far more interested in what you say than how you say it.

When's your birthday?
C'est quand ton   say kon ton
anniversaire?   a·nee·vair·sair

Do you go to school or kindergarten?
Tu vas à l'école ou au   tew va a lay·kol oo o
jardin d'enfants?   zhar·dun don·fon

What grade are you in?
Tu es dans quelle classe?   tew ay don kel klas

Do you like sport?
Tu aimes le sport?   tew em ler spor

Do you like school?
L'école te plaît?   lay·kol ter play

Do you learn English?
Tu apprends l'anglais?   tew a·pron long·glay

basics

vocabulaire de base

Yes.	*Oui.*	wee
No.	*Non.*	non
Please.	*S'il vous plaît.*	seel voo play
Thank you	*Merci*	mair·see
(very much).	*(beaucoup).*	(bo·koo)
You're welcome.	*Je vous en prie.*	zher voo zon·pree
Excuse me.	*Excusez-moi.*	ek·skew·zay·mwa
Sorry.	*Pardon.*	par·don

greetings

salutations

A kiss on each cheek remains a common greeting in France, though between men (and when meeting a man or a woman for the first time) a handshake is more usual.

Hello.	*Bonjour.*	bon·zhoor
Hi.	*Salut.*	sa·lew
Good morning/ afternoon.	*Bonjour.*	bon·zhoor
Good evening/night.	*Bonsoir.*	bon·swar
See you later.	*À bientôt.*	a byun·to
Goodbye.	*Au revoir.*	o rer·vwar

How are you?
    Comment allez-vous? pol   ko·mon ta·lay·voo
    Ça va? inf   sa va

Fine. And you?
    Bien, merci. Et vous/toi? pol/inf   byun mair·see ay voo/twa

What's your name?

Comment vous appelez-vous? pol	ko·mon voo za·play·voo
Comment tu t'appelles? inf	ko·mon tew ta·pel

My name is ...

Je m'appelle ... zher ma·pel ...

I'd like to introduce you to ...

Je vous présente ... zher voo pray·zont ...

I'm pleased to meet you.

Enchanté(e). m/f on·shon·tay

The French can seem very formal about addressing people they don't know. They use *Monsieur*, *Madame* or *Mademoiselle* where English speakers would use no term of address at all.

Mr/Sir	*Monsieur (M)*	mer·syer
Ms/Mrs	*Madame (Mme)*	ma·dam
Miss	*Mademoiselle (Mlle)*	mad·mwa·zel
Doctor	*Docteur*	dok·ter

getting friendly

When talking to people familiar to you, or to children, it's usual to use the informal form of you, *tu* tew, rather than the plural or polite form, *vous* voo. The verb ending also changes. Phrases in this book are generally in the polite form, but where you see inf, you have a casual option to use where appropriate. If you feel you've become familiar enough to start using the informal form, you can ask if it's OK to use it:

Est-ce que je peux vous tutoyer?	es·ker zher per voo tew·twa·yay

See also **personal pronouns** in the **grammar** chapter, page 17.

making conversation

Sport and culture are safe areas of conversation and food is a sure way to get a French person speaking, but money talk (prices, income, etc) is best avoided.

Do you speak English?
Parlez-vous anglais?   par·lay·voo ong·glay

Do you live here?
Vous habitez ici?   voo za·bee·tay ee·see

Do you like it here?
Ça vous plaît ici?   sa voo play ee·see

I love it here.
Ça me plaît beaucoup ici.   sa mer play bo·koo ee·see

Where are you going?
Où allez-vous?   oo a·lay·voo

What are you doing?
Que faites-vous?   ker fet·voo

Are you waiting (for a bus)?
Attendez-vous   a·ton·day·voo
(un bus)?   (um bews)

Can I have a light?
Vous avez du feu?   voo za·vay dew fer

local talk		
Hey!	*Hé!*	ay
Great!	*Formidable!*	for·mee·da·bler
No problem.	*Pas de problème.*	pa der pro·blem
Sure.	*D'accord.*	da·kor
Maybe.	*Peut-être.*	per·te·trer
No way!	*Pas question!*	pa kay·styon
It's OK.	*C'est bien.*	say byun
OK.	*Bien.*	byun

What do you think (about ...)?
Que pensez-vous (de ...)?   ker pon·say·voo (der ...)

What's this called?
Comment ça s'appelle?   ko·mon sa sa·pel

Can I take a photo (of you)?
Je peux (vous) prendre   zher per (voo) pron·drer
en photo?   on fo·to

That's (beautiful), isn't it?
C'est (beau), non?   say (bo) non

Are you here on holiday?
Vous êtes ici pour   voo zet ee·see poor
les vacances?   lay va·kons

I'm here ...	*Je suis ici ...*	zher swee zee·see ...
for a holiday	*pour les vacances*	poor lay va·kons
on business	*pour le travail*	poor ler tra·vai
to study	*pour les études*	poor lay zay·tewd
with my family	*avec ma famille*	a·vek ma fa·mee·yer
with my partner	*avec mon/ma*	a·vek mon/ma
	partenaire m/f	par·ter·nair

This is my first trip (to France).
C'est la première fois   say la prer·myair fwa
que je viens (en France).   ker zher vyun (on frons)

How long are you here for?
Vous êtes ici depuis quand?   voo·zet ee·see der·pwee kon

I'm here for ... days/weeks.
Je reste ici ...   zher rest ee·see ...
jours/semaines.   zhoor/ser·men

Have you ever been (to England)?
Est-ce-que vous êtes déjà allé   es·ker voo zet day·zha a·lay
(en Angleterre)?   (on ong·gler·tair)

Do you want to come out with me?
Voulez-vous sortir   voo·lay·voo sor·teer
avec moi?   a·vek mwa

This is my ...	*Voici mon/ma ...* m/f	vwa·see mon/ma ...
child	*enfant* m&f	on·fon
colleague	*collègue* m&f	ko·leg
friend	*ami(e)* m/f	a·mee
husband	*mari* m	ma·ree
partner	*partenaire* m&f	par·ter·nair
wife	*femme* f	fam

local talk

Look!	*Regardez!* pol	rer·gar·day
Listen (to this)!	*Écoutez (ceci)!* pol	ay·koo·tay (ser·see)
I'm ready.	*Je suis prêt(e).* m/f	zher swee pray(t)
Are you ready?	*Vous êtes prêt(e)?* m/f pol	voo zet pray(t)
Just a minute.	*Une minute.*	ewn mee·newt
Just joking!	*Je blaguais!*	zher bla·gay

nationalities

nationalités

Where are you from?

Vous venez d'où? pol	voo ver·nay doo
Tu viens d'où? inf	tew vyun doo

What part of ... do you come from?

D'où est-ce que vous venez en ...? pol	doo es·ker voo ver·nay on ...
D'où est-ce que tu viens en ...? inf	doo es·ker tew vyun on ...

I'm from ...	*Je viens ...*	zher vyun ...
Australia	*d'Australie*	dos·tra·lee
Canada	*du Canada*	dew ka·na·da
England	*d'Angleterre*	dong·gle·tair
New Zealand	*de la Nouvelle-Zélande*	der la noo·vel·zay·lond
the USA	*des USA*	day zew·es·a

For more countries, see the **dictionary**.

age

How old ...?	Quel âge ...?	kel azh ...
are you	avez-vous pol	a·vay·voo
	as-tu inf	a·tew
is your son/	a votre fils/	a vo·trer fees/
daughter	fille	fee·yer

I'm ... years old.
J'ai ... ans.   zhay ... on
Too old!
Trop vieux/vieille! m/f   tro vyer/vyay
I'm younger than I look.
Je ne fais pas mon âge.   zher ner fay pa mo nazh
He/She is ... years old.
Il/Elle a ... ans.   eel/el a ... on

For your age, see **numbers & amounts**, page 27.

occupations & study

What's your occupation?
Vous faites quoi   voo fet kwa
comme métier? pol   kom may·tyay
Tu fais quoi   tew fay kwa
comme métier? inf   kom may·tyay

I'm a ...	Je suis un(e) ... m/f	zher swee zun/zewn ...
businessperson	homme/femme	om/fem
	d'affaires m/f	da·fair
chef	cuisinier/	kwee·zee·nyay/
	cuisinière m/f	kwee·zee·nyair
student	étudiant(e) m/f	ay·tew·dyon(t)

I work in ...	Je travaille dans ...	zher tra·vai don ...
education	l'enseignement	lon·sen·yer·mon
health	la santé	la son·tay
sales &	la vente et le	la vont ay ler
marketing	marketing	mar·kay·teeng

I'm ...	Je suis ...	zher swee ...
retired	retraité(e) m/f	rer·tray·tay
self-employed	indépendant(e) m/f	un·day·pon·don(t)
unemployed	chômeur/	sho·mer/
	chômeuse m/f	sho·merz

What are you studying?

Que faites-vous	ker fet·voo
comme études? pol	kom ay·tewd
Que fais-tu comme études? inf	ker fay·tew kom ay·tewd

I'm studying ...	Je fais des	zher fay day
	études ...	zay·tewd ...
engineering	d'ingénieur	dun·zhay·nyer
French	de français	der fron·say
media	des médias	day may·dya

For more occupations and fields of study, see the **dictionary**.

family

la famille

Do you have	Vous avez ...? pol	voo·za·vay ...
a ...?	Tu as ...? inf	tew a ...
I have a ...	J'ai ...	zhay ...
I don't have a ...	Je n'ai pas ...	zher nay pa ...
boyfriend	un petit ami	um per·tee ta·mee
brother	un frère	un frair
child	un/une enfant m/f	un/ewn on·fon
family	une famille	ewn fa·mee·yer
father	un père	um pair
girlfriend	une petite amie	ewn per·tee ta·mee
husband	un mari	um ma·ree
mother	une mère	ewn mair
partner	un/une	um/ewn
	partenaire m/f	par·ter·nair
sister	une sœur	ewn ser
wife	une femme	ewn fam

This is my ...

Voici mon/ma/mes ... m/f/pl	vwa·see mon/ma/may ...

Are you married?

Est-ce que vous êtes   es·ker voo zet mar·yay
marié(e)? m/f pol
Est-ce que tu es marié(e)? m/f inf   es·ker tew ay mar·yay

Do you live with your parents?

Vous habitez chez vos   voo za·bee·tay shay vo
parents? pol   pa·ron
Tu habites chez tes parents? inf   tew a·beet shay tay pa·ron

I live with someone.

Je vis avec quelqu'un.   zher vee a·vek kel·kun

I live with my ...

J'habite avec mon/   zha·beet a·vek mon/
ma/mes ... m/f/pl   ma/may ...

I'm ...   *Je suis ...*   zher swee ...
  single   *célibataire* m&f   say·lee·ba·tair
  married   *marié(e)* m/f   mar·yay
  separated   *séparé(e)* m/f   say·pa·ray

tracing roots & history

la généalogie

(I think) My ancestors came from this area.

(Je crois que) Mes   (zher krwa ker) may
ancêtres venaient de cette   zon·se·trer ver·nay der set
région.   ray·zhyon

I'm looking for my relatives.

Je cherche des personnes   zher shairsh day pair·son
de ma famille.   der ma fa·mee·yer

I have/had a relative who lived around here.

J'ai/J'avais un parent   zhay/zha·vay un pa·ron
qui habitait par ici.   kee a·bee·tay par ee·see

Where's the cemetery?

Où est le cimetière?   oo ay ler seem·tyair

He/She served near here.

Il/Elle a servi près d'ici.   eel/el a sair·vee pray dee·see

farewells

Tomorrow is my last day here.
Demain je passe ma   der·mun zher pas ma
dernière journée ici.   dair·nyair zhoor·nay ee·see

Let's swap addresses.
Échangeons nos adresses.   ay·zhon·zhon no za·dres

Here's my ...	*Voici mon ...*	vwa·see mon ...
What's your ...?	*Quel est votre ...?* pol	kel ay vo·trer ...
	Quel est ton ...? inf	kel ay ton ...
address	*adresse*	a·dress
email	*e-mail*	ay·mel
fax number	*numéro*	new·may·ro
	de fax	der faks
mobile number	*numéro*	new·may·ro
	de portable	der por·ta·bler
phone number	*numéro de*	new·may·ro der
	téléphone	tay·lay·fon
work number	*numéro*	new·may·ro
	au travail	tra·vai

If you ever visit	*Si vous voyagez*	see voo vwa·ya·zhay
(Laos), ...	*au (Laos), il faut ...* pol	o (low) eel fo ...
	Si tu voyages	see tew vwa·yazh
	au (Laos), il faut ... inf	o (low) eel fo ...
come and	*nous rendre*	noo ron·drer
visit us	*visite*	vee·zeet
you can stay	*séjourner*	say·zhoor·nay
with me	*chez moi*	shay mwa

Keep in touch!
Reste en contact! inf   rest on kon·takt

Are you on Facebook?
Es-tu sur Facebook? inf   ay·tew sewr fays·book

It's been great meeting you!
Ravi d'avoir fait   ra·vee da·vwar fay
ta connaissance! inf   ta ko·nay·sons

chatty souls

You might find yourself keeping in touch with French-speaking friends via Internet chat rooms. The conversations are marked by lots of abbreviations – here are a few to get you started:

bcp	*beaucoup*	bo·koo	a lot
c	*c'est*	say	it's
g	*j'ai*	zhay	I have
j	*je*	zher	I
jta	*je t'aime*	zher tem	I love you
k	*quoi*	kwa	what
m	*moi*	mwa	me
mdr	*mort de rire*	mor der reer	laugh out loud
pq	*pourquoi*	poor·kwa	why
pcq	*parce que*	pars ker	because
stp	*s'il te plait*	seel ter play	please
t	*tu*	tew	you
tlm	*tout le monde*	too ler mond	everyone

In this section, most phrases are given in an informal form. If you're unsure about what this means, see the box on page 88.

common interests

intérêts en commun

What do you do in your spare time?

Que fais-tu pendant tes loisirs?
ker fay·tew pon·don tay lwa·zeer

Do you like ...?	*Aimes-tu ...?*	em·tew ...
I like ...	*J'aime ...*	zhem ...
I don't like ...	*Je n'aime pas ...*	zher nem pa ...
art	*l'art*	lar
cooking	*cuisiner*	kwee·zee·nay
hiking	*la randonnée*	la ron·do·nay
photography	*voyager*	vwa·ya·zhay

For sporting interests, see **sports**, page 121, and the **dictionary**.

music

musique

Do you like to ...?	*Aimes-tu ...?*	em·tew ...
go to concerts	*aller aux concerts*	a·lay o kon·sair
listen to music	*écouter de la musique*	ay·koo·tay der la mew·zeek
play an instrument	*jouer d'un instrument*	zhoo·ay dun uns·trew·mon

Have you heard the latest album by ...?

As tu entendu le dernier album de ...?
a tew on·ton·dew ler dair·nyay al·bom der ...

Which ... do	Quels ...	kel ...
you like?	aimes-tu?	em·tew
bands	groupes	groop
music	genres de	zhon·rer der
	musique	mew·zeek
Which radio	Quelle station de	kel sta·syon der
station plays	radio passe de	ra·dyo pas der
... music?	la musique ...?	la mew·zeek ...
classical	classique	kla·seek
electronic	électronique	ay·lek·tro·neek

Where can I buy this music?

Où puis-je trouver ce type   oo pweezh troo·vay ser teep
de musique?   der mew·zeek

Off to a concert? See **buying tickets**, page 37, and **going out**, page 107.

cinema & theatre

cinéma & théâtre

I feel like	J'aimerais	zhem·ray
going to a ...	bien voir ...	byun vwar ...
ballet	un ballet	um ba·lay
comedy	une comédie	ewn ko·may·dee
film/movie	un film	un feelm
play	une pièce	ewn pyes
	de théâtre	der tay·a·trer

What's showing at the cinema tonight?

Qu'est-ce qui passe au   kes·kee pas o
cinéma ce soir?   see·nay·ma ser swar

Is it in English?

C'est en anglais?   say ton ong·glay

Does it have subtitles?

C'est sous-titré?   say soo·tee·tray

Is it dubbed in English/French?

Ce film est-il doublé   ser feelm ay·teel doo·blay
en anglais/français?   on ong·glay/fron·say

Is there a/an ...? — *Y a-t-il un ...?* — ya·teel un ...
- **cloakroom** — *vestiaire* — vest·yair
- **intermission** — *entracte* — on·trakt
- **programme** — *programme* — pro·gram

Where can I get a cinema/theatre guide?
Où pourrais-je trouver un programme de cinéma/théâtre? — oo poo·rezh troo·vay um pro·gram der see·nay·ma/tay·atrer

Are those seats taken?
Est-ce que ces places sont prises? — es·ker say plas son preez

Have you seen ...?
As-tu vu ...? — a·tew vew ...

Who's in it?
Qui joue dans ce film? — kee zhoo don ser feelm

Who directed it?
Qui a réalisé ce film? — kee a ray·a·lee·zay ser feelm

It stars ...
... est la vedette du film. — ... ay la ver·det dew feelm

Did you like the ...? — *As-tu aimé ...?* — a·tew ay·may ...
- **film** — *le film* — ler feelm
- **performance** — *la représentation* — la rer·pray·zon·ta·syon
- **play** — *la pièce* — la pyes

I thought it was ... — *Je l'ai trouvé ...* — zher lay troo·vay ...
- **excellent** — *excellent* — ek·say·lon
- **long** — *long* — long
- **OK** — *bien* — byun

I like ... — *J'aime les ...* — zhem lay...
I don't like ... — *Je n'aime pas les ...* — zher nem pa lay ...
- **action movies** — *films d'action* — feelm dak·syon
- **French films** — *films français* — feelm fron·say
- **sci-fi** — *films de science fiction* — feelm der syons·fik·syon

reading

What kind of books do you read?
Quel genre de   kel zhon·rer der
livres lis-tu?   lee·vrer lee·tew

Who's your favourite author?
Quel est ton auteur préféré?   kel ay ton o·ter pray·fay·ray

Which (French) author do you recommend?
Quel auteur (français)   kel o·ter (fron·say)
peux-tu recommander?   per·tew rer·ko·mon·day

Have you read ...?
As-tu lu ...?   a·tew lew ...

I read ...
Je lis ...   zher lee ...

I recommend ...
Je peux recommander ...   zher per rer·ko·mon·day ...

Where can I exchange books?
Où puis-je échanger   oo pweezh ay·shon·zhay
des livres?   day lee·vrer

For more on books and reading, see **shopping**, page 66.

happy days

Congratulations!
Félicitations!   fay·lee·see·ta·syon

Happy birthday!
Joyeux anniversaire!   zhwa·yerz a·nee·ver·sair

Merry Christmas!
Joyeux Nöel!   zhwa·yerz no·el

Happy Easter!
Joyeuses Pâques!   zhwa·yerz pak

feelings

Feelings are described with either nouns or adjectives: the nouns use 'have' in French (eg, 'I have hunger') and the adjectives use 'be' (like in English).

I'm ...	J'ai ...	zhay ...
I'm not ...	Je n'ai pas ...	zher nay pa ...
Are you ...?	Avez-vous ...? pol	a·vay voo ...
	As-tu ...? inf	a·tew ...
hot	*chaud*	sho
hungry	*faim*	fum
sleepy	*sommeil*	so·may

I'm ...	Je suis ...	zher swee ...
I'm not ...	Je ne suis pas ...	zher ner swee pa ...
Are you ...?	Êtes-vous ...? pol	et voo ...
	Es-tu ...? inf	ay·tew ...
disappointed	*déçu(e)* m/f	day·sew
happy	*heureux* m	er·reu
	heureuse f	er·reuz
sad	*triste* m&f	treest
satisfied	*satisfait(e)* m/f	sa·tees·fay(t)

If you're not feeling well, see **health**, page 175.

local talk		
Better luck next time.	*Ça ira mieux la prochaine fois.*	sa ee·ra myer la pro·shen fwa
How lucky!	*Quelle chance.*	kel shons
It's strange.	*C'est marrant.*	say ma·ron
No problem.	*Pas de problème.*	pa der pro·blem
Too bad.	*Tant pis.*	tom pee
What a shame.	*Quel dommage.*	kel do·mazh
What's up?	*Qu'est-ce qu'il ya?*	kes keel ya

opinions

Did you like it?
Cela vous a plu?   ser·la voo za plew

What did you think of it?
Qu'est-ce que vous   kes·ker voo
en avez pensé?   zon na·vay pon·say

I thought it was ... It's ...	Je l'ai trouvé ... C'est ...	zher lay troo·vay ... say ...
beautiful	beau	bo
better	mieux	myer
bizarre	bizarre	bee·zar
great	formidable	for·mee·da·bler
horrible	horrible	o·ree·bler
OK	bien	byun
strange	étrange	ay·tronzh
weird	bizarre	bee·zar
worse	pire	peer

a matter of degree

a little	un peu	um per
I'm a little sad.	*Je suis un peu triste.*	zher swee zum per treest

really	vraiment	vray·mon
I'm really sorry.	*Je suis vraiment navré.*	zher swee vray·mon na·vray

very	très	tray
I feel very vulnerable.	*Je me sens très vulnérable.*	zher mer son tray vewl·nay·ra·bler

politics & social issues

Who do you vote for?
Pour qui votez-vous?   poor kee vo·tay·voo

I support the	*Je soutiens*	zher soo·tyun
... party.	*le parti ...*	ler par·tee ...
I'm a member of	*Je suis membre*	zher swee mom·brer
the ... party.	*du parti ...*	dew par·tee ...
communist	*communiste*	ko·mew·neest
conservative	*conservateur*	kon·sair·va·ter
democratic	*démocrate*	day·mo·krat
green	*écologiste*	ay·ko·lo·zheest
labour	*travailliste*	tra·va·yeest
republican	*républicain*	ray·pew·blee·kun
social democratic	*social démocrate*	so·syal day·mo·krat
socialist	*socialiste*	so·sya·leest

Did you hear about ...?
Vous avez entendu   voo za·vay on·ton·dew
parler de ...?   par·lay der ...

I (don't) agree with ...
Je (ne) suis (pas) pour ....   zher (ner) swee (pa) poor ...

Do you agree with it?
Êtes-vous d'accord avec cela?   et·voo da·kor a·vek ser·la

---

from the big cheese

*'Comment est-il possible de gouverner un pays qui produit
plus de trois cent soixante-dix fromages différents?'*
Charles de Gaulle

ko·mon ay·teel po·see·bler der goo·vair·nay un pay·ee
kee pro·dwee plews der trwa·son swa·son·dees fro·mazh
dee·fay·ron

'How is it possible to govern a country which produces
more than 370 different cheeses?'

I'm ...	Je suis ...	zher swee ...
Are you ...?	Êtes-vous ...?	et·voo ...
against (it)	contre (cela)	kon·trer (ser·la)
in favour of (it)	pour (cela)	poor (ser·la)
How do people feel about ...?	Qu'est-ce qu'on pense ...?	kes·kom pons ...
abortion	de l'avortement	der la·vor·ter·mon
animal rights	des droits des animaux	day drwa day za·nee·mo
corruption	de la corruption	der la ko·rewp·syon
crime	de la criminalité	dew la kree·mee·na·lee·tay
the economy	de l'économie	der lay·ko·no·mee
education	de l'éducation	der lay·dew·ka·syon
the environment	de l'environnement	der lon·vee·ron·mon
equal opportunity	de l'égalité des chances	der lay·ga·lee·tay day shons
EU expansion	de l'élargissement de l'Union européenne	der lay·lar·zhees·mon der lew·nyon er·ro·pay·yen
euthanasia	de l'euthanasie	der ler·ta·na·zee
globalisation	de la globalisation	der la glo·ba·lee·za·syon
health care	du système de sécurité sociale	dew sees·taym der say·kew·ree·tay so·syal
human rights	des droits de l'homme	day drwa der lom
immigration	de l'immigration	der lee·mee·gra·syon
language nationalism	du nationalisme linguistique	dew na·syo·na·lees·mer lun·gwee·steek
party politics	de la politique de partis	der la po·lee·teek der par·tee
racism	du racisme	dew ra·sees·mer
sexism	du sexisme	dew sek·sees·mer
taxes	des impôts	day zum·po
terrorism	du terrorisme	dew tay·ro·rees·mer
unemployment	du chômage	dew sho·mazh
the war in ...	de la guerre en ...	der la gair on ...

the environment

Is there an environmental problem here?
Y a-t-il un problème   ya·teel un pro·blem
d'environnement ici?   don·vee·ron·mon ee·see

alternative energy sources	*sources* f pl *d'énergie alternatives*	soors day·nair·zhee al·tair·na·teev
biodegradable	*biodégradable*	byo·day·gra·da·bler
carbon dioxide emissions	*émissions* f pl *de CO2*	ay·mee·syon der say·o·der
climate change	*changement* m *climatique*	shon·zhe·mon klee·ma·teek
conservation	*conservation* f	kon·sair·va·syon
deforestation	*déforestation* f	day·fo·res·ta·syon
disposable	*jetable*	zher·ta·bler
drought	*sécheresse* f	say·shres
ecosystem	*écosystème* m	ay·ko·sees·tem
endangered species	*espèces* f *en voie de disparition*	es·pes on vwa der dees·pa·ree·syon
flood risk	*risques* m pl *d'inondation*	reesk dee·non·da·syon
global warming	*réchauffement* m *climatique*	ray·shof·mon klee·ma·teek
hunting	*chasse* f	shas
hydroelectricity	*hydro-électricité* f	ee·dro· ay·lek·tree·see·tay
irrigation	*irrigation* f	ee·ree·ga·syon
nuclear energy	*énergie* f *nucléaire*	ay·nair·zhee new·klay·air
nuclear testing	*essais* m pl *nucléaires*	ay say·say new·klay·air
ozone layer	*couche* f *d'ozone*	koosh do·zon
pesticides	*pesticides* m	pes·tee·seed
pollution	*pollution* f	po·lew·syon
recycling	*recyclage* m	rer·see·klazh
sustainable energy	*énergies* f pl *renouvelables*	ay·ner·zhee rer·noo·ver·la·bler
toxic waste	*déchets* m pl *toxiques*	day·shay tok·seek
water supply	*approvisionnement* f *en eau*	a·pro·vee·zyon·mon on no

Is this a protected ...?	C'est ... protégée?	set ... pro·tay·zhay
forest	une forêt	ewn fo·ray
species	une espèce	ewn es·pes

express yourself

The French language has an abundant store of wry turns of phrase. Throw some of these colourful expressions into an argument for dramatic effect:

N'y vas pas par quatre chemins!   nee va pa par ka·trer sher·mun
Come straight to the point!
(lit: don't go four ways)

Quelle salade!   kel sa·lad
What a pack of lies!
(lit: what a salad)

In this section, most phrases are given in an informal form. If
you're unsure about what this means, see the box on page 88.

where to go

où aller

What's on ...?	Qu'est-ce qu'on joue ...?	kes·kon zhoo ...
locally	dans le coin	don ler kwun
this weekend	ce week-end	ser week·end
today	aujourd'hui	o·zhoor·dwee
tonight	ce soir	ser swar
Where are the ...?	Où sont les ...?	oo son lay ...
clubs	clubs	klerb
discos	discothèques	dees·ko·tek
gay venues	boîtes gaies	bwat gay
places to eat	restaurants	res·to·ron
pubs	pubs	perb
Is there a local ... guide?	Y a-t-il un programme ...?	ya·teel un pro·gram ...
entertainment	des spectacles	day spek·ta·kler
film	des films	day feelm

What's there to do in the evenings?
Qu'est-ce qu'on
peut faire le soir?
kes·kon
per fair ler swar

Is there a local gay guide?
Y a-t-il un guide
des endroits gais?
ya·teel un geed
day zon·drwa gay

I'd like to go to a/the ...	Je voudrais aller ...	zher voo·dray a·lay ...
ballet	au ballet	o ba·lay
bar	au bar	o bar
cafe	au café	o ka·fay
cinema	au cinéma	o see·nay·ma
concert	à un concert	a ung kon·sair
karaoke bar	au karaoké	o ka·ra·o·kay
nightclub	en boîte	on bwat
opera	à l'opéra	a lo·pay·ra
pub	au pub	o perb
restaurant	au restaurant	o res·to·ron
theatre	au théâtre	o tay·a·trer

invitations

invitations

What are you doing ...?	Que fais-tu ...?	ker fay·tew ...
right now	maintenant	mun·ter·non
this evening	ce soir	ser swar
this weekend	ce week-end	ser week·end

Would you like to go (for a)...?	Tu voudrais aller ...?	tew voo·dray a·lay ...
I feel like going (for a) ...	J'ai envie d'aller ...	zhay on·vee da·lay ...
coffee	boire un café	bwar ung ka·fay
dancing	danser	don·say
drink	prendre un verre	pron·drer un vair
meal	manger	mon·zhay
out somewhere	sortir	sor·teer
walk	faire une promenade	fair ewn prom·nad

My round.	C'est ma tournée.	say ma toor·nay

Do you know a good restaurant?
Tu connais un bon restaurant?   tew ko·nay un bon res·to·ron

Do you want to come to the concert with me?
Tu veux aller au   tew ver a·lay o
concert avec moi?   kon·sair a·vek mwa

We're having a party.
Nous allons faire une fête.   noo za·lon fair ewn fet

You should come.
Tu dois venir.   tew dwa ver·neer

responding to invitations

Sure!
D'accord!   da·kor

Yes, I'd love to.
Je viendrai avec plaisir.   zher vyun·dray a·vek play·zeer

Where shall we go?
Où aller?   oo a·lay

No, I'm afraid I can't.
Non, désolé, je ne peux pas.   non day·zo·lay zher ner per pa

What about tomorrow?
Et demain?   ay der·mun

Sorry, I can't ...	*Désolé, je ne*	day·zo·lay zher ner
	... pas.	... pa
dance	*danse*	dons
sing	*chante*	shont

arranging to meet

What time shall we meet?
On se retrouve à quelle heure? on ser rer·troov a kel er

Where will we meet?
On se retrouve où? on ser rer·troov oo

I'll pick you up (at seven).
Je viendrai te chercher zher vyun·dray ter shair·shay
(à sept heures). (a set er)

I'll be coming later. Where will you be?
J'arriverai plus tard. zha·reev·ray plew tar.
Où seras-tu? oo se·ra·tew

If I'm not there by (nine), don't wait for me.
Si je ne suis pas là avant see zher ner swee pa la a·von
(neuf heures), ne m'attends pas. (ner ver) ner ma·ton pa

I'm looking forward to our meeting.
J'attends notre rendez-vous zha·ton no·trer ron·day·voo
avec impatience. a·vek un·pa·syons

Sorry I'm late.
Désolé d'être en retard. day·zo·lay de·trer on rer·tar

Never mind.
Ce n'est pas grave. ser nay pa grav

Let's meet at ...	*On peut se*	on per ser
	retrouver ...	rer·troo·vay ...
(eight o'clock)	*à (huit heures)*	a (wee ter)
the (entrance)	*devant (l'entrée)*	der·von (lon·tray)
Agreed/OK!	*D'accord!*	da·kor
I'll see you then.	*Allez, salut!*	a·lay sa·lew
See you later.	*À plus tard.*	a plew tar
See you tomorrow.	*À demain.*	a der·mun

nightclubs & bars

Are there any nightclubs here?
*Est-ce qu'il y a des boîtes
de nuit ici?*
es·keel ya day bwat
der nwee ee·see

Where can we go (salsa) dancing?
*Où est-ce qu'on peut
danser (la salsa)?*
oo es·kom per
don·say (la sal·sa)

What time does the show start?
*Le spectacle commence
à quelle heure?*
ler spek·ta·kler ko·mons
a kel er

How do I get there?
Comment y aller?
ko·mon ee a·lay

What's the cover charge?
C'est combien le couvert?
say kom·byun ler koo·vair

Come on!
Allez!
a·lay

What type of music do you like?
*Quel genre de musique
aimes-tu?*
kel zhon·rer der mew·zeek
em·tew

I like (reggae).
J'aime (le reggae).
zhem (ler ray·gay)

This place is great!
C'est formidable ici!
say for·mee·da·bler ee·see

I'm having a great time!
Je m'amuse bien!
zher ma·mewz byun

I don't like the music here.
*Je n'aime pas
la musique ici.*
zher nem pa
la mew·zeek ee·see

Let's go somewhere else.
Allons ailleurs.
a·lon za·yer

Do you want to ...?	*Tu veux bien ...?*	tew ver byun ...
go closer to	*t'approcher*	ta·pro·shay
the stage	*de la scène*	der la sen
sit at the	*t'asseoir au*	ta·swar o
front/back	*premier/*	prer·myay/
	dernier rang	dair·nyay rong

What a fantastic ...!	*Quel ...*	kel ...
	fantastique!	fon·ta·steek
concert	*concert*	kon·sair
group	*groupe*	groop

What a great singer!
Quel(le) chanteur/chanteuse kel shon·ter/shon·terz
formidable! m/f for·mee·da·bler

For more on bars, drinks and partying, see **eating out**, page 140.

drugs

la drogue

I don't take drugs.
Je ne touche pas à la drogue. zher ner toosh pa a la drog

I take ... occasionally.
Je prends du ... zher pron dew ...
occasionnellement. o·ka·zyo·nel·mon

Do you want to have a smoke?
Tu veux fumer? tew ver few·may

Do you have a light?
Vous avez du feu? voo za·vay dew fer

If the police are talking to you about drugs, see **police**, page 171, for useful phrases.

romance
l'amour

In this section, phrases are given in an informal form – if you're unsure about what this means, see the box on page 88.

asking someone out
inviter quelqu'un à sortir

Would you like to do something?
Est-ce que tu aimerais faire quelque chose? — es·ker tew em·ray fair kel·ker shoz

Yes, I'd love to.
Oui, j'aimerais bien. — wee zhem·ray byun

I'm sorry, I can't.
Non, je suis désolé(e), je ne peux pas. m/f — non zher swee day·zo·lay zher ner per pa

Not if you were the last person on earth!
Jamais de la vie! — zha·may der la vee

local talk

He/She is a ...	*C'est ...*	sayt ...
babe	*une nana*	ewn na·na
bitch	*une garce*	ewn gars
hot girl	*une fille chaude*	ewn fee·yer shod
hot guy	*un type chaud*	un teep sho
prick	*un con*	un kon
He/She gets around.	*Il/Elle a roulé sa bosse.*	eel/el a roo·lay sa bos

pick-up lines

You look like someone I know.
Tu me fais penser à   tew mer fay pon·say a
quelqu'un que je connais.   kel·kun ker zher ko·nay

Would you like a drink?
Si on buvait quelque chose?   see on bew·vay kel·ker shoz

What star sign are you?
Tu es de quel signe?   tew ay der kel see·nyer

Shall we get some fresh air?
Nous allons prendre l'air?   noo za·lon pron·drer lair

You're a fantastic dancer.
Tu danses vraiment bien.   tew dons vray·mom byun

Do you come here often?
Tu viens ici souvent?   tew vyun ee·see soo·von

Can I ...?	*Puis-je ...?*	pweezh ...
come in for	*entrer prendre*	on·tray pron·drer
a coffee	*un café*	ung ka·fay
dance with you	*danser avec toi*	don·say a·vek twa
see you again	*te revoir*	ter rer·vwar
sit here	*m'asseoir ici*	ma·swar ee·see
take you home	*te raccompagner*	ter ra·kom·pa·nyay

Do you have a ...?	*Est-ce que tu as ...?*	es·ker tew a ...
boyfriend	*un petit ami*	um per·tee ta·mee
fetish	*un fétiche*	un fay·teesh
girlfriend	*une petite amie*	ewn per·teet a·mee
light	*du feu*	dew fer

kiss me you fool

The word for 'a kiss' in French is *un baiser* un bay·zay, but the *un* word is the key here – without it, the word becomes a certain strong swear word. The verb 'kiss' is *embrasser* om·bra·say.

You have (a) beautiful ...	*Tu as ...*	tew a ...
body	*un beau corps*	um bo kor
eyes	*de beaux yeux*	der bo zyer
hands	*de belles mains*	der bel mun
laugh	*un beau sourire*	um bo soo·reer
personality	*une belle personnalité*	ewn bel pair·so·na·lee·tay

Will you take me home?
Tu veux bien me ramener à la maison?
tew ver byun mer ram·nay a la may·zon

Do you want to come inside for a while?
Tu veux entrer un instant?
tu ver on·tray un un·ston

rejections

Excuse me, I have to go now.
Excusez-moi, je dois partir maintenant.
ek·skyew·zay·mwa zher dwa par·teer mun·ter·non

No, thank you.
Non, merci.
non mair·see

I'd rather not.
Je n'ai pas très envie.
zher nay pa tray zon·vee

Your ego is out of control!
Tu es complètement imbu(e) de toi-même! m/f
tew ay kom·plet·mon um·bew der twa·mem

getting closer

I like you very much.
Je t'aime beaucoup. zher tem bo·koo

Do you like me too?
Tu m'aimes aussi? tew mem o·see

You're very attractive.
Tu es très beau/belle. m/f tew ay tray bo/bel

I'm interested in you.
Je m'intéresse zher mun·tay·res
vraiment à toi. vray·mon a twa

You're great.
Tu es formidable. tew ay for·mee·da·bler

Can I kiss you?
Je peux t'embrasser? zher per tom·bra·say

local talk

Leave me alone!
Laissez-moi tranquille! lay·say·mwa trong·keel

Don't touch me!
Ne me touchez pas! ner mer too·shay pa

I'm not interested.
Ça ne m'intéresse pas. sa ner mun·tay·res pa

Get lost!
Va te faire voir! va ter fair vwar

You're disturbing me.
Tu me gênes. tew mer zhen

sex

sexe

I want to make love to you.
Je veux faire l'amour avec toi.   zher ver fair la·moor a·vek twa

Let's use (a condom).
On va utiliser   on va ew·tee·lee·zay
(un préservatif).   (um pray·zair·va·teef)

I think we should stop now.
Il faut arrêter maintenant.   eel fo a·ray·tay mun·ter·non

Let's go to bed!
On va se coucher.   on va ser koo·shay

Kiss me.	*Embrasse-moi.*	om·bras·mwa
I want you.	*Je te veux.*	zher ter ver
Do you like this?	*Ça te plaît?*	sa ter play
I like that.	*J'aime ça.*	zhem sa
That's great.	*C'est sensationnel.*	say son·sa·syo·nel
I don't like that.	*Je n'aime pas ça.*	zher nem pa sa
Stop!	*Arrête!*	a·ret
Don't stop!	*N'arrête pas!*	na·ret pa
Oh yeah!	*Chouette alors!*	shwet a·lor
I'm coming.	*Je viens.*	zher vyun
Easy tiger!	*Vas-y mollo!*	va·zee mo·lo

That was ...	*C'était ...*	say·tay ...
amazing	*excellent*	ek·say·lon
great	*super*	sew·pair
weird	*bizarre*	bee·zar

romance

117

love

l'amour

I love you.
Je t'aime. — zher tem

Do you love me?
Tu m'aimes? — tew mem

Do you want to go out with me?
Veux-tu sortir avec moi? — ver·tew sor·teer a·vek mwa

Let's move in together!
Vivons ensemble! — vee·von on·som·bler

Will you marry me?
Veux-tu m'épouser? — ver·tew may·poo·zay

problems

les problèmes

Are you seeing someone else?
Il y a quelqu'un d'autre? — eel ya kel·kun do·trer

You're just using me for sex.
Je ne suis qu'un objet sexuel pour toi. — zher ner swee kun ob·zhay seks·wel poor twa

I don't think it's working out.
Je ne pense pas que ça marche. — zher ner pons pa ker sa marsh

We'll work it out.
Les choses finiront par s'arranger. — lay shoz fee·nee·ron par sa·ron·zhay

I never want to see you again.
Je ne veux plus te revoir. — zher ner ver plew ter rer·vwar

religion

la religion

What's your religion?
Quelle est votre religion? pol — kel ay vo·trer rer·lee·zhyon
Quelle est ta religion? inf — kel ay ta rer·lee·zhyon

I'm ...	*Je suis ...*	zher swee ...
I'm not ...	*Je ne suis pas ...*	zher ner swee pa ...
agnostic	*agnostique* m&f	ag·no·steek
atheist	*athée* m&f	a·tay
Buddhist	*bouddhiste* m&f	boo·deest
Catholic	*catholique* m&f	ka·to·leek
Christian	*chrétien(ne)* m/f	kray·tyun/kray·tyen
(Eastern)	*chrétien(ne)* m/f	kray·tyun/kray·tyen
Orthodox	*orthodoxe*	or·to·doks
Hindu	*hindou(e)* m/f	un·doo
Jewish	*juif/juive* m/f	zhweef/zhweev
Muslim	*musulman(e)* m/f	mew·zewl·mon/ mew·zewl·man
practising	*pratiquant(e)* m/f	pra·tee·kon(t)
Protestant	*protestant(e)* m/f	pro·tay·ston(t)
religious	*croyant(e)* m/f	krwa·yon(t)
I (don't) believe in ...	*Je (ne) crois (pas) ...*	zher (ner) krwa (pa) ...
destiny/fate	*au destin*	o day·stun
God	*en Dieu*	on dyer
Can I ... here?	*Puis-je ... ici?*	pweezh ... ee·see
Where can I ...?	*Où est-ce qu'on peut ...?*	oo es·kom per ...
attend mass	*aller à la messe*	a·lay a la mes
attend a service	*aller à l'office*	a·lay a lo·fees
pray	*faire mes/ses dévotions*	fair may/say day·vo·syon

cultural differences

How do you do this in your country?
Comment fait-on cela dans ko·mon fay·ton ser·la don
votre pays? vo·trer pay·ee

Is this a local or national custom?
Est-ce que c'est une coutume esk·ker say·tewn koo·tewm
locale ou nationale? lo·kal oo na·syo·nal

I didn't mean to do anything wrong.
Mes propos n'avaient rien may pro·po na·vay ryun
de blessant. der blay·son

I'm not used to this.
Je ne suis pas zher ner swee pa
habitué(e) à cela. m/f a·bee·tew·ay a ser·la

I don't mind watching, but I'd rather not join in.
Je veux bien regarder zher ver byun rer·gar·day
mais je ne veux pas may zher ner ver pa
participer. par·tee·see·pay

I'll try it.
Je vais essayer ça. zher vay ay·say·yay sa

I'm sorry,	*Je m'excuse, c'est*	zher mek·skewz say
it's against my ...	*contraire à ma ...*	kon·trair a ma ...
culture	*culture*	kewl·tewr
religion	*religion*	rer·lee·zhyon

This is very ...	*Ceci est très ...*	ser·see ay tray ...
different	*différent*	dee·fay·ron
fun	*amusant*	za·mew·zon
interesting	*intéressant*	zun·tay·ray·son

For phrases relating to cultural differences and food, see
vegetarian & special meals, page 150.

sporting interests

sports favoris

Do you like sport?
Vous aimez le sport?   voo zay·may ler spor

Yes, very much.
Oui, beaucoup.   wee bo·koo

Not really.
Pas vraiment.   pa vray·mon

I prefer watching sport.
Je préfère regarder le sport.   zher pray·fair rer·gar·day le spor

What sport do you play?
Quel sport faites-vous?   kel spor fet·voo

What sports do you like?
Quels sports aimez-vous?   kel spor ay·may·voo

I like ...	*J'aime ...*	zhem ...
basketball	*le basketball*	ler bas·ket·bol
rugby	*le rugby*	ler rewg·bee
running	*la course*	la koors
soccer	*le football*	ler foot·bol
squash	*le squash*	ler skwash
surfing	*le surf*	ler serf
Who's your favourite ...?	*Quel(le) est votre ... favori(te)?* m/f	kel ay vo·trer ... fa·vo·ree(t)
sportsperson	*sportif/ sportive* m/f	spor·teef/ spor·teev
team	*équipe* f	ay·keep

For more sports, see the **dictionary**.

going to a game

Would you like to go to a game?
Vous voulez aller voo voo·lay a·lay
voir un match? vwar um matsh

Who's playing?
Qui joue? kee zhoo

Who's winning?
Qui est en train de gagner? kee ay ton trun der ga·nyay

What was the final score?
Quel est le score final? kel ay ler skor fee·nal

It was a draw.
Ils ont fait match nul. eel zon fay matsh newl

That was a	C'était vraiment	say·tay vray·mon
... game.	un ... match.	um ... matsh
bad	mauvais	mo·vay
good	bon	bon
great	beau	bo

score!

What a ...!	Quel(le) ...! m/f	kel ...
goal	but m	bewt
hit	coup m	koo
kick	tir m	teer
pass	passe f	pas
performance	performance f	pair·for·mons

| What's the score? | | |
| Quel est le score? | | kel ay ler skor |

draw/even	match nul	matsh newl
love	égalité	ryun
match-point	balle de match	bal der matsh
nil/zero	zéro	zay·ro

playing sport

Do you want to play?
Vous voulez jouer?   voo voo·lay zhoo·ay

Can I join in?
Je peux participer?   zher per par·tee·see·pay

Yes, that'd be great.
Oui, ça serait excellent.   wee sa se·ray tek·say·lon

I have an injury.
Je suis blessé.   zher swee blay·say

Your/My point.
Un point pour vous/moi.   um pwun poor voo/mwa

Kick/Pass it to me!
Passez-le-moi!   pa·say·ler·mwa

You're a good player.
Vous jouez bien.   voo zhoo·ay byun

Thanks for the game.
Merci d'avoir joué   mair·see da·vwar zhoo·ay
avec moi.   a·vek mwa

Where's the best place to jog around here?
Où peut-on faire   oo per·ton fair
du jogging?   dew zho·geeng

Where's a	*Où y a t-il un/*	oo ee a teel un/
nearby ...?	*une ... par ici?* m/f	ewn ... par ee·see
gym	*gymnase* m	zheem·naz
swimming pool	*piscine* f	pee·seen
tennis court	*terrain* m	tay·run
	de tennis	der tay·nees

sports

Can I ..., please?	Puis-je ..., s'il vous plaît?	pweezh ... seel voo play
have a list of aerobic sessions	avoir une liste des cours d'aérobic	a·vwar ewn leest day koor da·ay·ro·beek
rent a locker	louer un casier	loo·way ung ka·zyay
see the gym	voir le gymnase	vwar ler zheem·naz

What's the charge per ...?	Quel est le prix ...?	kel ay ler pree ...
day	par jour	par zhoor
game	de la séance	der la say·ons
hour	de l'heure	der ler
visit	de la visite	der la vee·zeet

gender rules

Don't forget:

> when you see an m, it means 'masculine', so the article you use will be either *un* un or *le* ler.

> when you see an f, it means 'feminine', so the article you use will be either *une* ewn or *la* la.

For more information, see **gender** in the **grammar** chapter, page 16.

Can I hire a ...?	Puis-je louer ...?	pwee·zher loo·way ...
bicycle	un vélo	un vay·lo
court	un terrain de tennis	un tay·run der tay·nees
racquet	une raquette	ewn ra·ket

Do I have to be a member to attend?
Faut-il être membre? · fo·teel e·trer mom·brer

Is there a women-only session/pool?
Y a-t-il une séance/piscine pour les femmes? · ya·teel ewn say·ons/pee·seen poor lay fam

Where are the changing rooms?
Où sont les vestiaires? · oo son lay vays·tyair

cycling

Where does the race finish?
Où finit la course?   oo fee·nee la koors

Where does it pass through?
Ça passe par où?   sa pas par oo

Who's winning?
Qui est en train de gagner?   kee ay ton trun der ga·nyay

Is today's leg very hard?
Est-ce que l'étape   es·ker lay·tap
d'aujourd'hui   do·zhoor·dwee
est très difficile?   ay tray dee·fee·seel

My favourite cyclist is …
Mon coureur cycliste   mon koo·rer see·kleest
favori, c'est …   fa·vo·ree say …

cyclist	*cycliste* m&f	see·kleest
hill stage	*fortes côtes* f	fort kot
leg (in race)	*étape* f	ay·tap
time trial	*course* f *contre*	koors kon·trer
	la montre	la mon·trer
winner	*gagnant(e)* m/f	ga·nyon(t)
the yellow jersey	*le maillot* m *jaune*	ler ma·yo zhon

For phrases on getting around by bicycle, see **transport**, page 45.

extreme sports

Are you sure this is safe?
Êtes-vous sûr que   et·voo sewr ker
c'est sans danger?   say son don·zhay

Is the equipment secure?
Est-ce que l'équipement   es·ker lay·keep·mon
est solide?   ay so·leed

This is insane!
C'est fou, ça!   say foo sa

abseiling	*rappel* m	ra·pel
bungy-jumping	*saut* m *à l'élastique*	so a lay·las·teek
caving	*spéléologie* f	spay·lay·o·lo·zhee
mountain biking	*vélo* m *tout-terrain*	vay·lo too tay·run
parascending	*parachutisme* m	pa·ra·shew·tees·mer
	ascensionnel	a·son·syo·nel
rock-climbing	*varappe* f	va·rap
skydiving	*parachutisme* m	pa·ra·shew·tees·mer
	en chute libre	on shewt lee·brer
white-water rafting	*rafting* m	raf·teeng

For phrases on hiking, see **outdoors**, page 129, and **camping**, page 55.

soccer/football

He's a great (player).
C'est un (joueur)   say tun (zhoo·er)
formidable.   for·mee·da·bler

Which team is at the top of the league?
Quelle équipe est en   kel ay·keep ay
tête du championnat?   ton tet dew shom·pyo·na

What a terrible team!
Quelle équipe lamentable!   kel ay·keep la·mon·ta·bler

corner	corner m	kor·nair
foul	faute f	fot
free kick	coup m franc	koo frong
goalkeeper	gardien m	gar·dyun
	de but	der bewt
offside	hors jeu	or zher
penalty	penalty m	pay·nal·tee
penalty kick	tir m de	teer der
	penalty	pay·nal·tee

skiing

le ski

How much is a pass?
C'est combien le   say kom·byun ler
forfait-skieurs?   for·fay skee·er

I'd like to hire ...	J'aimerais louer ...	zhem·ray loo·way ...
(snow) boots	des après-skis	day za·pray·skee
goggles	des lunettes	day lew·net
	de protection	der pro·tek·syon
poles	des bâtons de ski	day ba·ton der skee
skis	des skis	day skee
a ski suit	une	ewn
	combinaison	kom·bee·nay·zon
	de ski	der skee

Is it possible to go	C'est possible	say po·see·bler
... here?	de faire ... ici?	der fair ... ee·see
Alpine skiing	du ski alpin	dew skee al·pun
cross-country	du ski de fond	dew skee der fon
skiing		
snowboarding	le surf	ler serf
	des neiges	day nezh
tobogganing	du toboggan	dew to·bo·gon

sports

127

Can I take lessons?
Est-ce que je peux   es·ker zher per
prendre des leçons?   pron·drer day ler·son

What level is that slope?
Quelle est la difficulté   kel ay la dee·fee·kewl·tay
de cette piste?   der set peest

What are the skiing conditions like ...?	*Quel est l'état des pistes ...?*	kel ay lay·ta day peest ...
at (Mt Blanc)	*au (Mont Blanc)*	o (mon blong)
further down	*plus bas*	plew ba
higher up	*plus haut*	plew o

Which are the ... slopes?	*Quelles sont les pistes ...?*	kel son lay peest ...
advanced	*pour skieurs de niveau avancé*	poor skee·er der nee·von a·von·say
beginner	*pour débutants*	poor day·bew·ton
intermediate	*pour skieurs de niveau moyen*	poor skee·er der nee·vo mwa·yun

cable car	*téléphérique* m	tay·lay·fay·reek
chairlift	*télésiège* m	tay·lay·syezh
instructor	*moniteur* m	mo·nee·ter
resort	*station* m *de ski*	sta·syon der skee
ski-lift	*remonte-pente* m	rer·mont·pont
sled/sledge	*luge* f	lewzh

hiking

les randonnées

Where can I ...?	*Où est-ce que je peux ...?*	oo es·ker zher per ...
buy supplies	*acheter des provisions*	ash·tay day pro·vee·zyon
find out about hiking trails	*me renseigner sur les sentiers à suivre*	mer ron·se·nyay sewr lay son·tyay a swee·vrer
find someone who knows this area	*trouver quelqu'un qui connaît la région*	troo·vay kel·kun kee ko·nay la ray·zhyon
get a map	*trouver une carte*	troo·vay ewn kart
hire hiking gear	*louer du matériel de randonnée*	loo·way dew ma·tay·ryel der ron·do·nay
Do I need to take ...?	*Est-ce qu'il faut apporter ...?*	es·keel fo a·por·tay ...
bedding	*du matériel de couchage*	dew ma·tay·ryel der koo·shazh
food	*des vivres*	day vee·vrer
water	*de l'eau*	der lo

How long is the trail?
Le chemin fait combien de kilomètres?   ler shmun fay kom·byun der kee·lo·me·trer

Do we need a guide?
A-t-on besoin d'un guide?   a·tom ber·zwun dun geed

Are there guided treks?
Est-ce qu'il y a des marches organisées?   es·keel ya day marsh or·ga·nee·zay

Is it safe?
C'est sans danger? — say son don·zhay

Is there a hut there?
Y a-t-il une cabane là-bas? — ya·teel ewn ka·ban la·ba

When does it get dark?
À quelle heure fait-il nuit? — a kel er fay·teel nwee

Where's the nearest village?
Où est le village le plus proche? — oo ay ler vee·lazh ler plew prosh

Which is the ... route?	*Quel est l'itinéraire ...?*	kel ay lee·tee·nay·rair ...
easiest	*le plus facile à suivre*	ler plew fa·seel a swee·vrer
most interesting	*le plus intéressant*	ler plew zun·tay·ray·son
shortest	*le plus court*	ler plew koor

Where have you come from?
Vous êtes parti d'où? — voo zet par·tee doo

How long did it take?
Ça a pris combien de temps? — sa a pree kom·byun der tom

Does this path go to ...?
Est-ce que ce sentier mène à ...? — es·ker ser son·tyay men a ...

Can we go through here?
On peut passer par ici? — on per pa·say par ee·see

Is the water OK to drink?
Est-ce que l'eau est potable? — es·ker lo ay po·ta·bler

I'm lost.
Je suis perdu(e). m/f — zher swee pair·dew

Baignade Interdite!	be·nyad un·ter·deet	**No Swimming!**

at the beach

à la plage

Where's the ... beach?	*Où est la plage ...?*	oo ay la plazh ...
nearest	*la plus proche*	la plew prosh
nudist	*nudiste*	der new·deest
public	*publique*	pewb·leek

Is it safe to ... here?	*On peut ... sans danger?*	on per ... son don·zhay
dive	*plonger*	plon·zhay
swim	*nager*	na·zhay

What time is ... tide?	*À quelle heure est la marée ...?*	a kel er ay la ma·ray ...
high	*haute*	ot
low	*basse*	bas

How much for a an ...?	*Combien coûte ...?*	kom·byun koot ...
chair	*une chaise longue*	ewn shez longk
hut	*une cabine de bain*	ewn ka·been der bun
umbrella	*un parasol*	um pa·ra·sol

outdoors

weather

What's the weather like?
Quel temps fait-il? kel tom fay·teel

What's the weather forecast?
Quelles sont les prévisions kel son lay pray·vee·zyon
météo? may·tay·yo

(Today) It's ... *(Aujourd'hui)* (o·zhoor·dwee)
 Il fait ... eel fay ...
  cold *froid* frwa
  (very) hot *(très) chaud* (tray) sho
  windy *du vent* dew von

It's raining. *Il pleut.* eel pler
It's snowing. *Il neige.* eel nezh
It's cloudy. *Le temps est couvert.* ler tom ay koo·vair

flora & fauna

flore & faune

What ... is that? *Quel(le) est ...? m/f* kel ay ...
  animal *cet animal m* say ta·nee·mal
  bird *cet oiseau m* say wa·zo
  flower *cette fleur f* set fler
  tree *cet arbre m* say tar·brer

What's it used for? *Ça sert à quoi?* sa sair a kwa

Is it ...? *C'est ...?* say ...
  common *commun* ko·mun
  dangerous *dangereux* donzh·rer
  endangered *menacé de* mer·na·say der
 disparition dees·pa·ree·syon
  poisonous *vénéneux* vay·nay·ner
  protected *protégé* pro·tay·zhay

For geographical and agricultural terms and names of animals and plants, see the **dictionary**.

132

FOOD > eating out

Petit déjeuner per·tee day·zher·nay (breakfast) typically consists of bread and jam and a coffee or hot chocolate – pastries, yogurt and cereals might also be taken. *Déjeuner* day·zher·nay (lunch) is the main meal of the day and may involve a number of courses. *Dîner* dee·nay (dinner) is eaten around 8pm, and is a light version of lunch. Bread and wine feature at both lunch and dinner.

key language

vocabulaire de base

breakfast	*petit déjeuner* m	per·tee day·zher·nay
lunch	*déjeuner* m	day·zher·nay
dinner	*dîner* m	dee·nay
snack	*casse-croûte* m	kas·kroot
eat	*manger*	mon·zhay
drink	*boire*	bwar
daily special	*suggestion* f *du jour*	sew·zhes·tyon dew zhoor
set menu	*menu* m	mer·new
I'd like ...	*Je voudrais ...*	zher voo·dray ...
I'm starving!	*Je meurs de faim!*	zher mer der fum
Enjoy your meal!	*Bon appétit!*	bon na·pay·tee

finding a place to eat

où manger?

Can you recommend a ...?	*Est-ce que vous pouvez me conseiller ...?*	es·ker voo poo·vay mer kon·say·yay ...
bar	*un bar*	um bar
cafe	*un café*	ung ka·fay
restaurant	*un restaurant*	un res·to·ron

Where would you go for a celebration?
On va où pour faire la fête? on va oo poor fair la fet

Where would you go for ...?	*Où est-ce qu'on trouve ...?*	oo es kon troov ...
a cheap meal	*les restaurants bon marché*	lay res·to·ron bom mar·shay
local specialities	*les spécialités locales*	lay spay·sya·lee·tay lo·kal

I'd like to reserve a table for ...	*Je voudrais réserver une table pour ...*	zher voo·dray ray·zair·vay ewn ta·bler poor ...
(eight) o'clock	*(vingt) heures*	(vungt) er
(two) people	*(deux) personnes*	(der) pair·son

I'd like ..., please.	*Je voudrais ..., s'il vous plaît.*	zher voo·dray ... seel voo play
a table for (five)	*une table pour (cinq) personnes*	ewn ta·bler poor (sungk) pair·son
a table in the (non-)smoking area	*une table dans un endroit pour (non-)fumeurs*	ewn ta·bler don zun on·drwa poor (non-)few·mer
the wine list	*la carte des vins*	la kart day vun

Do you have ...?	*Est-ce que vous avez ...?*	es·ker voo za·vay ...
children's meals	*des repas enfants*	day rer·pa on·fon
a menu in English	*une carte en anglais*	ewn kart on ong·glay

Are you still serving food?
On peut toujours passer des commandes? om per too·zhoor pa·say day ko·mond

How long is the wait?
Il faut attendre combien de temps? eel fo a·ton·drer kom·byun der tom

at the restaurant

Can I see the menu, please?
Est-ce que je peux voir   es·ker zher per vwar
la carte, s'il vous plaît?   la kart seel voo play

What would you recommend?
Qu'est-ce que vous conseillez?   kes·ker voo kon·say·yay

I'll have what they're having.
Je prendrai la même   zher pron·dray la mem
chose qu'eux.   shoz ker

What's in that dish?
Quels sont les ingrédients?   kel son lay zun·gray·dyon

---

listen for ...

noo som kom·play
  Nous sommes complets.   **We're fully booked.**

noo na·von plew der ta·bler
  Nous n'avons plus   **We have no tables.**
  de tables.

oo voo·lay·voo voo zas·war
  Où voulez-vous vous   **Where would you like to**
  asseoir?   **sit?**

say fair·may
  C'est fermé.   **We're closed.**

um mo·mon
  Un moment.   **One moment.**

voo day·zee·ray
  Vous désirez?   **What can I get for you?**

voo voo·lay bwar kel·ker shoz on a·ton·don
  Vous voulez boire quelque   **Would you like a drink**
  chose en attendant?   **while you wait?**

vwa·la
  Voilà!   **Here you go!**

Does it take long to prepare?
Est-ce que la préparation va es·ker la pray·pa·ra·syon va
prendre beaucoup de temps? pron·drer bo·koo der tom

Is it self-serve?
C'est self-service? say self·sair·vees

Is service included in the bill?
Le service est compris? ler sair·vees ay kom·pree

Are these complimentary?
C'est gratuit ça? say gra·twee sa

We're just having drinks.
C'est juste pour des boissons. say zhewst poor day bwa·son

I'd like ...	*Je voudrais ...*	zher voo·dray ...
a local speciality	*une spécialité locale*	ewn spay·sya·lee·tay lo·kal
a meal fit for a king	*un repas digne d'un roi*	un rer·pa dee·nyer dun rwa

at the table

à table

Please bring ...	*Apportez-moi ..., s'il vous plaît.*	a·por·tay·mwa ... seel voo play
the bill	*l'addition*	la·dee·syon
a (wine)glass	*un verre (à vin)*	un vair (a vun)
toothpicks	*des cure-dents*	day kewr·don

I didn't order this.
Ce n'est pas ce que j'ai ser nay pa ser ker zhay
commandé. ko·mon·day

listen for ...

ay·may·voo ...	
Aimez-vous ...?	**Do you like ...?**
kel kwee·son	
Quelle cuisson?	**How would you like it cooked?**
zher voo kon·say ...	
Je vous conseille ...	**I suggest ...**

talking food

I love this dish.
J'adore ce plat.   zha·dor ser pla

We love the local cuisine.
Nous adorons la   noo za·do·ron la
cuisine locale.   kwee·zeen lo·kal

That was delicious!
C'était délicieux!   say·tay day·lee·syer

My compliments to the chef.
Mes compliments au chef.   may kom·plee·mon o shef

I'm full.
Je n'ai plus faim.   zher nay plew fum

Are you sure that wasn't horse?
Vous êtes certain que ce   voo·zet sair·tun ker ser
n'était pas du cheval?   nay·tay pa dew sher·val

This is ...	C'est ...	say ...
burnt	*brûlé*	brew·lay
(too) cold	*(trop) froid*	(tro) frwa
superb	*superbe*	sew·pairb

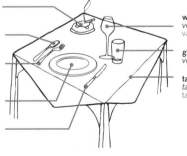

ashtray
cendrier m
son·dree·yay

spoon
cuillère f
kwee·yair

fork
fourchette f
foor·shet

plate
assiette f
a·syet

knife
couteau m
koo·to

wineglass
verre m *à vin*
vair a vun

glass
verre m

table
table f
ta·bler

eating out

137

meals

> breakfast

bacon	*bacon* m	bay·kon
bread	*pain* m	pun
butter	*beurre* m	ber
cereal	*céréales* m pl	say·ray·al
cheese	*fromage* m	fro·mazh
cornflakes	*cornflakes* m pl	korn·flayks
egg	*œuf* m	erf
jam	*confiture* f	kon·fee·tewr
margarine	*margarine* f	mar·ga·reen
milk	*lait* m	lay
muesli	*muesli* m	mewz·lee
omelette	*omelette* f	om·let
(with cheese)	*(au fromage)*	(o fro·mazh)
toast	*pain* m *grillé*	pung gree·yay

> light meals

What's that called?
    Ça s'appelle comment?   sa sa·pel ko·mon

I'd like ...,	*Je voudrais ...,*	zher voo·dray ...
please.	*s'il vous plaît.*	seel voo play
one slice	*un morceau*	um mor·so
(of pizza)	*(de pizza)*	(der peed·za)
a sandwich	*un sandwich*	un sond·weetsh
that one	*ça*	sa

For typical dishes see the **culinary reader**, page 153, and for other food items see the **dictionary**.

methods of preparation

I'd like it ...	J'aime ça ...	zhem sa ...
I don't want it ...	Je ne veux pas ça ...	zher ner ver pa sa ...
boiled	bouilli	boo·yee
broiled	grillé	gree·yay
fried	frit	free
grilled	grillé	gree·yay
mashed	en purée	on pew·ray
medium	à point	a pwun
rare	saignant	say·nyon
re-heated	réchauffé	ray·sho·fay
steamed	à la vapeur	a la va·per
well-done	bien cuit	byun kwee
with the dressing on the side	avec la sauce à côté	a·vek la sos a ko·tay
without dressing/ sauce	sans sauce	son sos

For other specific meal requests, see **vegetarian & special meals**, page 149.

you might read ...

Amuse-gueule	a·mewz·gerl	Appetizers
Soupes	soop	Soups
Entrées	on·tray	Entrees
Salades	sa·lad	Salads
Plat Principal	pla prun·see·pal	Main Course
Desserts	day·sair	Desserts
Apéritifs	a·pay·ree·teef	Aperitifs
Spiritueux	spee·ree·twer	Spirits
Bières	byair	Beers
Vins Mousseux	vum moo·ser	Sparkling Wines
Vins Blancs	vum blong	White Wines
Vins Rouges	vun roozh	Red Wines
Vins de Dessert	vun der day·sair	Dessert Wines

condiments

I'd like ...,	Je voudrais ...,	zher voo·dray ...
please.	s'il vous plaît.	seel voo play
ketchup	le ketchup	ler ketsh·erp
pepper	le poivre	ler pwa·vrer
salt	le sel	ler sel
tomato sauce	la sauce tomate	la sos to·mat
vinegar	le vinaigre	ler vee·nay·grer

in the bar

Excuse me.	Excusez-moi.	ek·skew·zay·mwa
I'm next.	C'est mon tour.	say mon toor
I'll have (a gin).	Je prends (un gin).	zher pron (un zheen)

Same again, please.
La même chose, s'il vous plaît.   la mem shoz seel voo play

No ice, thanks.
Pas de glaçons, merci.   pa der gla·son mair·see

I'll buy you a drink.
Je vous offre un verre.   zher voo zo·frer un vair

What would you like?
Qu'est-ce que vous voulez?   kes·ker voo voo·lay

It's my round.
C'est ma tournée.   say ma toor·nay

You can get the next one.
La prochaine fois c'est vous   la pro·shen fwa say voo
qui payerez la tournée.   kee pay·ray la toor·nay

How much alcohol does this contain?
Quelle est la teneur   kel ay la te·ner
alcoolique?   al·ko·leek

Do you serve meals here?
Faites-vous les repas ici?   fet·voo lay rer·pa ee·see

nonalcoholic drinks

... mineral water	*eau minérale ...*	o mee·nay·ral ...
sparkling	*gazeuse*	ga·zerz
still	*non-gazeuse*	nong·ga·zerz
orange juice	*jus* m *d'orange*	zhew do·ronzh
soft drink	*boisson* f	bwa·son
	non-alcoolisée	non·al·ko·lee·zay
(hot) water	*eau* f *(chaude)*	o (shod)
(cup of) tea ...	*(un) thé ...*	(un) tay ...
(cup of) coffee ...	*(un) café ...*	(ung) ka·fay ...
with milk	*au lait*	o lay
without/	*sans/avec*	son/a·vek
with sugar	*sucre*	sew·krer

alcoholic drinks

beer	*bière* f	byair
brandy	*cognac* m	ko·nyak
champagne	*champagne* m	shom·pan·yer
cocktail	*cocktail* m	kok·tel
a shot of ...	*un petit verre de ...*	um per·tee vair der ...
gin	*gin*	zheen
rum	*rhum*	rom
tequila	*tequila*	tay·kee·la
vodka	*vodka*	vod·ka
whisky	*whisky*	wees·kee

a bottle of	*une bouteille*	ewn boo·tay
... wine	*de vin ...*	der vun ...
a glass of ... wine	*un verre de vin ...*	un vair der vun ...
dessert	*de dessert*	der day·sair
red	*rouge*	roozh
rose	*rosé*	ro·zay
sparkling	*mousseux*	moo·ser
table	*de table*	der ta·bler
white	*blanc*	blong
a ... of beer	*... de bière*	... der byair
glass	*un verre*	un vair
large bottle	*une grande bouteille*	ewn grond boo·tay
pint	*un demi*	un der·mee
small bottle	*une petite bouteille*	ewn per·teet boo·tay

one too many?

Thanks, but I don't feel like it.
Je n'en ai pas envie,   zher non ay pa on·vee
merci.   mair·see

No thanks, I'm driving.
Non merci, je conduis.   non mair·see zher kon·dwee

I don't drink alcohol.
Je ne bois pas d'alcool.   zher ner bwa pa dal·kol

This is hitting the spot.
C'est justement ce qu'il   say zhewst·mon ser keel
me faut.   mer fo

I'm tired, I'd better go home.
Je suis fatigué,   zher swee fa·tee·gay
je dois rentrer.   zher dwa ron·tray

Where's the toilet?
Où sont les toilettes?   oo son lay twa·let

I'm feeling drunk.
Je suis ivre.   zher swee zee·vrer

I feel fantastic!
Je me sens vachement bien!   zher mer son vash·mon byun

I really, really love you.
Je t'aime vraiment beaucoup.   zher tem vray·mon bo·koo

santé!

Blend right into the crowd with these handy drinking phrases:

Cheers!	*Santé!*	son·tay
To the chef!	*Au chef!*	o shef
Here's to everyone!	*À tout le monde!*	a too ler mond
Here's to France!	*À la France!*	a la frons
Have another!	*Encore un coup!*	ong·kor ung koo
Skol, skol, skol!	*Cul sec!*	kew sec

No, it isn't the alcohol talking.
Non, c'est moi qui dis ça,   non say mwa kee dee sa
ce n'est pas l'alcool qui parle.   ser nay pa lal·kol kee parl

I think I've had one too many.
Je pense que j'ai bu   zher pons ker zhay bew
un coup de trop.   ung koo der tro

Can you call a taxi for me?
Pouvez-vous appeler   poo·vay·voo a·play
un taxi pour moi?   un tak·see poor mwa

I don't think you should drive.
Je ne pense pas que vous   zher ner pons pa ker voo
êtes en état de conduire.   zet on ay·ta der kon·dweer

I'm pissed.
Je suis bourré.   zher swee boo·ray

I feel ill.
Je me sens malade.   zher mer son ma·lad

Maybe a Bloody Mary will make me feel better.
Peut-être qu'un Bloody   per·te·trer kum bla·dee
Mary me fera du bien.   may·ree mer fer·ra dew byun

---

listen for ...

kes·ker voo der·zee·ray pron·drer
Qu'est-ce que vous   **What'll it be?**
desirez prendre?

zher pons ker sa sew·fee
Je pense que ça suffit.   **I think you've had enough.**

key language

vocabulaire de base

cooked	*cuit(e)* m/f	kwee(t)
dried	*sec/sèche* m/f	sek/sesh
fresh	*frais/fraîche* m/f	fray/fresh
frozen	*surgelé(e)* m/f	sewr·zher·lay
old	*vieux/vieille* m/f	vyer/vyay
raw	*cru(e)* m/f	krew
smoked	*fumé(e)* m/f	few·may
stale	*rassis(e)* m/f	ra·see(z)

buying food

acheter de la nourriture

How much is (a kilo of cheese)?
C'est combien (le kilo   say kom·byun (ler kee·lo
de fromage)?   der fro·mazh)

What's the local speciality?
Quelle est la spécialité locale?   kel ay la spay·sya·lee·tay lo·kal

What's that?
Qu'est-ce que c'est, ça?   kes·ker say sa

Can I taste it?
Je peux goûter?   zher per goo·tay

bakers' boules

The word for 'baker', *boulanger* boo·lon·zhay, comes
from *boule* bool, 'ball': the shape of the first loaves of
bread. Bread is still made in the shape of a *boule*.

How much?	Combien?	kom·byun
I'd like ...	Je voudrais ...	zher voo·dray ...
(200) grams	(deux cents) grammes	(der son) gram
(two) kilos	(deux) kilos	(der) kee·lo
(three) pieces	(trois) morceaux	(trwa) mor·so
(six) slices	(six) tranches	(sees) tronsh
some of that/those	de ça	der sa
Do you have ...?	Est-ce que vous avez ...?	es·ker voo za·vay ...
anything	quelque chose	kel·ker shoz
cheaper	de moins cher	der mwun shair
other kinds	autre chose	o·trer shoz

For other useful amounts, see **numbers & amounts**, page 28.

listen for ...

eel non rest plew
Il n'en reste plus.

There's none left.

ker pwee·zher fair poor voo
Que puis-je faire pour vous?

Can I help you?

ong·kor kel·ker shoz
Encore quelque chose?

Would you like anything else?

sa fay (sungk er·ro)
Ça fait (cinq euros).

That's (five euros).

sa say (tung ka·mom·bair)
Ça, c'est (un camembert).

That's (a camembert).

voo day·zee·ray
Vous désirez?

What would you like?

zher non ay plew
Je n'en ai plus.

I don't have any.

FOOD

146

Where can I find the ... section?	*Où est-ce qu'on trouve le rayon ...?*	oo es kon troov ler ray·yon ...
dairy	*des produits laitiers*	day pro·dwee lay·tyay
frozen goods	*des surgelés*	day sewr·zher·lay
fruit and vegetable	*des fruits et légumes*	day frwee ay lay·gewm
meat	*viande*	vyond
poultry	*volaille*	vo·lai

Can I have a bag, please?
Puis-je avoir un sac, s'il vous plaît? — pweezh a·vwar un sak, seel voo play

Where is the health-food section?
Où se trouve le rayon bio? — oo ser troov ler ray·yon bee·yo

Where is the health-food store?
Où se trouve la boutique bio? — oo ser troov la boo·teek bee·yo

For food items see the **culinary reader**, page 153, and the **dictionary**.

cooking utensils

ustensiles de cuisine

bottle opener	*ouvre-bouteilles* m	oo·vrer·boo·tay
bowl	*bol* m	bol
can opener	*ouvre-boîtes* m	oo·vrer·bwat
chopping board	*planche* f à découper	plonsh a day·koo·pay
corkscrew	*tire-bouchon* m	teer·boo·shon
fork	*fourchette* f	foor·shet
fridge	*réfrigérateur* m	ray·free·zhay·ra·ter
frying pan	*poêle* f à frire	pwal a freer
knife	*couteau* m	koo·to
oven	*four* m	foor
plate	*assiette* f	a·syet
saucepan	*casserole* f	kas·rol
spoon	*cuillère* f	kwee·yair
toaster	*grille-pain* m	gree·pun

vive le cheese!

There are over 400 kinds of cheese in France, from subtle cream cheeses to pungent, whiplash-inducing mould cheeses. Like wines, some cheeses are particular to certain regions and have been awarded an *appellation d'origine* a·pe·la·syon do·ree·zheen, which guarantees the cheese's origin. Cheeses can be broadly grouped into the following styles:

... cheese	fromage ...	fro·mazh ...
goat's milk	de chèvre	der she·vrer
hard	à pâte dure	a pat dewr
sheep's milk	de brebis	der brer·bee
soft	à pâte molle	a pat mol

Here are three fine examples:

> *Brebis des Pyrénées* brer·bee der pee·ray·nay cheese made with ewe's milk, from the Basque region
> *Coulommiers* koo·lom·yay soft, creamy cheese of the Brie family
> *Pont l'Evêque* pon·lay·vek soft and runny cow's milk cheese with a strong and pungent taste

vegetarian & special meals

les repas végétariens & les régimes

ordering

Is there a ... restaurant near here?
*Y a-t-il un restaurant
... par ici?*
ya·teel un res·to·ron
... par ee·see

Do you have ... food?
Vous faites les repas ...?
voo fet lay rer·pa ...

halal	*halal* m&f	a·lal
kosher	*casher* m&f	ka·shair
vegetarian	*végétarien(ne)* m/f	vay·zhay·ta·ryun
		vay·zhay·ta·ryen

**Can I order this
without ... in it?**
*Je peux commander
ça sans ...?*
zher per ko·mon·day
sa son ...

**Could you prepare
a meal without ...?**
*Pouvez-vous
préparer
un repas sans ...?*
poo·vay·voo
pray·pa·ray
un rer·pa son ...

butter	*du beurre*	dew ber
eggs	*des œufs*	day zer
meat stock	*du*	dew
	bouillon gras	boo·yon gra

listen for ...

say kee·zee·nay avek der la vyond
*C'est cuisiné avec de
la viande.*
It has meat in it.

voo poo·vay mon·zhay ...?
Vous pouvez manger ...?
Can you eat ...?

zher vay der·mon·day o kwee·zee·nyay/shef
*Je vais demander au
cuisinier/chef.*
**I'll check with the
cook/chef.**

Is this ...?	C'est un produit ...?	say tun pro·dwee ...
free of animal produce	qui n'est pas d'origine animale	kee nay pa do·ree·zheen a·nee·mal
free-range	de ferme	der fairm
genetically modified	qui contient des organismes génétiquement modifiés	kee kon·tyun day zor·ga·nees·mer zhay·nay·teek·mom mo·dee·fyay
gluten-free	sans gluten	son glew·ten
halal	halal	a·lal
kosher	casher	ka·shair
low in sugar	à faible teneur en sucre	a fe·bler ter·ner on sew·krer
low-fat	allégé	a·lay·zhay
organic	biologique	byo·lo·zheek
salt-free	sans sel	son sel

special diets & allergies

régimes & allergies alimentaires

I'm ...	Je suis ...	zher swee ...
Buddhist	bouddhiste m&f	boo·deest
Hindu	hindou(e) m/f	un·doo
Jewish	juif/juive m/f	zhweef/zhweev
Muslim	musulman(e) m/f	mew·zewl·mon/ mew·zewl·man
vegan	végétalien(ne) m/f	vay·zhay·ta·lyun/ vay·zhay·ta·lyen
vegetarian	végétarien(ne) m/f	vay·zhay·ta·ryun/ vay·zhay·ta·ryen

I'm allergic to ...	Je suis allergique ...	zher swee za·lair·zheek ...
animal products	aux aliments d'origine animale	o za·lee·mon do·ree·zheen a·nee·mal
caffeine	à la caféine	a la ka·fay·een
dairy produce	aux produits laitiers	o pro·dwee lay·tyay
eggs	aux œufs	o zer
fish	au poisson	o pwa·son
gelatin	à la gélatine	a la zhay·la·teen
genetically modified food	à la nourriture contenant des organismes génétiquement modifiés	a la noo·ree·tewr kon·ter·non day zor·ga·nees·mer zhay·nay·teek·mom mo·dee·fyay
gluten	au gluten	o glew·ten
honey	au miel	o myel
MSG	au glutamate de sodium	o glew·ta·mat der so·dyom
pork	au porc	o por
poultry	à la volaille	a la vo·lai
red meat	à la viande rouge	a la vyond roozh
seafood	aux fruits de mer	o frwee der mair
shellfish	aux crustacés	o krew·sta·say
wheat flour	à la farine de blé	a la fa·reen der blay

going nuts

There is no single word to translate 'nuts'. You have to say which kind of nut you mean, for example *noix* nwa, 'walnut', *cacahuète* ka·ka·wet, 'peanut', or *noisette* nwa·zet, 'hazelnut'.

I don't eat/drink ...
   Je ne mange/bois pas ...   zher ner monzh/bwa pa ...

I'm on a special diet.
   Je suis un régime.   zher swee un ray·zheem

I can't eat it for ...	*Je ne mange*	zher ner monzh
	pas ça ...	pa sa ...
health reasons	*pour des raisons*	poor day ray·zon
	de santé	der son·tay
philosophical	*pour des raisons*	poor day ray·zon
reasons	*philosophiques*	fee·lo·zo·feek
religious reasons	*à cause de*	a koz der
	ma religion	ma rer·lee·zhyon

y oh y

If you see a consonant followed by a y in the phonetic guide for a word or phrase, remember that it's a consonant sound, like the 'y' in 'you' – it's never a vowel sound. For more on vowels and consonants, see **pronunciation**, page 9.

This miniguide to French cuisine is designed to help you navigate menus. French nouns, and adjectives affected by gender, have their gender indicated by ⓜ or ⓕ. If it's a plural noun, you'll also see pl.

A

abats ⓜ a·ba *giblets*
— **de boucherie** der boo·shree *offal*

abricot ⓜ ab·ree·ko *apricot*

addition ⓕ a·dee·syon
bill · check

agneau ⓜ a·nyo *lamb*
— **de lait** ⓜ der lay
baby lamb · spring lamb

aiguillette ⓕ ay·gwee·yet
long & thin slice of meat, usually poultry breast, especially duck

ail ⓜ ai *garlic*

aile ⓕ ayl *wing (bird or poultry)*

aïoli ⓜ ay·o·lee *garlic flavoured mayonnaise sauce, served cold*

à la a la *served with · in the style of*

alcool ⓜ al·kol *alcohol*

aligot ⓜ a·lee·go *mashed potatoes, garlic & melted cheese (Auvergne)*

alouette ⓕ al·wet *lark*

alsacienne al·zas·yen '
Alsatian style' – dish usually garnished with sauerkraut, pork, sausages or simmered with wine & mushrooms

amande ⓕ a·mond *almond*
— **de mer** der mair
queen or bay scallop

américaine a·may·ree·ken
'American style' – generally a dish of fish or shellfish, particularly lobster, flamed in brandy & simmered in white wine & tomatoes

amuse-gueule ⓜ a·mewz·gerl
cocktail snack or appetiser

ananas ⓜ a·na·nas *pineapple*

anchoïade ⓕ on·sho·yad
dip of pureed anchovies mixed with garlic & olive oil (Provence)

anchois ⓜ on·shwa *anchovy*

ancienne on·syen
'old style' – depending on the meat used, can be served in a cream sauce with mushrooms, vegetables, onions or shallots, and/or with wine & herbs

andouille ⓕ on·doo·yer *smoked sausage made of pork tripe usually eaten cold*

andouillette ⓕ on·doo·yet
smaller version of andouille

aneth ⓜ a·net *dill*

anglaise ong·glayz
'English style' – usually boiled meat or vegetables · breaded & fried vegetables, meat, fish or poultry

anguille ⓕ ong·gee·yer *eel*

anis ⓜ a·nees *anis · aniseed*

appellation d'origine contrôlée (AOC) ⓕ a·pe·la·syon do·ree·zheen kon·tro·lay (a o say)
refers to officially recognised produce with a guarantee of origin

artichaut ⓜ ar·tee·sho *artichoke*

asperge ⓕ a·spairzh *asparagus*

assiette ⓕ a·syet *plate*
— **anglaise** ong·glayz
assorted cold meats & gherkins
— **de charcuterie** der shar·kew·tree
assorted pork & other meat products, including sausages, hams, pates & rillettes
— **variée** va·ree·ay *assorted vegetables and/or meat or fish products*

assorti(e) ⓜ/ⓕ a·sor·tee *assorted*

au o *served as in* • *in the style of*

aubergine ① o·bair·zheen *eggplant*

avocat ⓜ a·vo·ka *avocado*

B

baba au rhum ⓜ ba·ba o rom *small sponge cake, often with raisins, soaked in a rum-flavoured syrup after baking*

bacon ⓜ bay·kon *bacon*
— **fumé** few·may *smoked bacon*
— **maigre** may·grer *lean bacon*

baguette ① ba·get *long & crispy loaf of bread* • *chopstick*

ballottine ① ba·lo·teen *boned meat, stuffed & poached*
— **de volaille** der vo·lai *poultry ballottine stuffed with forcemeat*

banane ① ba·nan *banana*

barbue ① bar·bew *brill or barbel, a carp-like fish*

barquette ① bar·ket *small boat-shaped shell made of shortcrust pastry (sometimes puff pastry) with sweet or savoury fillings*

basilic ⓜ ba·zee·leek *basil*

basquaise bas·kayz *'Basque style' – usually prepared with tomatoes & sweet or red peppers*

bavarois ⓜ ba·va·rwa *Bavarian – a cold mousse-like dessert of cream and/or fruit puree*

bavaroise ① ba·va·rwaz *syrupy tea that can be set into ice cream*

bavette ① ba·vet *'bib apron' – flank steak*

béarnaise ① bay·ar·nayz *white sauce made of wine or vinegar beaten with egg yolks & flavoured with herbs*

bécasse ① bay·kas *woodcock, a game bird*

Béchamel ① bay·sha·mel *milk-based sauce*

belon ⓜ ber·lon *round pinkish oyster*

Bercy bair·see *'Bercy style' – butter, white wine & shallot sauce*

betterave ① be·trav *beetroot*

beurre ⓜ ber *butter*
— **blanc** blong *white sauce made of a vinegar & white wine reduction blended with softened butter & shallots*
— **noir** nwar *'black butter' – butter browned until nearly burned, sometimes flavoured with capers & parsley*
— **ravigote** ra·vee·got *butter with herbs*

bien cuit(e) ⓜ/① byun kwee(t) *well-done*

bière ① bee·yair *beer*
— **blonde** blond *light-coloured or pale beer* • *lager*
— **en bouteille** on boo·tay *bottled beer*
— **brune** brewn *dark beer or stout*
— **lager** la·ger *lager*
— **pression** pre·syon *draught* • *draft beer* • *beer on tap*

bifteck ⓜ beef·tek *steak*

bio(logique) byo(·lo·zheek) *organic*

biscuit ⓜ bees·kwee *biscuit* • *cookie*

bisque ① beesk *spicy shellfish soup or chowder, with cream & Cognac*

blanc de blanc blong der blong *white wine made of white grapes with white juice*

blanc de volaille ⓜ blong der vo·lai *boned breast of fowl, cooked without browning*

blanquette de veau ① blong·ket der vo *veal stew in white sauce enriched with cream*

blé ⓜ blay *wheat*

bleu ⓜ bler *blue-veined cheese, often used to flavour dishes or sauces* • *nearly raw beef* • *fish boiled in vinegar bouillon*

bœuf ⓜ berf *beef*
— **bourguignon** boor·geen·yon *chunks of beef marinated in red wine, spices & herbs, stewed with mushrooms, onions & bacon*
— **en daube** on dob *chunks of beef & chopped ham flamed in Armagnac brandy & stewed with red wine, onions, garlic, vegetables & herbs*
— **miroton** mee·ro·ton *pre-cooked boiled beef slices, usually left over from pot-au-feu, gently stewed with onions*
— **à la mode** a la mod *larded chunks of beef, braised in wine, either served hot with carrots & onions, or cold in aspic*

boisson ⓕ bwa·son *drink • beverage*
— **non alcoolisée** non al·ko·lee·zay *soft drink*

bombe glacée ⓕ bom·ber gla·say *ice cream dessert – two different ice creams moulded together in a cone shape, decorated with candied fruits, candied (glazed) chestnuts & Chantilly cream*

bonbon ⓜ bom·bon *sweet/candy*

bordelaise bor·der·layz *red wine sauce with shallots, beef juices, thyme & sometimes boletus mushrooms*

bouchée ⓕ boo·shay *various types of cocktail snacks or small puffs with a variety of fillings, served hot or cold*

boucherie ⓕ boo·shree *butcher's shop*

boudin ⓜ boo·dun *smooth sausage, may be grilled or pan-fried*
— **blanc** blong *white veal, pork or chicken sausage*
— **noir** nwar *black pork blood sausage (see also sanguette)*

bouillabaisse ⓕ bwee·ya·bes *soup traditionally made of assorted fish stewed in a broth with garlic, orange peel, fennel, tomatoes &*

saffron. Modern versions include lobster & shrimps. The broth & the fish may be served separately, with croutons & rouille. (Marseilles)

bouillon ⓜ boo·yon *broth • stock*

boulangerie ⓕ boo·lon·zhree *bakery*

boulette ⓕ boo·let *small meatball or croquette (often leftovers) sauteed, browned or poached in a broth*

boulghour ⓜ bool·goor *bulgur wheat*

bouquet garni ⓜ boo·kay gar·nee *mix of herbs tied together – usually parsley, bay leaf & thyme*

bourguignonne boor·gee·nyon *'Burgundy style' – dishes may include button mushrooms, bacon & pearl onions or shallots, braised in red wine*

bourride ⓕ boo·reed *fish soup or stew using firm whitefish like monkfish*

bouteille ⓕ boo·tay *bottle*

brandade de morue ⓕ bron·dad der mo·rew *salt cod pureed with milk, olive oil, garlic & sometimes mashed potatoes*

brebis ⓕ brer·bee *ewe (female sheep)*

brème ⓕ brem *bream*

brioche ⓕ bree·yosh *small roll or cake made of yeast, flour, eggs & butter, sometimes flavoured with nuts, currants or candied fruits*

broche ⓕ brosh *spit roast*

brochet ⓜ bro·shay *pike*

brochette ⓕ bro·shet *grilled skewer of meat, fish or vegetables*

brocoli ⓜ bro·ko·lee *broccoli*

brouillé(e) ⓜ/ⓕ broo·yay *scrambled*

brûlot ⓜ brew·lo *sugar flamed in brandy & added to coffee*

brut ⓜ brewt *extra dry (Champagne)*

bûche de Noël ⓕ bewsh der no·el *traditionally served for Christmas – a rolled sponge cake filled & covered with butter-cream (usually chocolate, vanilla or coffee flavoured) or ice cream*

C

cabillaud ⓜ ka·bee·yo *cod*

cacahuete ⓜ ka·ka·wet *peanut*

cacao ⓜ ka·ka·o *cocoa*

café ⓜ ka·fay *cafe • coffee*

caille ⓕ kay·yer *quail*

caillette ⓕ kay·yet *rissole or meatball*

calmar ⓜ kal·mar *squid*

canard ⓜ ka·nar *duck*
  — **à l'orange** a lo·ronzh
  *duck braised with Cognac &
  Cointreau, served with oranges & an
  orange-based sauce*
  — **à la rouennaise** a la roo·en·nayz
  stuffed duck in a red wine sauce

cannelé ⓜ ka·ner·lay *brioche-like
  pastry made with corn flour, often
  spelled canallé (Bordeaux)*

cannelle ⓕ ka·nel *cinnamon*

câpre ⓕ kap·rer *caper*

carbonnade ⓕ kar·bo·nad *selection of
  char-grilled meats (often pork)*
  — **de bœuf** der berf
  *stew of beef slices, onions & herbs,
  simmered in beer (Northern France)*

carotte ⓕ ka·rot *carrot*

carpe ⓕ karp *carp*

carré ⓜ ka·ray *loin or rib*
  — **d'agneau** da·nyo *rack of lamb*
  — **de porc (au chou)** der por (o shoo)
  loin of pork (with cabbage)

carte ⓕ kart *menu*
  — **des vins** day vun *wine list*

cassate ⓕ ka·sat *ice cream combining
  different flavours, often studded
  with candied fruits*

casse-croûte ⓜ kas·kroot *snack*

cassis ⓜ ka·sees *blackcurrant (liqueur)*

cassoulet ⓜ ka·soo·lay
  *casserole or stew with beans & meat
  (southwest France)*

céleri ⓜ sayl·ree *celery*

cendre son·drer *baked in the embers*

cépage ⓜ say·pazh *grape or vine variety*

cèpe ⓕ sep *wild mushroom of the
  boletus family known for its full
  flavour & meaty texture*

céréale ⓕ say·ray·al *cereal or grain*

cerf ⓜ ser *venison • stag deer*

cerise ⓕ ser·reez *cherry*

cervelas ⓜ sair·ver·la *fat pork sausage
  cured with garlic & eaten hot*

cervelle ⓕ sair·vel *brain*

champignon ⓜ shom·pee·nyon
  mushroom
  — **de Paris** der pa·ree
  button mushroom

chanterelle ⓕ shon·trel
  boletus mushroom – same as girolle

Chantilly ⓕ shon·tee·yee *sweetened
  whipped cream flavoured with vanilla*

chapon ⓜ sha·pon *capon, castrated cock*

charbonnade ⓕ shar·bo·nad
  char-grilled meat

charcuterie ⓕ shar·kew·tree *variety of
  pork products that are cured, smoked
  or processed, including sausages,
  hams, pates & rillettes • the shop
  where these products are sold*

charlotte ⓕ shar·lot *dessert of bread
  slices or sponge fingers, lining a
  deep, round mould, filled with fruits,
  whipped cream or a fruit mousse*

chasselas ⓜ sha·sla *type of white grape*

chasseur sha·ser
  *'hunter' – sauce of white wine with
  mushrooms, shallots & bacon cubes*

châtaigne ⓕ shar·tayn·yer *chestnut*

chateaubriand ⓜ sha·to·bree·yon
  thick fillet or rump steak

chaud(e) ⓜ/ⓕ sho(d) *hot • warm*

chaud-froid ⓜ sho·frwa
  *'hot-cold' – a piece of poached or
  roasted meat, poultry or fish that,*

while cooling, is coated with a white creamy sauce that solidifies

chaudrée ① sho-dray *Atlantic fish stew*

chef de cuisine ⓜ shef der kwee-zeen *chef*

cheval ⓜ sher-val *horse • horsemeat*

chèvre ① she-vrer
goat • goat's milk cheese

chevreuil ⓜ sher-vrer-yer *venison*

chicorée ① shee-ko-ray *chicory/endive*

chipolata ① shee-po-la-ta
chipolata, a small sausage

chocolat ⓜ sho-ko-la *chocolate*
— **chaud** sho *hot chocolate*

chou ⓜ shoo *cabbage*
— **de Bruxelles** der brew-sel
Brussels sprout
— **rouge** roozh *red cabbage*

chou-fleur ⓜ shoo-fler *cauliflower*

choucroute ① shoo-kroot *sauerkraut*

ciboule ① see-bool *spring onion • shallot*

cidre ⓜ see-drer *cider*

citron ⓜ see-tron *lemon*

citron pressé ⓜ see-tron pray-say
freshly squeezed lemon juice

citronnade ① see-tro-nad *lemon squash • lemonade*

citrouille ① see-troo-yer *pumpkin*

civelle ① see-vel *small eel or alevin, generally served fried*

civet ⓜ see-vay *stew usually containing game marinated in red wine*

clam ⓜ klam *clam*

cochon ⓜ ko-shon *pig*
— **de lait** der lay *suckling pig*

cocktail ⓜ kok-tel *cold starter of shellfish & raw vegetables or fruits*

cœur ⓜ ker *heart*
— **de filet** der fee-lay *tenderloin steak*

coing ⓜ kwung *quince*

commande ① ko-mond *order*

compote ⓜ kom-pot *stewed fruit*

compris(e) ⓜ/① kom-pree(z) *included*

concombre ⓜ kong-kom-brer *cucumber*

confiserie ① kon-feez-ree
confectionery (sweets in general) • sweet shop or candy store

confit ⓜ kon-fee
preserved meat, usually duck, goose or pork. The meat is cooked in fat until it is tender, then potted & covered with the fat to preserve it.

confiture ① kon-fee-tewr *jam*

congolais ⓜ kong-go-lay
small coconut meringue cake

consommation ① kon-so-ma-syon
consumption • the general term for food & drink ordered in a cafe

consommé ⓜ kon-so-may *clarified meat, poultry or fish-based broth used as a base for sauces & soups*
— **à la printanière** a la prun-tan-yair
consommé with spring vegetables

contre-filet ⓜ kon-trer-fee-lay
beef sirloin roast

coq ⓜ kok *cockerel • rooster*
— **de bruyère** der brwew-yair *grouse*

coque ① kok *cockle*

coquelet ⓜ ko-klay *young cockerel*

coquillage ⓜ ko-kee-yazh *shellfish*

coquille Saint-Jacques ① ko-kee-yer
sun-zhak *scallop*

corbeille de fruits ① kor-bay-yer der
frwee *basket of assorted fruits*

cornichon ⓜ kor-nee-shon *gherkin*

côte ① kot *chop containing eye fillet*

côtelette ① kot-let *cutlet • chop*

coulis ⓜ koo-lee *fruit or vegetable puree, usually used as a sauce*

courge ① koorzh *gourd or marrow*

courgette ① koor-zhet
zucchini • baby marrow

couvert ⓜ koo-vair
number of people in a group at a restaurant • cover charge
— **gratuit** gra-twee *no cover charge*

— vin et service compris vun ay sair·vees kom·pree *price includes wine, service & cover charges*

crabe ⓜ krab *crab*

crème ⓕ krem *cream • a dessert with cream • a cream-based soup*
— anglaise ong·glayz *custard*
— crue krew
raw or unpasteurised cream
— fouettée fwe·tay *whipped cream*
— fraîche fresh *naturally thickened cream, has a slightly sour tang*
— glacée gla·say *ice cream*

crêpe ⓕ krep *large, paper-thin pancake served with various fillings*
— flambée flom·bay *pancake flamed with brandy or other liqueur*
— Suzette sew·zet *pancake with tangerine or orange sauce & brandy*

cresson ⓜ kray·son *watercress*

crevette grise ⓕ krer·vet greez
tiny shrimp
— rose ⓕ krer·vet roz *small shrimp*

croissant ⓜ krwa·son
flaky crescent-shaped roll, usually served for breakfast

croquant ⓜ kro·kon
butter cookie or biscuit

croque-madame ⓕ krok·ma·dam
grilled or pan-fried ham & cheese sandwich, topped with a fried egg

croquembouche ⓕ kro·kom·boosh
grand dessert of cream puffs dipped in caramel & assembled into a large pyramid shape

croque-monsieur ⓜ krok·mers·yer
grilled or pan-fried ham & cheese sandwich

croustade ⓕ kroo·stad *puff pastry shell filled with stewed fish, seafood, meat, poultry, mushrooms or vegetables*

croûte ⓕ kroot *crust • a puff pastry case filled with various savoury foods*

croûte (en —) kroot (on —) *'in crust' – food cooked enclosed in pastry*

croûton ⓜ kroo·ton *small piece of bread toasted or fried until crisp, used to garnish salads or soups*

cru ⓜ krew *growth • referring to a particular vineyard & its wine*

cru(e) ⓜ/ⓕ krew *raw*

crudités ⓕ pl krew·dee·tay *selection of raw vegetables served sliced, grated or diced with dressing as an entree*

crustacé ⓜ krew·sta·say *shellfish*

cuire kweer *to cook*

cuisine ⓕ kwee·zeen *cooking • kitchen*
— bourgeoise boor·zhwaz *French home cooking of the highest quality*
— campagnarde kom·pan·yard
country or provincial cooking, using the finest ingredients & most refined techniques to prepare traditional rural dishes

cuisse ⓕ kwees *thigh • leg*

cuit(e) ⓜ/ⓕ kwee(t) *cooked*
— au four o foor *baked*

cul de veau ⓜ kew der vo
veal fillet or rump steak

cuvée ⓕ kew·vay *blend of wine from various vineyards in the making of champagne – also refers to the vintage*

D

darne ⓜ darn *slice of a large raw fish, such as hake, salmon or tuna*

datte ⓕ dat *date*

daube ⓕ dob *beef, poultry or game stewed in a rich wine-laden broth*

déjeuner ⓜ day·zher·nay *lunch*

demi der·mee
half • beer glass size, about 0.33L
— -glace ·glas
rich brown stock & gravy
— -sel ⓜ ·sel *slightly salty*
— -sec ⓜ ·sek *slightly sweet (of wine)*

dieppoise dyep·waz *'Dieppe style' – soup generally consisting of fish, shrimp, mussels, mushrooms, vegetables, herbs & cream, cooked in cider*

digestif ⓜ dee·zhe·steef *digestive • drink served after a meal*

dijonnaise dee·zho·nez *'Dijon style' – dishes containing mustard or served with a mustard-based sauce (Burgundy)*

dinde/dindon ⓜ/ⓕ dund/dun·don *turkey*

diplomate ⓜ dee·plo·mat *trifle – sponge fingers steeped in milk or liqueur, put into a mould & filled with custard & candied fruits*

dodine de canard ⓕ do·deen der ka·nar *boned duck stuffed with forcemeat, rolled, cooked & served with a spicy sauce*

domaine ⓜ do·mayn *vineyard • used on a wine label, it indicates a wine of exceptional quality*

dos ⓜ do *back • meatiest portion of fish*

doux/douce ⓜ/ⓕ doo(s) *mild • sweet • soft • without salt (butter)*

duxelles ⓕ dewk·sel *finely chopped mushrooms sauteed in butter with shallots or onions, used as a seasoning or a sauce*

E

eau ⓕ o *water*
— **minérale** mee·nay·ral *mineral water*
— **du robinet** dew ro·bee·nay *tap water*
— **de source** der soors *spring water*

eau-de-vie ⓕ o·der·vee *'water of life' – clear fruit or nut brandy*

écrevisse ⓕ ay·krer·vees *crayfish*
— **à la nage** a la nazh *crayfish simmered in white wine, usually served with bread & butter as an entree*

émincé ⓜ ay·mun·say *thinly sliced meat*

endive ⓕ on·deev *chicory (UK) • endive (US)*
— **à la bruxelloise** a la brew·sel·waz *chicory/endive leaves rolled in a slice of ham & covered with cheese sauce*

entrecôte ⓕ on·trer·kot *rib steak*
— **chasseur** sha·ser *pan-broiled steak with a brown sauce made of white wine, mushrooms & tomatoes*
— **marchand de vin** mar·shon der vun *steak poached in red wine, shallots & onions*

entrée ⓕ on·tray *the course before the plat principal (main course)*

entremets ⓜ on·trer·may *cream-based sweet or dessert*

épaule ⓕ ay·pol *shoulder*

épinard ⓜ ay·pee·nar *spinach*

escabèche ⓕ es·ka·besh *highly-seasoned marinade used to flavour & preserve small fish*

escalope ⓕ es·ka·lop *thin boneless slice of meat, usually from the top round*
— **viennoise** vyen·waz *breaded veal escalope or cutlet*

escargot ⓜ es·kar·go *snail*

espadon ⓜ es·pa·don *swordfish*

espagnole es·pan·yol *'Spanish style' – generally including tomatoes, pimentos, capsicum, onion, garlic & rice*

estomac ⓜ es·to·ma *stomach*

estouffade ⓕ es·too·fad *meat, usually beef or pork, stewed in wine with carrots & herbs (southern France)*

estragon ⓜ es·tra·gon *tarragon*

étouffé(e) ⓜ/ⓕ ay·too·fay/ay·tew·vay *food steamed or braised in a tightly-sealed vessel with minimal liquid*

extra-sec ⓜ ek·stra·sek *very dry (of wine)*

F

faisan ⓜ fer·zon *pheasant*

fait(e) maison ⓜ/ⓕ fe(t) may·zon *home-made, of the house*

farce ⓕ fars *forcemeat • stuffing*

farci(e) ⓜ/ⓕ far·see *stuffed*

faux-filet ⓜ fo·fee·lay *beef sirloin*

fenouil ⓜ fer·noo·yer *fennel*

feuilletage ⓜ fer·yer·tazh *puff pastry*

feuilleté ⓜ fer·yer·tay *puff pastry usually filled with fruit, cheese, mushrooms, meat, seafood or poultry*

fève ⓕ fev *broad or Lima bean*

ficelle ⓕ fee·sel *long thin baguette • a tender cut of meat, often beef or duck poached in rich broth*

figue ⓕ feeg *fig*

filet ⓜ fee·lay *fillet of meat or fish*

financière fee·non·syair *food served with a rich dressing of pike dumplings, truffles, mushrooms & Madeira wine*

fines herbes ⓕ pl feen zairb *mixture of chopped fresh herbs consisting of tarragon, parsley, chervil & chives*

flageolet ⓜ fla·zho·lay *kidney bean*

flamande fla·mond *'Flemish style' – usually food with braised carrots, cabbage, turnips & sometimes bacon, potatoes or sausage, sometimes simmered in beer*

flambé(e) ⓜ/ⓕ flom·bay *dish with liqueur spooned or poured over it & ignited*

flamiche ⓕ fla·meesh *tart filled with leeks, eggs & cream, & sometimes pumpkin & Maroilles cheese (Picardy)*

flan ⓜ flon *open-top tart with various fillings • dessert made of baked custard flavoured with caramel*
— **parisien** pa·ree·zyun *tart filled with a vanilla cream*

florentine flo·ron·teen *'Florence style' – commonly dishes containing spinach & sometimes a cream sauce*

flûte ⓕ flewt *long bread roll, similar to baguette*

foie ⓜ fwa *liver*
— **gras** gra *fatted goose or duck liver. The birds are force-fed to speed the fattening process.*

fondue ⓕ fon·dew *usually a pot of melted cheeses, or hot oil or broth, that diners dip meat or bread in*
— **bourguignonne** boor·geen·yon *bite-size pieces of beef cooked in boiling oil & dipped in a variety of sauces*
— **chocolat** sho·ko·la *fruits & pieces of cake dipped in hot melted chocolate*
— **savoyarde** sa·vwa·yard *bread dipped in hot melted cheeses flavoured with white wine, garlic & cherry brandy (Savoy)*

forestière fo·re·styair *generally food sauteed with mushrooms & bacon, or with a Cognac-based sauce*

four ⓜ foor *oven*

fourchette ⓕ foor·shet *fork*

frais/fraîche ⓜ/ⓕ fray/fresh *fresh*

fraise ⓕ frez *strawberry*

framboise ⓕ from·bwaz *raspberry • raspberry liqueur*

frappé ⓜ fra·pay *syrup/liquid poured over crushed ice*

frappé(e) ⓜ/ⓕ fra·pay *chilled • iced*

friand ⓜ free·yon *pastry stuffed with minced sausage meat, ham & cheese, or almond cream*

friandise ⓕ free·on·deez *titbit • delicacy • sweets or candy*

fricadelle ⓕ free·ka·del *small fried mincemeat patty or meatball*

fricandeau ⓜ free·kon·do *veal fillet simmered in white wine, vegetables herbs & spices • a pork pate*

fricassée ⓕ free·ka·say *lamb, veal or poultry served in a thick creamy sauce, often with mushrooms & onions • quickly pan-fried foods, sometimes with wild mushrooms*

frit(e) ⓜ/ⓕ free(t) *fried*

frites ⓕ pl freet *chips • French fries*

friture ⓕ free·tewr *deep-fried food, often fish like whitebait*

froid(e) ⓜ/ⓕ frwa(d) *cold*

fromage ⓜ fro·mazh *cheese*
 — **blanc** blong *cream cheese*
 — **frais** fray *fermented dairy product similar to curds or cottage cheese*
 — **de tête** der tet
 brawn • head cheese (usually pork)

fromagerie ⓕ fro·ma·zhree *cheese shop*

fruit ⓜ frwee *fruit*
 — **confit** kon·fee
 candied or glazed fruit
 — **glacé** gla·say *candied or glazed fruit*
 — **de mer** der mair *seafood*

fumé(e) ⓜ/ⓕ few·may *smoked*

fumet ⓜ few·may *aromatic broth used in soups & sauces*

G

galantine ⓕ ga·lon·teen *pressed cold meat, usually poultry, stuffed with forcemeat, served cold as an entree*

galette ⓕ ga·let
 crêpe made with buckwheat flour • flat plain cake of brioche-type dough or puff pastry, with a variety of fillings • small short butter cookies
 — **sarrasin** sa·ra·zun
 buckwheat flour crêpe

gamba ⓕ gom·ba *king prawn*

garbure ⓕ gar·bewr *thick cabbage soup with salted pork, potatoes, vegetables, spices, herbs & sometimes confit d'oie. May be covered with bread slices & cheese, then browned in the oven.*

garni(e) ⓜ/ⓕ gar·nee *garnished*

gâteau ⓜ ga·to *cake*

gaufre ⓕ go·frer *waffle*

gelée ⓕ zher·lay *aspic or fruit jelly*

genièvre ⓕ zher·nye·vrer *juniper*

génoise ⓕ zhay·nwaz *very rich sponge cake, eaten as is or used as the foundation for other cake preparations*

gésier ⓜ zhay·zyay *poultry entrails*

gibelotte de lapin ⓕ zhee·blot der la·pun *rabbit stewed in wine sauce with bacon, potatoes, mushrooms, garlic, onion & herbs*

gibier ⓜ zheeb·yay *game*
 — **en saison** on say·zon
 game in season

gigot ⓜ zhee·go
 leg, generally of lamb or mutton

gigue ⓕ zheeg *haunch*

gingembre ⓜ zhun·zhom·brer *ginger*

girolle ⓕ zhee·rol *boletus mushroom – same as chanterelle mushroom*

glace ⓕ glas *ice • ice cream*

glacé(e) ⓜ/ⓕ gla·say *glazed • iced*

glaçon ⓜ gla·son *ice cube*

graisse ⓕ gres *grease • fat • suet*

grand cru ⓜ gron krew
 wine of exceptional quality

grand vin ⓜ gron vun
 wine of exceptional quality

grand(e) ⓜ/ⓕ gron(d) *large • big*

granité ⓜ gra·nee·tay *granular-textured fruit-flavoured water-ice or sorbet*

gras-double ⓜ gra·doo·bler *tripe – may be cooked in water, moulded in a rectangular block, or cut in strips & braised with tomatoes or onions*

grecque grek *'Greek style' – foods prepared with olive oil, onions, lemon, & sometimes tomato, peppers or fennel added*

grenadin ⓜ grer·na·dun
 veal (or sometimes poultry) fillet, wrapped in a thin slice of bacon

grenouille ① grer·noo·yer *frog*
  cuisses de — kwees der *frogs' legs*
grillade ① gree·yad *mixed grill*
grillé(e) ⓜ/① gree·yay *grilled*
grillons ⓜ gree·yon *chunks of fatty pork or duck cooked until crisp*
griotte ① gree·yot *morello cherry*
grive ① greev *thrush*
groseille ① gro·zay·yer *(red) currant*
  — à maquereau a ma·kro *gooseberry*

H

haché(e) ⓜ/① ha·shay *minced • chopped*
hareng ⓜ a·rung *herring*
  — fumé few·may *smoked herring • kipper*
haricot ⓜ a·ree·ko *bean*
  — blanc blong *white haricot or kidney bean*
  — rouge roozh *red kidney bean*
  — vert vair *green bean • French or string bean*
haute cuisine ① ot kwee·zeen *'high cuisine' – classic French style of cooking originating in the spectacular feasts of French kings. It's typified by super-rich, elaborately prepared & beautifully presented multi-course meals.*
herbe ① airb *herb*
hollandaise o·lon·dez *emulsified oil & egg yolk sauce, flavoured with fresh lemon juice*
homard ⓜ o·mar *Atlantic lobster*
  — à l'armoricaine/à l'américaine a lar·mo·ree·ken/a la·may·ree·ken *lobster simmered in white wine, tomatoes, shallots, garlic, pepper, flamed in Cognac or whisky & served with a lobster coral (roe) sauce*

  — Newburg nyoo·boorg *lobster cut into sections, cooked in Madeira wine & served with creamy sauce*
  — Thermidor ter·mee·dor *lobster sauteed in butter, served in its shell with a white wine & Bechamel sauce flavoured with shallots, herbs, spices & mustard, sprinkled with cheese & browned*
hors-d'œuvre ⓜ or·der·vrer *appetiser*
huile ① weel *oil*
huître ① wee·trer *oyster*

I

île flottante ① eel flo·tont *dessert of egg whites floating on a custard surface, coated with caramel sauce*
indienne un·dyen *'Indian style' – generally a dish flavoured with curry*
infusion ① un·few·zyon *herbal tea*

J

jalousie ① zha·loo·zee *latticed flaky pastry filled with almond paste & jam*
jambon ⓜ zhom·bon *ham*
  — de Bayonne der bay·yon *fine raw, slightly salty ham (Basque)*
  — de canard der ka·nar *cured or smoked duck breast*
  — chaud sho *baked ham*
  — cru krew *raw ham*
jardinière zhar·dee·nyair *'gardener's style' – dish of cooked vegetables*
jarret ⓜ zha·ray *knuckle or shank*
joue ① zhoo *cheek*
julienne ① zhew·lyen *usually vegetables, sometimes ham or chicken breast, cut in long, fine strips, cooked in butter or served raw*
jus ⓜ zhew *juice • gravy*

K

kascher ka·shair *kosher*

kir ⓜ keer
white wine sweetened with cassis
— royal rwa·yal
champagne with cassis

kirsch ⓜ keersh
cherry eau-de-vie or brandy

kriek ⓕ kreek
Belgian beer flavoured with cherries

kugelhopf ⓜ kew·gerl·hopf *chocolate,
almond & sultana cake (Alsace)*

L

lait ⓜ lay *milk*
— cru krew *raw or unpasteurised
milk used to make certain cheeses*
— écrémé ay·kray·may *skimmed milk*

laitance ⓕ lay·tons *soft roe*

laitue ⓕ lay·tew *lettuce*

langouste ⓕ long·goost *spiny lobster •
rock lobster (Mediterranean)*

langoustine ⓕ long·goo·steen *scampi •
Dublin Bay prawn • langoustine*

langue ⓕ long *tongue*

lapin ⓜ la·pun *rabbit*
— de garenne der ga·ren *wild rabbit*

lard ⓜ lar *bacon*
— fumé few·may *smoked bacon*
— maigre may·grer *lean bacon*

lardon ⓜ lar·don *bacon cube*

légume ⓜ lay·gewm *vegetable*

légumes jardinière ⓜ pl
lay·gewm zhar·dee·nyair
*diced fresh vegetables (usually
carrots, turnips, beans & cauliflower)
with butter, chervil & cream*

lentille ⓕ lon·tee·yer *lentil*

lièvre ⓜ lye·vrer *hare*
— en civet on see·vay
jugged hare (hare stew)

limande ⓕ lee·mond *lemon sole • dab*

limonade ⓕ lee·mo·nad *lemonade*

longe ⓕ lonzh *loin*
— de veau farcie der vo far·see
stuffed loin of veal

lorraine lo·ren *'Lorraine style' –
generally a dish garnished with red
cabbage & potato croquettes, or
bacon slices & Gruyère cheese*

lyonnaise lee·o·nez *'Lyon style' – dish
generally including onions cooked
golden brown, seasoned with wine,
garlic & parsley*

M

madeleine ⓕ mad·len
*small shell-shaped cake, generally
flavoured with lemon but also
almonds or cinnamon.*

madère ma·dair
*'Madeira style' – dishes served
with a sauce flavoured with sweet
Madeira (Portuguese fortified wine)*

magret ⓜ ma·gray
*breast meat from a fattened mallard
or Barbary duck specially raised for
foie gras (see jambon de canard)*

maigre may·grer *lean, or without meat*

maïs ⓜ ma·ees *corn/maize*

maison (de la —) may·zon (der la —)
speciality of the restaurant

mange-tout ⓜ monzh·too *snow pea*

maquereau ⓜ ma·kro *mackerel*

marc ⓜ mar *drink made from distilled
grape skins & pulp left over after
being pressed for wine*

marcassin ⓜ mar·ka·sun *young boar*

marchand de vin mar·shon der vun
*wine merchant • 'wine merchant
style' – dish cooked with (red) wine*

marengo ⓜ ma·rung·go *stewed
chicken or veal served over toast &
garnished with crayfish or shrimps*

marinade ① ma·ree·nad

marinade – a highly flavoured liquid which may include wine or vinegar, oil, aromatic vegetables & herbs, that meat, fish or vegetables are steeped in to be flavoured & tenderised

mariné(e) ⑩/① ma·ree·nay marinated

marinière ma·ree·nyair 'mariner's style' – usually mussels or other seafood, simmered in white wine with onions parsley, thyme & bay leaves

marmelade ① mar·mer·lad

thick puree of fresh fruits stewed in sugar or compote

marron ⑩ ma·ron

chestnut (see also châtaigne)

massepain ⑩ mas·pun

marzipan – almond paste

matelote ① mat·lot fish stew (often eel) with wine, onions, shallots, garlic & sometimes mushrooms

mayonnaise ① ma·yo·nez mayonnaise

melon ⑩ mer·lon melon

menthe ① mont mint

menu ⑩ mer·new

generally means a set meal at a fixed price (menu à prix fixe)

— de dégustation

der day·gew·sta·syon

tasting menu – special menu giving a small sample of several dishes

merguez ① mair·gez

spicy red sausage made from beef or mutton, originally from North Africa

merveille ① mair·vay·yer fried pastry shapes, sprinkled with sugar

meunière mer·nyair

lightly sauteed in butter, usually with lemon juice & chopped parsley

meurette ① mer·ret red wine sauce

michette ① mee·shet

savoury bread stuffed with cheese, olives, onions & anchovies (Nice)

miel ⑩ myel honey

mignon ⑩ meen·yon small piece of tenderloin of beef, pork or veal

mijoté(e) ⑩/① mee·zho·tay simmered

millas ⑩ mee·las cornflour & goose fat cake eaten with a meat course

— de Bordeaux der bor·do

custard & cherry tart

mille-feuille ⑩ meel·fer·yer

'1000 leaves' – flaky pastry layered with custard or thick cream filling

mirabelle ① mee·ra·bel small yellow plum, used in tarts as well as liqueurs & plum brandy (Alsace, Lorraine)

miroton ⑩ mee·ro·ton

slices of pre-cooked beef, usually leftovers, simmered with onions, often served as stew

mode (à la —) mod (a la —)

'of the fashion' – often means made according to a local recipe (see also bœuf à la mode)

moelle ① mwal bone marrow

mont-blanc ⑩ mon blong

canned chestnut puree with or without a meringue base, topped with crème Chantilly

morceau ⑩ mor·so morsel or piece

morille ① mo·ree·yer morel mushroom, a wild mushroom, with a honeycomb cap & hollow stem

Mornay (sauce —) ① mor·nay

Bechamel sauce with Gruyère cheese, sometimes enriched with egg yolks

morue ① mo·rew cod

moule ① mool mussel

mousseline ① moos·leen fine puree or forcemeat lightened with whipped cream • a variation of hollandaise sauce made with whipped cream

mousseron ⑩ moos·ron

blewit – fleshy wild mushroom

mousseux ⓜ moo·ser
  sparkling • sparkling wine
moutarde ⓕ moo·tard *mustard*
mouton ⓜ moo·ton *mutton*
mulet ⓜ mu·lay *mullet*
mûre ⓕ mewr *blackberry*
muscat ⓜ mew·ska
  type of grape • a sweet dessert wine
museau ⓜ mew·zo *muzzle or snout •*
  pork brawn or head cheese
myrtille ⓕ meer·tee·yer
  bilberry or European blueberry

N

nature na·tewr *plain*
navarin ⓜ na·va·run *mutton or lamb*
  stew with vegetables & herbs
navet ⓜ na·vay *turnip*
neige ⓕ nezh
  'snow' – stiff beaten egg white
noir(e) ⓜ/ⓕ nwar *black*
noisette ⓕ nwa·zet *hazelnut • a round,*
  boneless cut of lamb or venison
noix ⓕ nwa *nut • walnut*
  — du Brésil bray·zeel *brazil nut*
  — de coco der ko·ko *coconut*
normande nor·mond *'Norman style' –*
  usually a dish of meat, shellfish or
  vegetables, served with cream
note ⓕ not *bill or check (restaurant)*
nouilles ⓕ noo·yer *noodles*
nouvelle cuisine ⓕ noo·vel kwee·zeen*
  food prepared & presented to
  emphasise the inherent textures &
  colours of the ingredients – features
  rather small portions served with
  light sauces

O

œuf ⓜ erf *egg*
  — brouillé broo·yay *scrambled egg*
  — à la coque a la kok *soft-boiled egg*
  — dur dewr *hard-boiled egg*
  — frit free *fried egg*

oie ⓕ wa *goose*
oignon ⓜ on·yon *onion*
olive ⓕ o·leev *olive*
omelette ⓕ om·let *omelette*
onglet ⓜ ong·glay *prime cut of beef*
orange ⓕ o·ronzh *orange*
  — pressée ⓕ pray·say
  freshly squeezed orange juice
oreille ⓕ o·ray·yer *ear*
orge ⓕ orzh *barley*
os ⓜ os *bone*
  — à moelle a mwal *marrow-bone*

P

pain ⓜ pun *bread*
palmier ⓜ pal·myay *sweet pastry*
  shaped like a heart or a palm leaf
palourde ⓕ pa·loord *medium-sized clam*
pamplemousse ⓜ pom·pler·moos
  grapefruit
pan-bagnat ⓜ pun ban·ya
  small round bread loaves, split or
  hollowed out, soaked with olive oil
  & filled with onions, vegetables,
  anchovies & black olives (Nice)
panaché ⓜ pa·na·shay
  shandy (beer & lemonade)
panais ⓜ pa·nay *parsnip*
pané(e) ⓜ/ⓕ pa·nay
  coated in breadcrumbs • breaded
panisse ⓕ pa·nees *pancake or patty of*
  chickpea flour, fried & served with
  certain meat dishes (Provence)
papillote ⓕ pa·pee·yot *dish cooked*
  encased in greaseproof paper or foil
parfait ⓜ par·fay *ice cream dessert,*
  often served in a tall glass, sometimes
  with custard, fruit, nuts & liqueur
Paris-Brest ⓜ pa·ree·brest
  ring-shaped cake of choux pastry,
  filled with butter-cream, decorated
  with flaked almonds & icing sugar
Parmentier ⓜ par·mon·tyay
  any dish containing potatoes

pastèque ① pas·tek *watermelon*

pastis ⑩ pa·stees *an aniseed-flavoured drink, drunk as an aperitif & always mixed with water*

patate douce ① pa·tat doos *sweet potato*

pâté ⑩ pa·tay *pate – thick paste, often pork. Sometimes called terrine.*
— **de foie gras** der fwa gra *goose or duck liver paste*
— **maison** may·zon *pate made according the restaurant's own recipe*

pâtes ① pl pat *pasta • noodles*

pâtisserie ① pa·tees·ree *pastries, cakes & other sweetmeats • the place where they are sold*

pavé ⑩ pa·vay *thickly-cut steak*

paysanne pay·zan *'peasant style' – dish containing various vegetables & wine, or assorted chopped vegetables, usually used to garnish a soup or an omelette*

pêche ① pesh *peach*

perche ① persh *perch*

perdrix ① per·dree *partridge*

Périgourdine pay·ree·goor·deen *'Perigord style' – dish containing truffles & sometimes foie gras*

persil ⑩ pair·seel *parsley*

persillade ① pair·see·yad *mixture of chopped parsley & garlic, added to recipes at the end of cooking*

pet-de-nonne ⑩ pay·der·non *'nun's fart' – small deep fried fritter or choux pastry, served hot with sugar or with fruit coulis*

pied ⑩ pyay *foot • trotter*

pigeon ⑩ pee·zhon *pigeon*

pignon ⑩ pee·nyon *pine nut/kernel*

piment ⑩ pee·mon *pimento, small red pepper • allspice*

pintade ① pun·tad *guinea fowl*

pistache ① pees·tash *pistachio nut*

pistache (en —) pee·stash (on —) *dish prepared with garlic*

pistou ⑩ pee·stoo *pesto – basil & garlic paste*

plat ⑩ pla *plate • dish*
— **du jour** dew zhoor *speciality of the day*
— **principal** prun·see·pal *main course or dish*

plateau de fromage ⑩ pla·to der fro·mazh *cheese board or platter*

pleurote ⑩ pler·rot *pleurotus – mild white mushroom with tender flesh*

pluvier ⑩ plew·vyay *plover (small game bird)*

poché(e) ⑩/① po·shay *poached*

poêlé(e) ⑩/① pwa·lay *pan-fried*

point (à —) pwun (a —) *medium-well done meat, usually still pink*

poire ① pwar *pear*

poiré ⑩ pwa·ray *perry (pear cider)*

poireau ⑩ pwa·ro *leek*

pois ⑩ pwa *pea*
— **cassé** ka·say *split pea*
— **chiche** sheesh *chickpea*

poisson ⑩ pwa·son *fish*
— **d'eau douce** do doos *freshwater fish*
— **de mer** der mair *saltwater fish*

poissonnerie ① pwa·son·ree *fish shop*

poitrine ① pwa·treen *chest (meat from the chest area)*

poivre ⑩ pwa·vrer *pepper*

poivron ⑩ pwa·vron *capsicum or sweet pepper*

pomme ① pom *apple*

pomme de terre ① pom der tair *potato*

pomme chips pom sheeps *crisps or potato chips*

pomme duchesse pom dew·shes *deep-fried fritter of mashed potato, butter & egg yolk*

porc ⑩ por *pig • pork*

porto ⑩ por·to *port*

potage ⑩ po·tazh *usually a thickened soup of pureed vegetable base*

pot-au-feu ⓜ po·to·fer
beef, root vegetable & herb stockpot.
Traditionally, the stock is served as an
entree & the meat & vegetables are
served as a main course.

potée ⓕ po·tay
meat (usually pork) & vegetables
cooked in an earthenware pot

potimarron ⓜ po·tee·ma·ron
gourd – variety of squash

potiron ⓜ po·tee·ron *pumpkin*

pouding ⓜ poo·deeng *pudding*

poularde ⓕ poo·lard
pullet or fattened chicken

poulet ⓜ poo·lay *chicken*
  — chasseur sha·ser
  chicken sauteed in white wine with
  mushrooms, shallots & bacon
  — au pot o po *whole chicken filled*
  with giblets, ham & bread, stewed
  with vegetables

poulpe ⓕ poolp *octopus*

poussin ⓜ poo·sun *very young chicken*

praire ⓕ prair *clam*

praline ⓕ pra·leen
almonds, sometimes flavoured with
coffee or chocolate & a sugar coating

pré-salé ⓜ pray·sa·lay *lamb pastured*
in the salty meadows of the Atlantic
or the English Channel

premier cru prer·myay krew *high-*
quality wines from specific vineyards

primeur ⓜ pree·mer
spring or early vegetable or fruit

printanière prun·ta·nyair
dish often prepared or served with
fresh spring vegetables

produits ⓜ pl **de la mer** pro·dwee der
la mair *seafood*

profiterole ⓜ pro·fee·trol
small ball of choux pastry with
savoury or sweet fillings

provençale pro·von·sal *'Provence style'* –
dish usually cooked with olive oil,
tomatoes, garlic, onions, olives,
sweet peppers & various herbs

prune ⓕ prewn *plum*

pruneau ⓜ prew·no *prune*

puits ⓜ **d'amour** pwee da·moor
small puff pastry shell filled with
custard or jam & sprinkled with sugar

Q

quenelle ⓕ ker·nel *oval-shaped*
dumpling of fish or meat, forcemeat,
egg & flour, often served poached
  — de brochet der bro·shay
  pike dumpling

queue ⓕ ker *tail*

quiche ⓕ keesh *open-top tart with*
meat, fish or vegetable filling, baked
with beaten eggs & cream

R

raclette ⓕ ra·klet *hot melted cheese*
scraped from a block of cheese placed
in front of a vertical grill, served with
potatoes & gherkins (Savoy)

radis ⓜ ra·dee *radish*

ragoût ⓜ ra·goo *stew of meat, poultry*
or fish and/or vegetables

raie ⓕ ray *skate • ray*

raisin ⓜ ray·zun *grape*

rascasse ⓕ ras·kas *scorpion fish* –
grotesque but delicious fish essential
in bouillabaisse (Mediterranean)

ratatouille ⓕ ra·ta·too·yer
vegetable 'stew' – tomatoes,
zucchini, eggplant, sweet peppers &
onions, flavoured with garlic, herbs
& olive oil, served with lemon juice

reine ren
'queen's style' – a dish with poultry

religieuse ① rer·lee·zhyerz
double-decker choux pastry puff,
filled with coffee or chocolate-
flavoured custard & coated with icing

rémoulade ① re·moo·lad
classic sauce made by combining
mayonnaise with mustard, capers,
chopped gherkins, herbs &
anchovies, served chilled with grated
celery, or as an accompaniment to
cold meat or seafood

rillettes ① pl ree·yet coarsely shredded,
potted meat (usually pork), eaten as
a spread on toast or bread

rillons ⓜ ree·yon chunks of fatty pork
or duck cooked until crisp

ris de veau ⓜ ree der vo sweetbreads

rissole ① ree·sol fried or baked pastry
turnover, filled with a savoury filling
of meat, poultry or vegetables

riz ⓜ ree rice

rognon ⓜ ron·yon kidney

romarin ⓜ ro·ma·run rosemary

rosbif ⓜ ros·beef roast beef

rosette de Lyon ① ro·zet der lee·on
large pork sausage (like salami)

rôti ⓜ ro·tee roast

rouget ⓜ roo·zhay mullet

rouille ① roo·yer thick aïoli sauce

roulade ① roo·lad slice of meat or fish
rolled around stuffing • a rolled-up
vegetable souffle

roulé(e) ⓜ/① roo·lay rolled

S

sabayon ⓜ sa·ba·yon creamy dessert
of beaten eggs, sugar & wine or
liqueur, flavoured with lemon juice

sablé ⓜ sa·blay rich shortbread biscuit

safran ⓜ sa·fron saffron

saignant(e) ⓜ/① sen·yon(t)
rare (meat)

saisi(e) ⓜ/① say·zee seared

salade ① sa·lad salad • lettuce
— **composée** kom·po·zay mixed salad
— **verte** vairt green salad

salé(e) ⓜ/① sa·lay salted

salmis ⓜ sal·mee
game or poultry partially roasted,
then simmered in wine

sang ⓜ song blood

sanglier (sauvage) ⓜ song·glee·yay
(so·vazh) (wild) boar

sanguette ① song·get boudin sausage
(often flat) made from rabbit, duck
or goose blood (Périgord)

sauce ① sos sauce • gravy

saucisse ① so·sees sausage
— **de Francfort** der frongk·for
frankfurter
— **de Strasbourg** der straz·boor
knackwurst
— **de Toulouse** der too·looz
mild pork sausage

saucisson ⓜ so·see·son large sausage
usually air-dried & eaten cold
— **à l'ail** a lai garlic sausage
— **de Lyon** der lee·on long air-dried
pork sausage, flavoured with garlic &
pepper, or a boiling sausage similar
to saucisson à l'ail
— **sec** sek
air-dried sausage (like salami)

saumon ⓜ so·mon salmon

sauté(e) ⓜ/① so·tay sauteed

sauvage so·vazh wild

savarin ⓜ sa·va·run ring-shaped sponge
cake soaked with a rum syrup & filled
with custard or whipped cream &
fresh or poached fruits

savoie ① sav·wa light, airy cake made
with beaten egg whites

sec/sèche ⓜ/① sek/sesh dry

séché(e) ⓜ/① say·shay dried

seiche ① sesh cuttlefish

sel ⓜ sel salt

semoule ① ser·mool semolina

service ⓜ sair·vees *service (charge)*
— **compris** kom·pree *service included (often abbreviated as s.c. at the bottom of the bill)* – *service charge is built into the price of each dish. Pay the total at the bottom.*
— **en sus** on sews
service charge is calculated after the food & drink ordered is added up. Pay the total at the bottom.

serviette ⓕ sair·vyet *serviette • napkin*

sésame ⓜ say·zam *sesame*

sirop ⓜ see·ro *fruit syrup or cordial served mixed with water, soda or with carbonated mineral water*

soja ⓜ so·zha *soya bean*

solette ⓕ so·let *baby sole*

sorbet ⓜ sor·bay *sorbet*

soubise ⓕ soo·beez *dish served with creamed onion puree & rice*

soufflé ⓜ soof·lay *souffle*

soupe ⓕ soop
soup – *generally thick & hearty*

spéciale ⓕ spay·syal *top-quality oyster*

spécialité (de la maison) ⓕ
spay·sya·lee·tay (der la may·zon)
speciality of the house

steak ⓜ stek *steak*
— **tartare** tar·tar *steak tartare – raw minced beef served with raw onion, egg yolk, capers & parsley*

sucre ⓜ sew·krer *sugar*

sucré(e) ⓜ/ⓕ sew·kray *sweetened*

suprême de volaille ⓕ sew·prem der vo·lai *boned chicken breast with creamy sauce*

sur commande sewr ko·mond
to your special order

T

table d'hôte ⓕ ta·bler dot
meal at a set price & hour

taboulé ⓜ ta·boo·lay *tabouli* –
common salad of couscous with parsley & mint, tomatoes & onions, seasoned with olive oil & lemon juice

tapenade ⓕ ta·per·nad *savoury spread or dip of pureed olives, anchovies, capers, olive oil & lemon, eaten with bread or hard-boiled eggs*

tarte ⓕ tart *flan • tart*
— **aux fraises** o frez *strawberry tart*
— **Tatin** ta·tun
type of tart with pastry baked on top of fruit (usually apples)

tartiflette ⓕ tar·tee·flet
dish of potatoes, Reblochon cheese & sometimes bacon (Savoy)

tartine ⓕ tar·teen *slice of bread with any topping or garnish, such as butter, jam, honey, cream cheese*

tendron ⓜ ton·dron *cut of meat from the end of ribs to the breastbone*

terrine ⓕ tay·reen
preparation of meat, poultry, fish or game, baked in a ceramic dish called a terrine, & served cold

tête ⓕ tet *head*

thé ⓜ tay *tea*
— **au citron** o see·tron *tea with lemon*
— **au lait** o lay *tea with milk*
— **nature** na·tewr
plain tea (without milk)

thon ⓜ ton *tuna*

timbale ⓕ tum·bal
meat, fish, or seafood stew cooked in a pastry-case • rice or pasta with vegetables, cooked in a round or cup-shaped mould, served with sauce

tisane ⓕ tee·zan *herbal tea*
— **de camomille** der ka·mo·mee·yer *camomile tea*
— **de menthe** der mont *mint tea*
— **de tilleul** der tee·yerl
tea made with dried linden blossoms

tomate ⓕ to·mat *tomato*

topinambour ⓕ to-pee-nom-boor
Jerusalem artichoke

tournedos ⓜ toor-ner-do
thick round slice of beef fillet
— **Rossini** ro-see-nee *tournedos
garnished with foie gras & truffles,
served with Madeira wine sauce*

tourte ⓕ toort *sweet or savoury pie*

tourteau ⓜ toor-to *large crab*

tourtière ⓕ toor-tyair
sweet or savoury pie

tout compris too kom-pree
all-inclusive (price)

traiteur ⓜ tray-ter *caterer or
delicatessen selling prepared dishes*

tranche ⓕ tronsh *slice*

tranché tron-shay *sliced*

tripes ⓕ pl treep *tripe*
— **à la mode de Caen** a la mod der
kon *tripe simmered with cider, leeks
& carrots*

troquet ⓜ tro-kay *bistro • tavern •
cafe • small restaurant*

truffe ⓕ trewf *truffle*
— **en chocolat** on sho-ko-la
*melted chocolate enriched with
butter, cream & egg yolks, rolled into
small balls & covered with cocoa*

truite ⓕ trweet *trout*
— **au bleu** o bler *trout poached in
a court-bouillon broth of vinegar,
white wine, vegetables & herbs*

tuile ⓕ tweel *'tile' – fragile, wing-like
almond biscuit*

V

vache ⓕ vash *cow*

vanille ⓕ va-nee-yer *vanilla*

vapeur ⓕ va-per *steam*

vapeur (à la —) va-per (a la —) *steamed*

varié(e) ⓜ/ⓕ var-yay *assorted*

veau ⓜ vo *veal*

velouté ⓜ ver-loo-tay *rich, creamy
soup, usually prepared with
vegetables, shellfish or fish puree*

venaison ⓕ ver-nay-zon *venison*

verdure ⓕ vair-dewr *green vegetables*

viande ⓕ vyond *meat*
— **hachée** ha-shay *minced meat*
— **séchée** say-shay
*dried beef served in paper-thin slices
as hors d'œuvre*
— **froide** frwad *cold meat*

viennoiserie ⓕ vyen-wa-zree *baked
goods like croissants & brioches*

vin ⓜ vun *wine*
— **blanc** blong *white wine*
— **doux** doo *sweet, dessert wine*
— **mousseux** moo-ser *sparkling wine*
— **ordinaire** or-dee-nair *table wine*
— **de pays** der pay-yee *reasonable
quality & generally drinkable wine*
— **rouge** roozh *red wine*
— **sec** sek *dry wine*
— **de table** der ta-bler *table wine –
very cheap lower-quality wine*

vinaigre ⓜ vee-nay-grer *vinegar*

volaille ⓕ vo-lai *poultry • fowl*

vol-au-vent ⓜ vo-lo-von
*round puff-pastry cases filled with
a mixture of sauce & meat, poultry,
seafood or vegetables*

W

waterzoï ⓜ wa-ter-zoy
*chicken, or sometimes fish, poached
with shredded vegetables (especially
leeks) & served with a sauce of
broth, cream & egg yolks (northern
France)*

Y

yaourt ⓜ ya-oort *yoghurt*
— **à boire** a bwar *yoghurt drink*
— **brassé** bra-say
thick creamy yoghurt
— **maigre** may-grer *low-fat yoghurt*

SAFE TRAVEL > essentials
essentiels

emergencies

urgences

Help!	*Au secours!*	o skoor
Stop!	*Arrêtez!*	a·ray·tay
Go away!	*Allez-vous-en!*	a·lay·voo·zon
Thief!	*Au voleur!*	o vo·ler
Fire!	*Au feu!*	o fer
Watch out!	*Faites attention!*	fet a·ton·syon
Call the police!	*Appelez la police!*	a·play la po·lees

It's an emergency!
C'est urgent! say tewr·zhon

There's been an accident.
Il y a eu un accident. eel ya ew un ak·see·don

Do you have a first-aid kit?
Avez-vous une trousse a·vay·voo ewn troos
de première urgence? der prer·myair ewr·zhons

Can you help me, please?
Est-ce que vous pourriez es·ker voo poo·ryay
m'aider, s'il vous plaît? may·day seel voo play

Can I use the telephone?
Est-ce que je pourrais es·ker zher poo·ray
utiliser le téléphone? ew·tee·lee·zay ler tay·lay·fon

I'm lost.
Je suis perdu(e). m/f zher swee pair·dew

Where are the toilets?
Où sont les toilettes? oo son lay twa·let

police

police

Where's the police station?
Où est le commissariat oo ay ler ko·mee·sar·ya
de police? der po·lees

essentials

171

I want to report an offence.
Je veux signaler un délit.   zher ver see·nya·lay un day·lee

I've been raped.
J'ai été violé(e). m/f   zhay ay·tay vyo·lay

I've been assaulted.
J'ai été violenté(e). m/f   zhay ay·tay vyo·lon·tay

He/She has been raped.
Il/Elle a été violé(e). m/f   eel/el a ay·tay vyo·lay

He/She tried to rape me.
Il/Elle a essayé de   eel/el a ay·say·yay der
me violer.   mer vyo·lay

I've been robbed.
On m'a volé.   on ma vo·lay

He/She has been robbed.
Il/Elle s'est fait voler.   eel/el say fay vo·lay

He/She tried to rob me.
Il/Elle a essayé de   eel/el a ay·say·yay der
me voler.   mer vo·lay

It was him/her.
C'est lui/elle.   say lwee/el

---

the police may say ...

You'll be charged with ...	*On va vous inculper ...*	on va voo ung·kewl·pay ...
He/She will be charged with ...	*On va l'inculper ...*	on va lung·kewl·pay ...
anti-government activity	*d'activités antigouvernementales*	dak·tee·vee·tay on·tee·goo·vair·ner·mon·tal
disturbing the peace	*d'avoir troublé l'ordre public*	da·vwar troo·blay lor·drer pewb·leek
shoplifting	*de vol à l'étalage*	der vol a lay·ta·lazh

I've lost my ...	*J'ai perdu ...*	zhay pair·dew ...
My ... was/ were stolen.	*On m'a volé ...*	on ma vo·lay ...
backpack	*mon sac à dos*	mon sak a do
bags	*mes valises*	may va·leez
handbag	*mon sac à main*	mon sak a mun
money	*mon argent*	mon ar·zhon
passport	*mon passeport*	mom pas·por
wallet	*mon portefeuille*	mom por·ter·fer·yer

What am I accused of?
Je suis accusé(e) de quoi? m/f — zher swee a·kew·zay der kwa

I'm sorry.
Je suis désolé(e). m/f — zher swee day·zo·lay

I apologise.
Je m'excuse. — zher mek·skewz

I didn't realise I was doing anything wrong.
Je ne croyais pas que je faisais quelque chose de mal. — zher ner krwa·yay pa ker zher fer·zay kel·ker shoz der mal

I didn't do it.
Ce n'est pas moi qui l'ai fait. — ser nay pa mwa kee lay fay

I'm innocent.
Je suis innocent(e). m/f — zher swee zee·no·son(t)

I want to contact my embassy/consulate.
Je veux contacter mon ambassade/consulat. — zher ver kon·tak·tay mon om·ba·sad/kon·sew·la

Can I make a phone call?
Je peux téléphoner? — zher per tay·lay·fo·nay

Can I have a lawyer (who speaks English)?
Je peux avoir un avocat (qui parle anglais)? — zher per a·vwar un a·vo·ka (kee parl ong·glay)

Can we pay an on-the-spot fine?
Je peux payer l'amende
tout de suite?
zher per pay·yay la·mond
too der sweet

I have insurance.
J'ai une assurance.
zhay ewn a·sew·rons

Can I have a copy, please?
Puis-je en avoir un
exemplaire?
pwee·zhon a·vwar ung
neg·zom·plair

This drug is for personal use.
C'est uniquement pour
mon usage personnel.
say ew·neek·mom poor
mon ew·zazh pair·so·nel

I have a prescription for this drug.
On m'a prescrit cette drogue.
om ma pray·skree set drog

I understand.
Je comprends.
zher kom·pron

I don't understand.
Je ne comprends pas.
zher ner kom·pron pa

---

beware of the chickens!

As in any language, French words can have a number of meanings that can lead to some funny, or possibly strange, sentences. How about this for an account of a (sure, unlikely) run-in with the law:

Madame Aubergine a posé un papillon sur ma renault,
et les poulets m'ont ramené dans un panier à salade.
ma·dam o·bair·zheen a po·say un pa·pee·yon sewr ma
re·no ay lay poo·lay mon ra·me·nay dons un pan·yay a
sa·lad

(lit: Mrs Eggplant put a butterfly on my Renault, and
the chickens came and took me away in a salad
basket)

A more useful translation of this might be:

A parking inspector stuck a ticket on my car, then the
cops came and took me away in a paddy wagon.

Where's a	*Où y a t-il un/*	oo ee a teel un/
nearby ...?	*une ... par ici?* m/f	ewn ... par ee·see
(night) chemist	*pharmacie* f	far·ma·see
	(de nuit)	(der nwee)
dentist	*dentiste* m	don·teest
doctor	*médecin* m	mayd·sun
hospital	*hôpital* m	o·pee·tal
medical centre	*centre* m	son·trer
	médical	may·dee·kal
optometrist	*optométriste* m	op·to·may·treest

I need a doctor (who speaks English).
J'ai besoin d'un médecin   zhay ber·zwun dun mayd·sun
(qui parle anglais).   (kee parl ong·glay)

Could I see a female doctor?
Est-ce que je peux voir   es·ker zher per vwar
une femme médecin?   ewn fam mayd·sun

Can the doctor come here?
Est-ce que le médecin   es·ker ler mayd·sun
peut venir ici?   per ver·neer ee·see

I've run out of my medication.
Je n'ai plus de   zher nay plew der
médicaments.   may·dee·ka·mon

I don't want a blood transfusion.
Je ne veux pas de   zher ner ver pa der
transfusion sanguine.   trons·few·zyon song·geen

Please use a new syringe.
Je vous prie d'utiliser   zher voo pree dew·tee·lee·zay
une seringue neuve.   ewn ser·rungk nerv

I've been vaccinated for ...	Je me suis fait vacciner contre ...	zher mer swee fay vak·see·nay kon·trer ...
He/She has been vaccinated for ...	Il/Elle s'est fait vacciner contre ...	eel/el say fay vak·see·nay kon·trer ...
hepatitis	l'hépatite	lay·pa·teet
tetanus	le tétanos	ler tay·ta·nos
typhoid	la typhoïde	la tee·fo·eed
I need new ...	J'ai besoin de nouvelles ...	zhay ber·zwun der noo·vel ...
contact lenses	lentilles de contact	lon·tee·yer der kon·takt
glasses	lunettes	lew·net

My prescription is ...
Mon ordonnance indique ... mon or·do·nons on·deek ...

---

the doctor may say ...

What's the problem?
Qu'est-ce qui ne va pas? kes·kee ner va pas

Where does it hurt?
Où est-ce que vous avez mal? oo es·ker voo za·vay mal

I'd like to take your temperature.
Je voudrais prendre votre température. zher voo·dray pron·drer vo·trer tom·pay·ra·tewr

How long have you been like this?
Depuis quand êtes-vous dans cet état? der·pwee kon et·voo don say tay·ta

Have you had this before?
Cela vous est déjà arrivé? ser·la voo zay day·zha a·ree·vay

How long are you travelling for?
Quelle est la durée de votre voyage? kel ay la dew·ray der vo·trer vwa·yazh

the doctor may say ...

Do you ...?	*Est-ce que vous ...?*	es·ker voo ...
drink	*buvez*	bew·vay
smoke	*fumez*	few·may
take drugs	*vous droguez*	voo dro·gay

Are you ...?	*Êtes-vous ...?*	et·voo ...
allergic to	*allergique à*	za·lair·zheek a
anything	*quelque chose*	kel·ker shoz
pregnant	*enceinte*	zon·sunt

Are you sexually active?
Vous avez une vie sexuelle?
voo za·vay ewn vee sek·swel

Have you had unprotected sex?
Vous avez eu des rapports non protégés?
voo za·vay ew day ra·por non pro·tay·zhay

Are you on any medication?
Est-ce que vous prenez des médicaments?
es·ker voo prer·nay day may·dee·ka·mon

You need to be admitted to hospital.
Il faut vous faire hospitaliser.
eel fo voo fair os·pee·ta·lee·zay

Have it checked when you go home.
Consultez votre docteur en rentrant.
kon·sewl·tay vo·trer dok·ter on ron·tron

You should return home for treatment.
Vous devez rentrer chez vous pour suivre un traitement.
voo der·vay ron·tray shay voo poor swee·vrer un tret·mon

You're a hypochondriac. Go and enjoy your holiday!
Vous êtes un véritable malade imaginaire. Partez en vacances et amusez-vous!
voo zet un vay·ree·ta·bler ma·lad ee·ma·zhee·nair. par·tay on va·kons ay a·mew·zay·voo

symptoms & conditions

I'm sick.
Je suis malade. — zher swee ma·lad

My friend is sick.
Mon ami(e) est malade. m/f — mon a·mee ay ma·lad

It hurts here.
J'ai une douleur ici. — zhay ewn doo·ler ee·see

I've been injured.
J'ai été blessé(e). m/f — zhay ay·tay blay·say

I've been vomiting.
J'ai vomi. — zhay vo·mee

I can't sleep.
Je n'arrive pas à dormir. — zher na·reev pa a dor·meer

I have an infection.
J'ai une infection. — zhay ewn nun·fek·syon

I have a rash.
J'ai des démangeaisons. — zhay day day·mon·zhe·zon

I feel ...	Je me sens ...	zher mer son ...
anxious	inquiet/	un·kyay/
	inquiète m/f	un·kyet
better	mieux	myer
weak	faible	fe·bler
worse	plus mal	plew mal

I feel ...	J'ai ...	zhay ...
dizzy	des vertiges	day ver·teezh
hot and cold	chaud et froid	sho ay frwa
nauseous	des nausées	day no·zay
shivery	des frissons	day free·son

I have (a) ...	J'ai ...	zhay ...
diarrhoea	la diarrhée	la dya·ray
headache	mal à la tête	mal a la tet
sore throat	mal à la gorge	mal a la gorzh

I've recently had ...
J'ai eu récemment ...   zhay ew ray·sa·mon ...

He/She has recently had ...
Il/Elle a eu   eel/el a ew
récemment ...   ray·sa·mon ...

I'm on medication for ...
Je prends des   zher pron day
médicaments pour ...   may·dee·ka·mon poor ...

He/She is on medication for ...
Il/Elle prend des   eel/el pron day
médicaments pour ...   may·dee·ka·mon poor ...

bronchitis	*bronchite* f	bron·sheet
diabetes	*diabète* m	dya·bet
venereal disease	*maladie* f *vénérienne*	ma·la·dee vay·nay·ryen

women's health

la santé féminine

(I think that) I'm pregnant.
(Je pense que)   (zher pons ker)
Je suis enceinte.   zher swee zon·sunt

I'm on the Pill.
Je prends la pilule.   zher pron la pee·lewl

I haven't had my period for ... weeks.
Je n'ai pas eu mes règles   zher nay pa ew may re·gler
depuis ... semaines.   der·pwee ... ser·men

I've noticed a lump here.
J'ai remarqué une   zhay rer·mar·kay ewn
grosseur ici.   gro·ser ee·see

I have period pain.
J'ai des règles   zhay day ray·gler
douloureuses.   doo·loo·rer·zer

I need ...	*J'ai besoin ...*	zhay ber·zwun ...
contraception	*d'un contraceptif*	dun kon·trer·sep·teef
the morning-after pill	*de la pilule du lendemain*	de la pee·lewl dew lon·der·mun
a pregnancy test	*d'un test de grossesse*	dun test der gro·ses

abortion	*avortement* m	a·vor·ter·mon
mammogram	*mammographie* f	ma·mo·gra·fee
menstruation	*règles* f pl	re·gler
miscarriage	*fausse couche* f	fos koosh
pap smear	*frottis* m	fro·tee
premenstrual tension	*syndrome* m *prémenstruel*	sun·drom pray·mon·strew·el

the doctor may say ...

Are you using contraception?
Vous utilisez des   voo zew·tee·lee·zay
contraceptifs?   day kon·trer·sep·teef

Are you menstruating?
Vous avez vos règles?   voo za·vay vo re·gler

When did you last have your period?
C'était quand la   say·tay kon la
dernière fois que vous   dair·nyair fwa ker voo
avez eu vos règles?   za·vay ew vo re·gler

You're pregnant.
Vous êtes enceinte.   voo zet on·sunt

allergies

I'm allergic to ...	*Je suis*	zher swee
	allergique ...	za·lair·zheek ...
He/She's	*Il/Elle est*	eel/el ay
allergic to ...	*allergique ...*	ta·lair·zheek ...
antibiotics	*aux antibiotiques*	o zon·tee·byo·teek
anti-inflammatories	*aux anti-inflammatoires*	o zun·tee·un·fla·ma·twar
aspirin	*à l'aspirine*	a las·pee·reen
bees	*aux abeilles*	o za·bay·yer
codeine	*à la codéine*	a la ko·day·een
sulphur-based drugs	*aux sulfamides*	o sewl·fa·meed

I have a skin allergy.

J'ai une allergie	zhay ewn a·lair·zhee
de peau.	der po

For some food-related allergies, see **vegetarian & special meals**, page 151.

body talk

Here are a couple of colourful expressions referring to body parts:

I'm starving.

J'ai l'estomac dans	zhay les·to·ma don
les talons.	lay ta·lon
(lit: I have my stomach in my heels)	

I'm exhausted.

Je n'ai plus de jambes.	zher nay plew der zhomb
(lit: I don't have any more legs)	

parts of the body

My ... hurts.
 Mon/Ma ... me fait mal. m/f   mon/ma ... mer fay mal

I can't move my ...
 Je n'arrive pas à bouger   zher na·reev pa a boo·zhay
 mon/ma ... m/f   mon/ma ...

I have a cramp in my ...
 J'ai une crampe au ... m   zhay ewn kromp o ...
 J'ai une crampe à la ... f   zhay ewn kromp a la ...

My ... is swollen.
 Mon/Ma ... est enflé(e). m/f   mon/ma ... ay·ton·flay

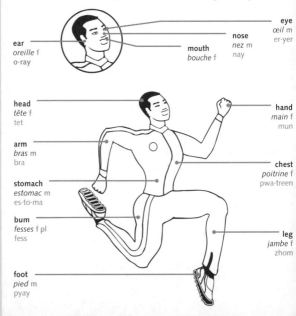

eye
œil m
er·yer

nose
nez m
nay

ear
oreille f
o·ray

mouth
bouche f

head
tête f
tet

arm
bras m
bra

stomach
estomac m
es·to·ma

bum
fesses f pl
fess

foot
pied m
pyay

hand
main f
mun

chest
poitrine f
pwa·treen

leg
jambe f
zhom

chemist

chez le pharmacien

I need something for ...
J'ai besoin d'un   zhay ber·zwun dun
médicament pour ...   may·dee·ka·mom poor ...

Do I need a prescription for ...?
J'ai besoin d'une   zhay ber·zwun dewn
ordonnance pour ...?   or·do·nons poor ...

How many times a day?
Combien de fois par jour?   kom·byun der fwa par zhoor

Will it make me drowsy?
Est-ce que ça peut provoquer   es·ker sa per pro·vo·kay
des somnolences?   day som·no·lons

For pharmaceutical items, see the **dictionary**.

listen for ...

a·vay·voo day·zha pree ser·see
   Avez-vous déjà   **Have you taken**
   pris ceci?   **this before?**

der fwa par zhoor (a·vek noo·ree·tewr)
   Deux fois par jour   **Twice a day (with food).**
   (avec nourriture).

ser·la ser·ra pray don (vung mee·newt)
   Cela sera prêt dans   **It'll be ready to pick up**
   (vingt minutes).   **in (20 minutes).**

tret·mon a swee·vrer zhews·ko boo
   Traitement à suivre   **You must complete**
   jusqu'au bout.   **the course.**

dentist

I have a ...	J'ai ...	zhay ...
broken tooth	une dent cassée	ewn don ka·say
cavity	une cavité	ewn ka·vee·tay
toothache	mal aux dents	mal o don

I've lost a ...	J'ai perdu ...	zhay pair·dew ...
I need a ...	J'ai besoin ...	zhay ber·zwun ...
crown	d'une couronne	dewn koo·ron
filling	d'un plombage	dun plom·bazh

My dentures are broken.
Mon dentier est cassé.   mon don·tyay ay ka·say

My orthodontic braces broke.
Mes bagues sont cassées.   may ba·ger son ka·say

My orthodontic braces fell off.
Mes bagues se sont   may ba·ger ser son
décollées.   day·ko·lay

My gums hurt.
Mes gencives me font mal.   may zhon·seev mer fon mal

I don't want it extracted.
Je ne veux pas que vous   zher ner ver pa ker voo
l'arrachiez.   la·rash·yay

Ouch!
Aïe!   a·ee

listen for ...

oo·vray too gron
Ouvrez tout grand.   **Open wide.**

run·say
Rinsez.   **Rinse!**

sa ne fer·ra pa der mal
Ça ne fera pas de mal.   **This won't hurt a bit.**

sa poo·ray fair un per mal
Ça pourrait faire un peu mal.   **This might hurt a little.**

SUSTAINABLE TRAVEL

As the climate change debate heats up, the matter of sustainability becomes an important part of the travel vernacular. In practical terms, this means assessing our impact on the environment and local cultures and economies – and acting to make that impact as positive as possible. Here are some basic phrases to get you on your way …

communication & cultural differences

I'd like to learn some of your local dialects.

J'aimerais apprendre	zhem·ray a·pron·dre
un peu de votre langue.	un per de vo·tre long

Would you like me to teach you some English?

Voulez-vous que je	voo·lay·voo ke zhe
vous apprenne	voo za·pren
un peu d'anglais? pol	un per dong·glay
Veux-tu que je t'apprenne	ver·tew ke zhe ta·pren
un peu d'anglais? inf	un per dong·glay

Is this a local or national custom?

Est-ce une coutume locale	es ewn koo·tewm lo·kal
ou nationale?	oo na·syon·nal

I respect your customs.

Je respecte vos coutumes.	zhe res·pekt vo koo·tewm

community benefit & involvement

What sorts of issues is this community facing?

A quelles difficultés est	a kel dee·fee·kewl·tay ay
confrontée cette	kon·fron·tay set
communauté?	ko·mew·no·tay

climate change	*changement* m *climatique*	shon·zhe·mon klee·ma·teek
freedom of religion in a secular society	*liberté* f *de religion dans une société séculaire*	lee·bair·tay de re·lee·zhyon don ewn so·syay·tay say·kew·lair
lack of drinkable water	*manque* m *d'eau potable*	mon·ke do po·ta·ble
malnutrition	*malnutrition* f	mal·new·tree·syon
racism	*racisme* m	ra·sees·me
unemployment	*chômage* m	sho·mazh

I'd like to volunteer my skills.
J'aimerais faire don de   zhem·ray fair don de
mes compétences.   may kom·pay·tons

Are there any volunteer programs available in the area?
Est-ce qu'il y a des   es keel ya day
programmes de bénévolat   pro·gram de bay·nay·vo·la
dans la région?   don la ray·zhyon

environment

Where can I recycle this?
Où est-ce que je peux   oo es ke zhe per
recycler ceci?   re·see·klay se·see

transport

Can we get there by public transport?
Peux-t-on s'y rendre en   pe·ton see ron·dre on
transport publique?   trons·por pewb·leek

Can we get there by bike?
Peux-t-on s'y rendre en vélo?   pe·ton see ron·dre on vay·lo

I'd prefer to walk there.
Je préfère y marcher.   zhe pray·fair ee mar·shay

accommodation

I'd like to stay at a locally run hotel.

J'aimerais loger dans un — zhem·ray lo·zhay don zun
hôtel géré localement. — o·tel zhay·ray lo·kal·mon

Are there any ecolodges here?

Est-ce qu'il y a des — es keel ya day
logements écologiques ici? — lozh·mon ay·ko·lo·zheek ee·see

Can I turn the air conditioning off and open the window?

Puis-je éteindre — pwee·zhe ay·tun·dre
l'air conditionné et — lair kon·dee·syon·nay ay
ouvrir la fenêtre? — oo·vreer la fe·nay·tre

There's no need to change my sheets.

Il n'y a pas besoin de — eel nee·ya pa be·zwun de
changer mes draps. — shon·zhay may dra

shopping

Where can I buy locally produced goods/souvenirs?

Où puis-je acheter des — oo pwee·zhe ash·tay day
marchandises/souvenirs — mar·shon·deez/soov·neer
produits localement? — pro·dwee lo·kal·mon

Do you sell Fair Trade products?

Est-ce que vous vendez — es ke voo von·day
des produits commerce — day pro·dwee ko·mairs
équitable? — ay·kee·ta·ble

food

Do you sell …?	*Est-ce que vous vendez …?*	es ke voo von·day …
locally produced food	*de la nourriture produite localement*	de la noo·ree·tewr pro·dweet lo·kal·mon
organic produce	*des produits organiques*	day pro·dwee or·ga·neek

Can you tell me which traditional foods I should try?

Pouvez-vous me dire quelle poo·vay·voo me deer kel
nourriture traditionnelle noo·ree·tewr tra·dee·syon·nel
je dois goûter? zhe dwa goo·tay

sightseeing

Are cultural tours available?

Offrez-vous des tours o·fray·voo day toor
culturels? kewl·tew·rel

Does your company ...?	*Est-ce que votre companie ...?*	es ke vo·tre kom·pa·nee ...
donate money to charity	*fait des dons aux charités*	fay day don o sha·ree·tay
hire local guides	*utilise des guides locaux*	ew·tee·leez day geed lo·ko
visit local businesses	*visite les commerces locaux*	vee·zeet lay kom·mairs lo·ko

Nouns in this dictionary have their gender indicated by ⓜ or ⓕ. If it's a plural noun, you'll also see pl. Where a word that could be either a noun or a verb has no gender indicated, it's a verb.

A

A

a/an *un(e)* ⓜ/ⓕ un/ewn
a little *un peu* ⓜ um per
a lot (of) *beaucoup (de)* bo·koo (der)
aboard *à bord* a bor
abortion *avortement* ⓜ a·vor·ter·mon
about *environ* on·vee·ron
above *au-dessus* o·der·sew
abroad *à l'étranger* a lay·tron·zhay
accept *accepter* ak·sep·tay
accident *accident* ⓜ ak·see·don
accommodation *logement* ⓜ lozh·mon
account *compte* ⓜ kont
ache *douleur* ⓕ doo·ler
achievement *réussite* ⓕ ray·ew·seet
acid (drug) *acide* ⓜ a·seed
across *de l'autre côté* ⓜ
    der lo·trer ko·tay don
act *jouer* zhoo·ay
activist *militant/militante* ⓜ/ⓕ
    mee·lee·ton(t)
actor *acteur/actrice* ⓜ/ⓕ ak·ter/ak·trees
acupuncture *acupuncture* ⓕ
    a·kew·pongk·tewr
adaptor *adaptateur* ⓜ a·dap·ta·ter
addicted (to drugs) *drogué* dro·gay
addiction *dépendance* ⓕ day·pon·dons
additional *supplémentaire*
    sew·play·mon·tair
address *adresse* ⓕ a·dres
administration *administration* ⓕ
    ad·mee·nee·stra·syon
admire *admirer* ad·mee·ray
admission (price) *prix* ⓜ *d'entrée*
    pree don·tray
admit *admettre* ad·me·trer
adult *adulte* ⓜ/ⓕ a·dewlt
advertisement *publicité* ⓕ
    pewb·lee·see·tay
advice *conseil* ⓜ kon·say

aerobics *aérobic* ⓜ a·ay·ro·beek
aerogram *aérogramme* ⓜ a·ay·ro·gram
aeroplane *avion* ⓜ a·vyon
affair *liaison* ⓕ lyay·zon
Africa *Afrique* ⓕ a·freek
after *après* a·pray
afternoon *après-midi* ⓜ a·pray·mee·dee
aftershave *après-rasage* ⓜ
    a·pray·ra·zazh
again *encore* ong·kor
against *contre* kon·trer
age *âge* ⓜ azh
aggressive *agressif/agressive* ⓜ/ⓕ
    a·gray·seef/a·gray·seev
agree *être d'accord* e·trer da·kor
agriculture *agriculture* ⓕ
    a·gree·kewl·tewr
ahead *en avant* on a·von
AIDS *SIDA* ⓜ see·da
air *air* ⓜ air
air-conditioned *climatisé*
    kee·ma·tee·zay
airline *ligne* ⓕ *aérienne*
    lee·nyer a·ay·ryen
airmail *par avion* par a·vyon
airplane *avion* ⓜ a·vyon
airport *aéroport* ⓜ a·ay·ro·por
airport tax *taxe* ⓕ *d'aéroport*
    taks da·ay·ro·por
aisle (on plane) *couloir* ⓜ koo·lwar
alarm clock *réveil* ⓜ ray·vay
alcohol *alcool* ⓜ al·kol
alive *vivant(e)* ⓜ/ⓕ vee·von(t)
all *tout* too
allergy *allergie* ⓕ a·lair·zhee
allow *permettre* pair·me·trer
almost *presque* pres·ker
alone *tout(e) seul(e)* ⓜ/ⓕ too(t) serl

already *déjà* day·zha
also *aussi* o·see
altar *autel* ⓜ o·tel
alternative *alternative* ⓕ al·tair·na·teev
altitude *altitude* ⓕ al·tee·tewd
always *toujours* too·zhoor
amateur *amateur* ⓜ a·ma·ter
amazing *stupéfiant(e)* ⓜ/ⓕ stew·pay·fyon(t)
ambassador *ambassadeur/ambassadrice* ⓜ/ⓕ om·ba·sa·der/om·ba·sa·drees
ambulance *ambulance* ⓕ om·bew·lons
among *parmi* par·mee
amount (money) *somme* ⓕ som
ancient *antique* on·teek
and *et* ay
angry *fâché(e)* ⓜ/ⓕ fa·shay
animal *animal* ⓜ a·nee·mal
ankle *cheville* ⓕ sher·vee·yer
annual *annuel(le)* ⓜ/ⓕ a·nwel
another *un/une autre* ⓜ/ⓕ un/ewn o·trer
answer *réponse* ⓕ ray·pons
answer *répondre* ray·pon·drer
ant *fourmi* ⓕ foor·mee
antibiotics *antibiotiques* ⓜ on·tee·byo·teek
antinuclear *anti-nucléaire* on·tee·new·klay·air
antique *antiquité* ⓕ on·tee·kee·tay
antiseptic *antiseptique* ⓜ on·tee·sep·teek
any *n'importe quel/quelle* ⓜ/ⓕ num·port kel
anyone *n'importe qui* num·port kee
anything *n'importe quoi* num·port kwa
anywhere *n'importe où* num·port oo
apartment *appartement* ⓜ a·par·ter·mon
appendix *appendice* a·pun·dees
appointment *rendez-vous* ⓜ ron·day·voo
approximately *à peu près* a per pray
April *avril* ⓜ a·vreel
archaeology *archéologie* ⓕ ar·kay·o·lo·zhee
architect *architecte(e)* ⓜ/ⓕ ar·shee·tekt
architecture *architecture* ar·shee·tek·tewr
argue *se disputer* ser dees·pew·tay

argument *débat* ⓜ day·ba
arm *bras* ⓜ bra
armchair *fauteuil* ⓜ fo·ter·yee
aromatherapy *aromathérapie* ⓕ a·ro·ma·tay·ra·pee
around *autour* o·toor
arrest *arrêter* a·ray·tay
arrivals *arrivées* ⓕ a·ree·vay
arrive *arriver* a·ree·vay
art *art* ⓜ ar
art gallery *galerie* ⓕ gal·ree
artist *artiste* ⓜ/ⓕ ar·teest
as *comme* kom
ashtray *cendrier* ⓜ son·dree·yay
Asia *Asie* ⓕ a·zee
ask (a question) *poser* po·zay
ask for (something) *demander* der·mon·day
aspirin *aspirine* ⓕ as·pee·reen
ass (bum) *cul* ⓜ kew
asthma *asthme* ⓜ as·mer
at *à* a
athletics *athlétisme* ⓜ at·lay·tees·mer
atmosphere *atmosphère* ⓕ at·mos·fair
attached *attaché(e)* ⓜ/ⓕ a·ta·shay
auction *vente* ⓕ *aux enchères* vont o zon·shair
August *août* ⓜ oot
aunt *tante* ⓕ tont
Australia *Australie* ⓕ o·stra·lee
Austria *Autriche* ⓕ o·treesh
automatic *automatique* o·to·ma·teek
automatic teller machine (ATM) *guichet* ⓜ *automatique de banque (GAB)* gee·shay o·to·ma·teek der bonk
autumn *automne* ⓜ o·ton
avenue *avenue* ⓕ av·new
awful *affreux/affreuse* ⓜ/ⓕ a·frer/a·frerz

B

B&W (film) *noir et blanc* nwar ay blong
baby *bébé* ⓜ bay·bay
baby food *bouillie* ⓕ boo·yee
baby powder *talc* ⓜ talk
back (body) *dos* ⓜ do
backpack *sac* ⓜ *à dos* sak a do

bad *mauvais(e)* ⓜ/ⓕ mo·vay(z)
bag *sac* ⓜ sak
baggage *bagages* ⓜ ba·gazh
baggage allowance *franchise* ⓕ fron·sheez
baggage claim *retrait* ⓜ *des bagages* rer·tray day ba·gazh
bakery *boulangerie* ⓕ boo·lon·zhree
balance (account) *solde* ⓜ sold
balcony *balcon* ⓜ bal·kon
ball (tennis/football) *balle/ballon* ⓕ/ⓜ bal/ba·lon
ballet *ballet* ⓜ ba·lay
band (music) *bande* ⓕ bond
bandage *pansement* ⓜ pons·mon
Band-Aid *sparadrap* ⓜ spa·ra·dra
bank *banque* ⓕ bonk
bank account *compte* ⓜ *bancaire* kont bong·kair
bank draft *traite* ⓕ *bancaire* tret bong·kair
banknote *billet* ⓜ *de banque* bee·yay der bonk
baptism *baptême* ⓜ ba·tem
bar *bar* ⓜ bar
bar work *travail* ⓜ *dans un bar* tra·vai don zun bar
baseball *baseball* ⓜ bez·bol
basic *fondamental* fon·da·mon·tal
basket *panier* ⓜ pan·yay
basketball *basket(ball)* ⓜ bas·ket(·bol)
bastard *salaud* ⓜ sa·lo
bath *baignoire* ⓕ be·nywar
bath (have a) *(prendre un) bain* ⓜ (pron·drer un) bun
bathing suit *maillot* ⓜ *de bain* may·yo der bun
bathroom *salle* ⓕ *de bain* sal der bun
battery *pile* ⓕ peel
battery (car) *batterie* ⓕ bat·ree
be *être* e·trer
beach *plage* ⓕ plazh
beautiful *beau/belle* ⓜ/ⓕ bo/bel
beauty salon *salon* ⓜ *de beauté* sa·lon der bo·tay
because *parce que* pars ker
become *devenir* derv·neer
bed *lit* ⓜ lee

bed linen *draps* ⓜ dra
bedding *literie* ⓕ leet·ree
bedroom *chambre* ⓕ *à coucher* shom·brer a koo·shay
bee *abeille* ⓕ a·bay
beer *bière* ⓕ byair
before *avant* a·von
begin *commencer* ko·mon·say
behind *derrière* dair·yair
Belgium *Belgique* ⓕ bel·zheek
belief *croyance* ⓕ krwa·yons
believe *croire* krwar
below *sous* soo
beside *à côté de* a ko·tay der
best *le/la meilleur(e)* ⓜ/ⓕ ler/la may·yer
bet *pari* ⓜ pa·ree
bet *parier* par·yay
better *meilleur(e)* ⓜ/ⓕ may·yer
between *entre* on·trer
bib *bavoir* ⓜ ba·vwar
bible *bible* ⓕ bee·bler
bicycle *vélo* ⓜ vay·lo
big *grand(e)* ⓜ/ⓕ gron(d)
bigger *plus grand(e)* ⓜ/ⓕ plew gron(d)
biggest *le/la plus grand(e)* ⓜ/ⓕ ler/la plew gron(d)
bike *vélo* ⓜ vay·lo
bike chain *chaîne* ⓕ *de bicyclette* shen der bee·see·klet
bike path *piste* ⓕ *cyclable* peest see·kla·bler
bill (restaurant) *addition* ⓕ a·dee·syon
bird *oiseau* ⓜ wa·zo
birth certificate *acte* ⓜ *de naissance* akt der nay·sons
birthday *anniversaire* ⓜ a·nee·vair·sair
bitch *salope* ⓕ sa·lop
bite *mordre* mor·drer
bite (dog) *morsure* ⓕ mor·sewr
bite (insect) *piqûre* ⓕ pee·kewr
bitter *amer/amère* ⓜ/ⓕ a·mair
black *noir(e)* ⓜ/ⓕ nwar
blanket *couverture* ⓕ koo·vair·tewr
blessing *grâce* ⓕ gras
blind *aveugle* a·ver·gler
blister *ampoule* ⓕ om·pool
blocked *bloqué(e)* ⓜ/ⓕ blo·kay
blood *sang* ⓜ son

blood group *groupe* ⓜ *sanguin*
groop song·gun

blood pressure *tension* ⓕ *artérielle*
ton·syon ar·tay·ryel

blood test *analyse* ⓕ *de sang*
a·na·leez der son

blue *bleu(e)* ⓜ/ⓕ bler

board (a plane, ship) *monter à bord de*
mon·tay a bor der

boarding house *pension* ⓕ pon·syon

boarding pass *carte* ⓕ *d'embarquement*
kart dom·bar·ker·mon

boat *bateau* ⓜ ba·to

body *corps* ⓜ kor

bone *os* ⓜ os

book *livre* ⓜ leev·rer

book (make a booking) *réserver*
ray·zair·vay

booked up *complet/complète* ⓜ/ⓕ
kom·play/kom·plet

bookshop *librairie* ⓕ lee·bray·ree

boot (footwear) *botte* ⓕ bot

border *frontière* ⓕ fron·tyair

bored (be) *s'ennuyer* son·nwee·yay

boring *ennuyeux/ennuyeuse* ⓜ/ⓕ
on·nwee·yer/on·nwee·yerz

born *né(e)* ⓜ/ⓕ nay

borrow *emprunter* om·prun·tay

botanic garden *jardin* ⓜ *botanique*
zhar·dun bo·ta·neek

both *tous les deux* too lay der

bottle *bouteille* ⓕ boo·tay

bottle opener *ouvre-bouteille* ⓜ
oo·vrer·boo·tay

boulevard *boulevard* ⓜ bool·var

bowl *bol* ⓜ bol

box *boîte* ⓕ bwat

boxer shorts *boxer-short* ⓜ bok·sair·short

boxing *boxe* ⓕ boks

boy *garçon* ⓜ gar·son

boyfriend *petit ami* ⓜ per·tee ta·mee

bra *soutien-gorge* ⓜ soo·tyung·gorzh

Braille *braille* ⓕ bra·yer

brakes *freins* ⓜ frun

brave *courageux/courageuse* ⓜ/ⓕ
koo·ra·zher/koo·ra·zherz

bread *pain* ⓜ pun

break *casser* ka·say

break down *tomber en panne*
tom·bay on pan

breakfast *petit déjeuner* ⓜ
per·tee day·zher·nay

breast *sein* ⓜ sun

breathe *respirer* res·pee·ray

brewery *brasserie* ⓕ bra·ser·ree

bribe *pot-de-vin* ⓜ po·der·vun

bribe *suborner* sew·bor·nay

bridge *pont* ⓜ pon

briefcase *serviette* ⓕ sair·vyet

brilliant *génial(e)* ⓜ/ⓕ zhay·nyal

bring (a person) *amener* am·nay

bring (a thing) *apporter* a·por·tay

brochure *brochure* ⓕ bro·shewr

broken *cassé(e)* ⓜ/ⓕ ka·say

broken down (tombé) en panne
(tom·bay) on pan

bronchitis *bronchite* ⓕ bron·sheet

brother *frère* ⓜ frair

brown *brun/brune* ⓜ/ⓕ brun/brewn

bruise *bleu* ⓜ bler

brush *brosse* ⓕ bros

bucket *seau* ⓜ so

Buddhist *bouddhiste* boo·deest

budget *budget* ⓜ bew·dzay

buffet *buffet* ⓜ bew·fay

bug (insect) *insecte* ⓜ un·sekt

build *construire* kon·strweer

building *bâtiment* ⓜ ba·tee·mon

burn *brûlure* ⓕ brew·lewr

burn *brûler* brew·lay

bus (city) (auto)bus ⓜ (o·to)bews

bus (intercity) (auto)car ⓜ (o·to)kar

bus station *gare* ⓕ *routière* gar roo·tyair

bus stop *arrêt* ⓜ *d'autobus*
a·ray do·to·bews

business *affaires* ⓕ a·fair

business class *classe* ⓕ *affaires* klas a·fair

business man/woman *homme/femme*
d'affaires ⓜ/ⓕ om/fam da·fair

business trip *voyage* ⓜ *d'affaires*
vwa·yazh da·fair

busker *musicien(ne)* ⓜ/ⓕ *des rues*
mew·zee·syun/mew·zee·syen day rew

busy *occupé(e)* ⓜ/ⓕ o·kew·pay

but *mais* may

butcher's shop *boucherie* ⓕ boosh·ree

butterfly *papillon* ⓜ pa·pee·yon
button *bouton* ⓜ boo·ton
buy *acheter* ash·tay
by *par* par

C

cable *câble* ⓜ ka·bler
cable car *téléphérique* ⓕ tay·lay·fay·reek
cafe *café* ⓜ ka·fay
cake shop *pâtisserie* ⓕ pa·tees·ree
calculator *calculatrice* ⓕ kal·kew·la·trees
calendar *calendrier* ⓜ ka·lon·dree·yay
call *appeler* a·play
camera *appareil* ⓜ *photo* a·pa·ray fo·to
camp *camp* ⓜ kon
camping ground *camping* ⓜ kom·peeng
camping store *magasin* ⓜ *pour équipement de camping* ma·ga·zun poor ay·keep·mon der kom·peeng
campsite *terrain* ⓜ *de camping* tay·run der kom·peeng
can (be able) *pouvoir* poo·vwar
can (have permission) *pouvoir* poo·vwar
can (tin) *boîte* ⓕ bwat
can opener *ouvre-boîte* ⓜ oo·vrer·bwat
Canada *Canada* ⓜ ka·na·da
cancel *annuler* a·new·lay
cancer *cancer* ⓜ kon·sair
candle *bougie* ⓕ boo·zhee
capitalism *capitalisme* ⓜ ka·pee·ta·lees·mer
car *voiture* ⓕ vwa·tewr
car hire *location* ⓕ *de voitures* lo·ka·syon der vwa·tewr
car owner's title *carte grise* ⓕ kart greez
car registration *immatriculation* ⓕ ee·ma·tree·kew·la·syon
caravan *caravane* ⓕ ka·ra·van
care for (someone) *soigner* swa·nyay
career *carrière* ⓕ kar·ryair
careful *soigneux/soigneuse* ⓜ/ⓕ swa·nyer/swa·nyerz
Careful! *Attention!* a·ton·syon
caring *aimant(e)* ⓜ/ⓕ ay·mon(t)
carpark *parking* ⓜ par·keeng
carpenter *menuisier* ⓜ mer·nwee·zyay
carry *porter* por·tay

carton (for yoghurt) *pot* ⓜ po
carton (for ice cream) *boîte* ⓕ bwat
cartoon *dessin* ⓜ *animé* day·sun a·nee·may
cash *argent* ⓜ ar·zhon
cash (a cheque) *encaisser* ong·kay·say
cash register *caisse* ⓕ *(enregistreuse)* kes (on·rer·zhee·strerz)
cashier *caissier/caissière* ⓜ/ⓕ kay·syay/kay·syair
cassette *cassette* ⓕ ka·set
castle *château* ⓜ sha·to
casual work *travail* ⓜ *intermittent* tra·vai un·tair·mee·ton
cat *chat* ⓜ sha
catch *attraper* a·tra·pay
cathedral *cathédrale* ⓕ ka·tay·dral
Catholic *catholique* ka·to·leek
cause *cause* ⓕ koz
caution *prudence* ⓕ prew·dons
cave *grotte* ⓕ grot
CD *CD* ⓜ say·day
celebration *fête* ⓕ fet
cemetery *cimetière* ⓜ seem·tyair
cent *cent* ⓜ sent
centimetre *centimètre* ⓜ son·tee·me·trer
centre *centre* ⓜ son·trer
ceramic *céramique* ⓕ say·ra·meek
certain *certain(e)* ⓜ/ⓕ sair·tun/·ten
certificate *certificat* ⓜ sair·tee·fee·ka
chain *chaîne* ⓕ shen
chair *chaise* ⓕ shez
chairlift (skiing) *télésiège* ⓜ tay·lay·syezh
champagne *champagne* ⓜ shom·pa·nyer
championship *championnat* ⓜ shom·pyo·na
chance *hasard* ⓜ a·zar
change *changer* shon·zhay
change (money) *échanger* ay·shon·zhay
change (coins) *monnaie* ⓕ mo·nay
changing room (in shop) *cabine* ⓕ *d'essayage* ka·been day·say·yazh
channel *chaîne* ⓕ shen
charming *charmant(e)* ⓜ/ⓕ shar·mon(t)

chat *bavarder* ba·var·day
chat up *draguer* dra·gay
cheap *bon marché* ⓜ bon mar·shay
cheat *tricheur/tricheuse* ⓜ/ⓕ
  tree·sher/tree·sherz
check *vérifier* vay·ree·fyay
check (banking) *chèque* ⓜ shek
check (bill) *addition* ⓕ la·dee·syon
check-in (desk) *enregistrement*
  on·rer·zhee·strer·mon
checkpoint *contrôle* ⓜ kon·trol
cheese *fromage* fro·mazh
chef *chef de cuisine* ⓜ
  shef der kwee·zeen
chemist *pharmacie* ⓕ far·ma·see
chemist (person) *pharmacien(ne)* ⓜ/ⓕ
  far·ma·syun/far·ma·syen
cheque (banking) *chèque* ⓜ shek
chess *échecs* ⓜ ay·shek
chess board *échiquier* ⓜ ay·shee·kyay
chest *poitrine* ⓕ pwa·treen
chicken *poulet* ⓜ poo·lay
child *enfant* ⓜ&ⓕ on·fon
child seat *siège* ⓜ *pour enfant*
  syezh poor on·fon
childminding *garderie* ⓕ gard·ree
children *enfants* ⓜ&ⓕ pl on·fon
chiropractor *chiropracteur* ⓜ
  kee·ro·prak·ter
chocolate *chocolat* ⓜ sho·ko·la
choice *choix* ⓜ shwa
choose *choisir* shwa·zeer
Christian *chrétien(ne)* ⓜ/ⓕ
  kray·tyun/kray·tyen
Christian name *prénom* ⓜ pray·non
Christmas *Noël* ⓜ no·el
Christmas Day *jour* ⓜ *de Noël*
  zhoor der no·el
Christmas Eve ⓕ *veille de Noël*
  vay der no·el
church *église* ⓕ ay·gleez
cigar *cigare* ⓜ see·gar
cigarette *cigarette* ⓕ see·ga·ret
cigarette lighter *briquet* ⓜ bree·kay
cinema *cinéma* ⓜ see·nay·ma
circle *cercle* ⓜ sair·kler
circus *cirque* ⓜ seerk
citizen *citoyen(ne)* ⓜ/ⓕ
  see·twa·yun/see·twa·yen

citizenship *citoyenneté* ⓕ see·twa·yen·tay
city *ville* ⓕ veel
city centre *centre-ville* ⓜ son·trer·veel
city hall *mairie* ⓕ may·ree
civil rights *droits* ⓜ pl *civils*
  drwa see·veel
class *classe* ⓕ klas
classical *classique* kla·seek
clean *propre* pro·prer
clean *nettoyer* net·wa·yay
cleaning *nettoyage* ⓜ net·wa·yazh
clear *clair(e)* ⓜ/ⓕ klair
client *client(e)* ⓜ/ⓕ klee·on(t)
cliff *falaise* ⓕ fa·lez
climb *monter* mon·tay
cloak *cape* ⓕ kap
cloakroom *vestiaire* ⓕ vays·tyair
clock *pendule* ⓕ pon·dewl
close *proche* prosh
close *fermer* fair·may
closed *fermé(e)* ⓜ/ⓕ fair·may
clothes line *corde à linge* ⓕ kord a lunzh
clothing *vêtements* ⓜ vet·mon
clothing store *magasin* ⓜ *de*
  vêtements ma·ga·zun der vet·mon
cloud *nuage* ⓜ nwazh
cloudy *nuageux/nuageuse* ⓜ/ⓕ
  nwa·zher/nwa·zherz
clutch *embrayage* om·bray·yazh
coach *entraîneur* ⓜ on·tray·ner
coast *côte* ⓕ kot
coat *manteau* ⓜ mon·to
cocaine *cocaïne* ⓕ ko·ka·een
cockroach *cafard* ⓜ ka·far
cocktail *cocktail* ⓜ kok·tel
coffee *café* ⓜ ka·fay
coins *pièces* ⓕ pyes
cold *froid(e)* ⓜ/ⓕ frwa(d)
colleague *collègue* ⓜ/ⓕ ko·leg
collect (stamps etc) *collectionner*
  ko·lek·syo·nay
collect call *appel* ⓜ *en PCV*
  a·pel on pay·say·vay
collection *accumulation* ⓕ
  a·kew·mew·la·syon
college *institut universitaire* ⓜ
  un·stee·tew ew·nee·vair·see·tair
college (vocational) *école professionnelle*
  ⓕ ay·kol pro·fay·syo·nel

colour *couleur* ① koo·ler
comb *peigne* ⑩ pe·nyer
combination *combinaison* ①
kom·bee·nay·zon
come *venir* ver·neer
comedy *comédie* ① ko·may·dee
comfortable *confortable* kon·for·ta·bler
comic (magazine) *bande dessinée* ①
bond day·see·nay
commission *commission* ① ko·mee·syon
common *commun(e)* ⑩/①
ko·mun/ko·mewn
communism *communisme* ⑩
ko·mew·nees·mer
communist *communiste* ko·mew·neest
community *communauté* ①
ko·mew·no·tay
companion *compagnon/compagne* ⑩/①
kom·pa·nyon/kom·pa·nyer
company *entreprise* ① on·trer·preez
compass *boussole* ① boo·sol
competition *compétition* ①
kom·pay·tees·yon
complain *se plaindre* ser plun·drer
complaint *plainte* ① plunt
complimentary (free) *gratuit(e)* ⑩/①
gra·twee(t)
computer *ordinateur* ⑩ or·dee·na·ter
computer game *jeu* ⑩ *électronique*
zher ay·lek·tro·neek
concert *concert* ⑩ kon·sair
concussion *commotion* ① *cérébrale*
ko·mo·syon say·ray·bral
conditioner (hair) *après-shampooing* ⑩
a·pray·shom·pwung
condom *préservatif* ⑩ pray·zair·va·teef
conductor (bus) *receveur* ⑩ rer·ser·ver
conference (big) *congrès* ⑩ kong·gray
conference (small) *colloque* ⑩ ko·lok
confession (religious) *confession* ①
kon·fay·syon
confirm (a booking) *confirmer*
kon·feer·may
congratulations *félicitations*
fay·lee·see·ta·syon!
connection *rapport* ⑩ ra·por
conservative *conservateur/conservatrice*
⑩/① kon·sair·va·ter/kon·sair·va·trees
constipation *constipation* ①
kon·stee·pa·syon

consulate *consulat* ⑩ kon·so·la
contact lenses *verres de contact* ⑩
vair der kon·takt
contraceptive *contraceptif* ⑩
kon·trer·sep·teef
contract *contrat* ⑩ kon·tra
convenience store *supérette* ① *de
quartier* sew·pay·ret der kar·tyay
convent *couvent* ⑩ koo·von
conversation *conversation* ①
kon·vair·sa·syon
cook *cuisinier/cuisinière* ⑩/①
kwee·zee·nyay/kwee·zee·nyair
cook *cuire* kweer
cool *frais/fraîche* ⑩/① fray/fresh
cooperate *coopérer* ko·o·pay·ray
cop *flic* ⑩ fleek
corkscrew *tire-bouchon* ⑩ teer·boo·shon
corner *coin* ⑩ kwun
correct *correct(e)* ⑩/① ko·rekt
corrupt *corrompu(e)* ⑩/① ko·rom·pew
cost *coût* ⑩ koo
cotton *coton* ⑩ ko·ton
cotton balls *ouate* ① *de coton*
wat der ko·ton
cough *toux* ① too
cough medicine *syrop* ⑩ *contre la toux*
see·ro kon·trer la too
count *compter* kon·tay
counter (at bar) *comptoir* ⑩ kon·twar
country *pays* ⑩ pay·ee
countryside *campagne* ① kom·pa·nyer
coupon *coupon* ⑩ koo·pon
court (legal) *tribunal* ⑩ tree·bew·nal
court (tennis) *court* ⑩ koor
cover charge *couvert* ① koo·vair
cow *vache* ① vash
crafts *artisanat* ⑩ ar·tee·za·na
crash *accident* ⑩ ak·see·don
crazy *fou/folle* ⑩/① foo/fol
cream *crème* ① krem
creche *crèche* ① kresh
credit *crédit* ⑩ kray·dee
credit card *carte* ① *de crédit*
kart der kray·dee
creek *crique* ① kreek
crime *délit* ⑩ day·lee
crop (gathered) *récolte* ① ray·kolt
crop (grown) *culture* ① kewl·tewr

cross *traverser* tra·vair·say
cross (angry) *fâché(e)* ⓜ/ⓕ fa·shay
cross (religious) *croix* ⓕ krwa
crowd *foule* ⓕ fool
crowded *bondé(e)* ⓜ/ⓕ bon·day
cry *pleurer* pler·ray
cup *tasse* ⓕ tas
cupboard *placard* ⓜ pla·kar
current *actuel(le)* ⓜ/ⓕ ak·twel
currency exchange *taux* ⓜ *de change* to der shonzh
current (electricity) *courant* ⓜ koo·ron
current affairs *actualité* ak·twa·lee·tay
custom *coutume* ⓕ koo·tewm
customer *client(e)* ⓜ/ⓕ klee·on(t)
customs *douane* ⓕ dwan
cut *couper* koo·pay
cute *mignon/mignonne* ⓜ/ⓕ mee·nyon/mee·nyon
cutlery *couverts* ⓜ koo·vair
CV *CV* ⓜ say·vay
cycle *faire du vélo* fair dew vay·lo
cycling *cyclisme* ⓜ see·lee·smer
cyclist *cycliste* ⓜ/ⓕ see·kleest

D

dad *papa* ⓜ pa·pa
daily *quotidien(ne)* ⓜ/ⓕ ko·tee·dyun/ko·tee·dyen
damage *dégâts* ⓜ day·ga
dance *danser* don·say
dancing *danse* ⓕ dons
dangerous *dangereux/dangereuse* ⓜ/ⓕ don·zhrer/don·zhrerz
dark *obscur(e)* ⓜ/ⓕ ob·skewr
dark (of colour) *foncé(e)* ⓜ/ⓕ fon·say
date (go out with) *sortir avec* sor·teer a·vek
date (appointment) *rendez-vous* ⓜ ron·day·voo
date (day) *date* ⓕ dat
date of birth *date* ⓕ *de naissance* dat der nay·sons
daughter *fille* ⓕ fee·yer
dawn *aube* ob
day *jour* ⓜ zhoor
day after tomorrow *après-demain* a·pray·der·mun

day before yesterday *avant-hier* a·von·tyair
dead *mort(e)* ⓜ/ⓕ mor(t)
deaf *sourd(e)* ⓜ/ⓕ soor(d)
deal (cards) *donner* do·nay
death *mort* ⓕ mor
December *décembre* ⓜ day·som·brer
decide *se décider* ser day·see·day
decision *décision* ⓕ day·see·zyon
deep *profond(e)* ⓜ/ⓕ pro·fon(d)
definite *bien déterminé* byun day·tair·mee·nay
deforestation *déboisement* ⓜ day·bwaz·mon
degree *diplôme* ⓜ dee·plom
delay *retard* ⓜ rer·tard
delicatessen *charcuterie* ⓕ shar·kew·tree
deliver *livrer* leev·ray
demand *exiger* eg·zee·zhay
democracy *démocratie* ⓕ day·mo·kra·see
demonstration *manifestation* ⓕ ma·nee·fay·sta·syon
Denmark *Danemark* ⓜ dan·mark
dental floss *fil* ⓜ *dentaire* feel don·tair
dentist *dentiste* ⓜ don·teest
deny *nier* nee·ay
deodorant *déodorant* ⓜ day·o·do·ron
depart (leave) *partir* par·teer
department store *grand magasin* ⓜ gron ma·ga·zun
departure *départ* ⓜ day·par
deposit *dépôt* ⓜ day·po
descendent *descendant(e)* ⓜ/ⓕ day·son·don(t)
desert *désert* ⓜ day·zair
design *concevoir* kon·ser·vwar
dessert *dessert* ⓜ day·sair
destination *destination* ⓕ des·tee·na·syon
destroy *détruire* day·trweer
detail *détail* ⓜ day·tai
development *développement* ⓜ day·vlop·mon
diabetes *diabète* ⓜ dya·bet
dial tone *tonalité* ⓕ to·na·lee·tay
diaper *couche* ⓕ koosh
diaphragm *diaphragme* ⓜ dya·frag·mer
diarrhoea *diarrhée* ⓕ dya·ray
diary *agenda* ⓜ a·zhun·da

dice *dés* ⓜ day
dictionary *dictionnaire* ⓜ deek·syo·nair
die *mourir* moo·reer
diesel *gas-oil* ⓜ gaz·wal
diet *régime* ⓜ ray·zheem
different *différent(e)* ⓜ/ⓕ dee·fay·ron(t)
difficult *difficile* dee·fee·seel
dining car *wagon-restaurant* ⓜ va·gon·res·to·ron
dinner *dîner* ⓜ dee·nay
diploma *diplôme* ⓜ dee·plom
direct *direct(e)* ⓜ/ⓕ dee·rekt
direct (a film) *réaliser* ray·a·lee·zay
direct-dial *composition* ⓕ *directe* kom·po·zees·yon dee·rekt
direction *direction* ⓕ dee·rek·syon
director (film) *réalisateur/réalisatrice* ⓜ/ⓕ ray·a·lee·za·ter/ray·a·lee·za·trees
dirty *sale* sal
disabled *handicapé(e)* ⓜ/ⓕ on·dee·ka·pay
disappointed *déçu(e)* ⓜ/ⓕ day·sew
disaster *désastre* ⓜ day·zas·trer
discount *remise* ⓕ rer·meez
discover *découvrir* day·koov·reer
discrimination *discrimination* ⓕ dee·skree·mee·na·syon
discuss *discuter* dee·skew·tay
disease *maladie* ⓕ ma·la·dee
dish *plat* ⓜ pla
dishonest *malhonnête* mal·o·net
disinfectant *désinfectant* ⓜ day·zun·fek·ton
disk (CD-ROM) *disque* ⓜ deesk
disk (floppy) *disquette* ⓕ dees·ket
distance *distance* ⓕ dees·tons
distributor *concessionnaire* ⓜ kon·say·syo·nair
disturb *déranger* day·ron·zhay
dive *plonger* plon·zhay
diving *plongée sous-marine* ⓕ plon·zhay soo·ma·reen
diving equipment *équipement* ⓜ *de plongée* ay·keep·mon der plon·zhay
divorced *divorcé(e)* ⓜ/ⓕ dee·vor·say
dizzy (be dizzy) *avoir la tête qui tourne* a·vwar la tet kee toorn
do *faire* fair
doctor *médecin* ⓜ mayd·sun

dog ⓜ *chien* shyun
dole *allocation* ⓕ *de chômage* a·lo·ka·syon der sho·mazh
doll *poupée* ⓕ poo·pay
door *porte* ⓕ port
dope (drugs) *drogue* ⓕ drog
dose *dose* ⓕ doz
double *double* doo·bler
double bed *grand lit* ⓜ gron lee
double room *chambre* ⓕ *pour deux personnes* shom·brer poor der pair·son
down *en bas* on ba
dozen *douzaine* ⓕ doo·zen
drama (theatre) *théâtre* ⓜ tay·a·trer
draw (picture) *dessiner* day·see·nay
dream *rêver* ray·vay
dress (oneself) *s'habiller* sa·bee·yay
dress *robe* ⓕ rob
drink *boisson* ⓕ bwa·son
drink *boire* bwar
drink (alcoholic) *verre* ⓜ vair
drive *conduire* kon·dweer
drivers licence *permis* ⓜ *de conduire* pair·mee der kon·dweer
drop *laisser tomber* lay·say tom·bay
drug *drogue* ⓕ drog
drug addiction *toxicomanie* ⓕ tok·see·ko·ma·nee
drug dealer *trafiquant* ⓜ *de drogue* tra·fee·kon der drog
drugs *drogue* ⓕ drog
drum *tambour* ⓜ tom·boor
drums *batterie* ⓕ ba·tree
drunk *ivre* ee·vrer
dry *sec/sèche* ⓜ/ⓕ sek/sesh
dry (clothes) *sécher* say·shay
duck *canard* ⓜ ka·nar
dummy (pacifier) *tétine* ⓕ tay·teen
during *pendant* pon·don
dust *poussière* ⓕ poo·syair
duty *devoir* ⓜ der·vwar

E

each *chaque* shak
ear *oreille* ⓕ o·ray
early *tôt* to
earn *gagner* ga·nyay

earrings *boucles* ① *d'oreille*
boo·kler do·ray
Earth *Terre* ① tair
earth (ground) *terre* ① tair
earthquake *tremblement* ⓜ *de terre*
trom·bler·mon der tair
east *est* ⓜ est
Easter *Pâques* pak
easy *facile* fa·seel
eat *manger* mon·zhay
economy *économie* ① ay·ko·no·mee
economy class *classe* ① *touriste*
klas too·reest
ecstasy (drug) *ecstasy* ⓜ ek·sta·zee
eczema *eczéma* ⓜ eg·zay·ma
edge *bord* ⓜ bor
editor *rédacteur/rédactrice* ⓜ/①
ray·dak·ter/ray·dak·trees
education *éducation* ① ay·dew·ka·syon
effect *effet* ⓜ ay·fay
eight *huit* weet
elderly *âgé(e)* ⓜ/① a·zhay
election *élection* ① ay·lek·syon
electrical store *magasin* ⓜ *qui vend*
des appareils électriques ma·ga·zun
kee von day za·pa·ray ay·lek·treek
electricity *électricité* ①
ay·lek·tree·see·tay
elevator *ascenseur* ⓜ a·son·ser
email *e-mail* ⓜ ay·mel
embarrass *gêner* zhay·nay
embarrassed *gêné(e)* ⓜ/① zhay·nay
embarrassing *gênant(e)* ⓜ/①
zhay·non(t)
embassy *ambassade* ⓜ om·ba·sad
embroidery *broderie* ① bro·dree
emergency *cas urgent* ⓜ ka ewr·zhon
emotional (person) *facilement ému*
fa·seel·mon ay·mew
employee *employé/employée* ⓜ/①
om·plwa·yay/om·plwa·yay
employer *employeur* ⓜ om·plwa·yer
empty *vide* veed
end *bout* ⓜ boo
end *finir* fee·neer
endangered species *espèce* ①
menacée de disparition es·pes
mer·na·say der dees·pa·rees·yon
energy *énergie* ① ay·nair·zhee

engaged *fiancé(e)* ⓜ/① fyon·say
engagement *fiançailles* ① fyon·sai
engine *moteur* ⓜ mo·ter
engineer *ingénieur* ⓜ un·zhay·nyer
engineering *ingénierie* un·zhay·nee·ree
England *Angleterre* ① ong·gler·tair
English *anglais(e)* ⓜ/① ong·glay(z)
enjoy (oneself) *s'amuser* sa·mew·zay
enough *assez* a·say
enter *entrer* on·tray
entertainment guide
programme ⓜ *des spectacles*
pro·gram day spek·tak·ler
enthusiastic *enthousiaste* on·tooz·yast
entry *entrée* ① on·tray
envelope *enveloppe* ① on·vlop
environment *environnement* ⓜ
on·vee·ron·mon
epilepsy *épilepsie* ① ay·pee·lep·see
equal *égale* ay·gal
equal opportunity *égalité* ① *des chances*
ay·ga·lee·tay day shons
equality *égalité* ① ay·ga·lee
equipment *équipement* ⓜ ay·keep·mon
escalator *escalier* ⓜ *roulant*
es·ka·lyay roo·lon
escape *échapper* ay·sha·pay
estate agency *agence* ① *immobilière*
a·zhons ee·mo·bee·lyair
euro *euro* ⓜ er·ro
Europe *Europe* ① er·rop
euthanasia *euthanasie* ① er·ta·na·zee
evening *soir* ⓜ swar
event *événement* ⓜ ay·ven·mon
every *chaque* shak
every day *tous les jours* too lay zhoor
everyone *tout le monde* too ler mond
everything *tout* too
exactly *exactement* eg·zak·ter·mon
exam *examen* ⓜ eg·za·mun
example *exemple* ⓜ eg·zom·pler
excellent *excellent(e)* ⓜ/① ek·say·lon
except *sauf* sof
excess (baggage) *excédent* ek·say·don
exchange *échange* ⓜ ay·shonzh
exchange *échanger* ay·shon·zhay
exchange rate *taux* ⓜ *de change*
to der shonzh
excluded *pas compris* pa kom·pree

exercise *exercice* ⓜ eg·zair·sees

exhaust (car) *pot* ⓜ *d'échappement*
po day·shap·mon

exhausted *épuisé(e)* ⓜ/ⓕ ay·pwee·zay

exhibition *exposition* ⓕ
ek·spo·zee·syon

exit *sortie* ⓕ sor·tee

expensive *cher/chère* ⓜ/ⓕ shair

experience *expérience* ⓕ eks·pair·yons

explain *expliquer* eks·plee·kay

exploitation *exploitation* ⓕ
eks·plwa·ta·syon

export *exporter* eks·por·tay

express (mail) *exprès* eks·pres

express mail (by) *par exprès*
par eks·pres

extension (visa) *prolongation* ⓕ
pro·long·ga·syon

extra *supplémentaire* sew·play·mon·tair

extraordinary *extraordinaire*
eks·tra·or·dee·nair

eye *œil* ⓜ er·yee

eyes *yeux* ⓜ yer

F

fabric *tissu* ⓕ tee·sew

face *visage* ⓜ vee·zazh

face cloth *gant* ⓜ *de toilette*
gon der twa·let

fact *fait* ⓜ fet

factory *usine* ⓕ ew·zeen

factory worker *ouvrier* ⓜ *d'usine/*
ouvrière ⓕ *d'usine* oo·vree·yay
dew·zeen/oo·vree·yair dew·zeen

failure *échec* ⓜ ay·shek

faith *foi* ⓕ fwa

fall *tomber* tom·bay

fall (autumn) *automne* ⓜ o·ton

false *faux/fausse* ⓜ/ⓕ fo/fos

family *famille* ⓕ fa·mee·yer

family name *nom* ⓜ *de famille*
non der fa·mee·yer

famous *célèbre* say·leb·rer

fan (machine) *ventilateur* ⓜ
von·tee·la·ter

fan (of person) *fan* ⓜ/ⓕ fan

fanbelt *courroie* ⓕ *de ventilateur*
koor·wa der von·tee·la·ter

far *lointain(e)* ⓜ/ⓕ lwun·tun/·ten

fare *tarif* ⓜ ta·reef

farm *ferme* ⓕ ferm

farmer *agriculteur/agricultrice* ⓜ/ⓕ
a·gree·kewl·ter/a·gree·kewl·trees

fascist *fasciste* fa·sheest

fashion *mode* ⓕ mod

fast *rapide* ra·peed

fat *gras/grasse* ⓜ/ⓕ gra/gras

fate *destin* ⓜ des·tun

father *père* ⓜ pair

father-in-law *beau-père* ⓜ bo·pair

faucet *robinet* ⓜ ro·bee·nay

fault (someone's) *faute* ⓕ fot

faulty *défectueux/défectueuse* ⓜ/ⓕ
day·fek·twer/day·fek·twerz

fax machine *fax* ⓜ faks

fear *peur* ⓕ per

February *février* ⓜ fayv·ree·yay

feed *nourrir* noo·reer

feel (touch) *toucher* too·shay

feeling (physical) *sensation* ⓕ
son·sa·syon

feeling (emotion) *sentiment* ⓜ
son·tee·mon

female *femelle* fer·mel

fence *barrière* ⓕ bar·yair

fencing *escrime* ⓕ es·kreem

ferry *bac* ⓜ bak

festival *fête* ⓕ fet

fever *fièvre* ⓕ fyev·rer

few *peu* per

fiance *fiancé* ⓜ fyon·say

fiancee *fiancée* ⓕ fyon·say

fiction *fiction* ⓕ feek·syon

field *champ* ⓜ shom

fight *bagarre* ⓕ ba·gar

fill *remplir* rom·pleer

film (cinema) *film* ⓜ feelm

film (for camera) *pellicule* ⓕ
pay·lee·kewl

film speed *sensibilité* ⓕ *de la pellicule*
son·see·bee·lee·tay der la pay·lee·kewl

find *trouver* troo·vay

fine (penalty) *amende* ⓕ a·mond

finger *doigt* ⓜ dwa

finish *finir* fee·neer

fire *feu* ⓜ fer

firewood *bois* ⓜ *de chauffage*
bwa der sho·fazh

first *premier/première* ⓜ/ⓕ
prer·myay/prer·myair
first class *première classe* ⓕ
prer·myair klas
first-aid kit *trousse* ⓕ *à pharmacie*
troos a far·ma·see
fish *poisson* ⓜ pwa·son
fish shop *poissonnerie* ⓕ pwa·son·ree
fishing *pêche* ⓕ pesh
five *cinq* sungk
flag *drapeau* ⓜ dra·po
flannel (washing) *gant* ⓜ *de toilette*
gon der twa·let
flashlight *lampe* ⓕ *de poche*
lomp der posh
flat *plat(e)* ⓜ/ⓕ pla(t)
flavour *goût* ⓜ goo
flea *puce* ⓕ pews
fleamarket *marché* ⓜ *aux puces*
mar·shay o pews
flight *vol* ⓜ vol
flood *inondation* ⓕ ee·non·da·syon
flooding *inondation* ⓕ ee·non·da·syon
floor *plancher* ⓜ plon·shay
floor (storey) *étage* ⓜ ay·tazh
florist *fleuriste* ⓜ&ⓕ fler·reest
flower *fleur* ⓕ fler
flu *grippe* ⓕ greep
fly *mouche* ⓕ moosh
fly *voler* vo·lay
foggy *brumeux/brumeuse* ⓜ/ⓕ
brew·mer/brew·merz
follow *suivre* swee·vrer
food *nourriture* ⓕ noo·ree·tewr
food supplies *provisions* ⓕ pl
pro·vee·zyon
foot (pied) ⓜ pyay
football (soccer) *football* ⓜ foot·bol
footpath *sentier* ⓜ son·tyay
for *pour* poor
forecast *prévision* ⓕ pray·vee·zyon
forecast *prévoir* pray·vwar
foreign *étranger/étrangère* ⓜ/ⓕ
ay·tron·zhay/ay·tron·zhair
forest *forêt* ⓕ fo·ray
forever *pour toujours* poor too·zhoor
forget *oublier* oo·blee·yay
forgive *pardonner* par·do·nay
fork *fourchette* ⓕ foor·shet
fortnight *quinze jours* ⓜ pl kunz zhoor

fortune (money) *fortune* ⓕ for·tewn
fortune teller
diseuse ⓕ *de bonne aventure*
dee·zerz der bon a·von·tewr
foul (football) *faute* ⓕ fot
four *quatre* ka·trer
foyer (of cinema) *hall* ⓜ ol
fragile *fragile* fra·zheel
France *France* ⓕ frons
free (available) *disponible*
dees·po·nee·bler
free (gratis) *gratuit(e)* ⓜ/ⓕ gra·twee(t)
free (at liberty) *libre* lee·brer
freedom *liberté* ⓕ lee·bair·tay
freeze *geler* zher·lay
frequent *fréquent(e)* ⓜ/ⓕ fray·kon(t)
fresh *frais/fraîche* ⓜ/ⓕ fray/fresh
Friday *vendredi* von·drer·dee
fridge *réfrigérateur* ⓜ
ray·free·zhay·ra·ter
friend *ami/amie* ⓜ/ⓕ a·mee
friendly *amical(e)* ⓜ/ⓕ a·mee·kal
friendship *amitié* ⓕ a·mee·tyay
frog *grenouille* ⓕ grer·noo·yer
from *de* der
frost *gel* ⓜ zhel
frozen *gelé(e)* ⓜ/ⓕ zher·lay
fruit *fruit* ⓜ frwee
fruit picking *cueillette* ⓕ *de fruits*
ker·yet der frwee
fry *faire frire* fair freer
frying pan *poêle* ⓕ pwal
fuck *baiser* bay·zay
full *plein(e)* ⓜ/ⓕ plun/plen
full-time *à plein temps* a plun ton
fun (have fun) *s'amuser* sa·mew·zay
funeral *enterrement* ⓜ on·tair·mon
funny *drôle* ⓜ&ⓕ drol
furnished *meublé(e)* ⓜ/ⓕ mer·blay
furniture *meubles* ⓜ mer·bler
future *avenir* av·neer

G

game *jeu* ⓜ zher
game (football) *match* ⓜ matsh
garage *garage* ⓜ ga·razh
garbage *ordures* ⓕ pl or·dewr
garbage can *poubelle* ⓕ poo·bel
garden *jardin* ⓜ zhar·dun

gardening *jardinage* ⓜ zhar·dee·nazh
gas (for cooking) *gaz* ⓜ gaz
gas (petrol) *essence* ① ay·sons
gas cartridge *cartouche* ① *de gaz*
kar·toosh der gaz
gastroenteritis *gastro-entérite* ①
gastro·on·tay·reet
gate *barrière* ① bar·yair
gay *homosexuel(le)* ⓜ/① o·mo·sek·swel
general *général(e)* ⓜ/① zhay·nay·ral
generous *généreux/généreuse* ⓜ/①
zhay·nay·rer/zhay·nay·rerz
Germany *Allemagne* ① al·ma·nyer
get off (a train, etc) *descendre*
day·son·drer
gift *cadeau* ⓜ ka·do
gig *concert* ⓜ kon·sair
gipsy *bohémien/bohémienne* ⓜ/①
bo·ay·myun/bo·ay·myen
girl *fille* ① fee·yer
girlfriend *petite amie* ① per·teet a·mee
give *donner* do·nay
glandular fever
mononucléose ① *infectieuse*
mo·no·new·klay·oz un·fek·syerz
glass *verre* ⓜ vair
glasses (spectacles) *lunettes* ① pl
lew·net
gloves *gants* ⓜ pl gon
glue *colle* ① kol
go *aller* a·lay
go to bed *se coucher* ser koo·shay
go down (stairs, etc) *descendre*
day·son·drer
go out *sortir* sor·teer
go out with *sortir avec* sor·teer a·vek
go shopping *faire les courses*
fair lay koors
go window-shopping *faire du*
lèche-vitrines fair dew lesh·vee·treen
goal *but* ⓜ bewt
goalkeeper *gardien* ⓜ *de but*
gar·dyun der bewt
goat *chèvre* ① shev·rer
god *dieu* ⓜ dyer
goggles (skiing) *lunettes* ① pl lew·net
gold *or* ⓜ or
golf course *terrain* ⓜ *de golf*
tay·run der golf

good *bon/bonne* ⓜ/① bon/bon
goodbye *au revoir* ⓞ rer·vwar
government *gouvernement* ⓜ
goo·vair·ner·mon
gram *gramme* ⓜ gram
grandchild *petit-fils/petite-fille* ⓜ/①
per·tee fees/per·teet fee·yer
grandfather *grand-père* ⓜ grom·pair
grandmother *grand-mère* ① grom·mair
grandparents *grands-parents* ⓜ
grom·pa·ron
grass (lawn) *gazon* ⓜ ga·zon
grass (marijuana) *herbe* ① airb
grateful *reconnaissant(e)* ⓜ/①
rer·ko·nay·son(t)
grave *tombe* ① tomb
gray *gris(e)* ⓜ/① gree(z)
great (fantastic) *génial(e)* ⓜ/①
zhay·nyal
greedy (food) *gourmand(e)* ⓜ/①
goor·mon(d)
greedy (money) *avide* a·veed
green *vert(e)* ⓜ/① vair(t)
greengrocer *marchand* ⓜ *de légumes*
mar·shon der lay·gewm
grey *gris(e)* ⓜ/① gree(z)
grocery *épicerie* ① ay·pee·sree
grow *pousser* poo·say
g-string *cache-sexe* ① kash·seks
guaranteed *garanti(e)* ⓜ/① ga·ron·tee
guess *deviner* der·vee·nay
guesthouse *pension* ① *(de famille)*
pon·syon (der fa·mee·yer)
guide (person) *guide* ⓜ geed
guide dog *chien* ⓜ *d'aveugle*
shyun da·ver·gler
guidebook *guide* ⓜ geed
guided tour *visite* ① *guidée*
vee·zeet gee·day
guilty *coupable* koo·pa·bler
guitar *guitare* ① gee·tar
gun *pistolet* ⓜ pees·to·lay
gym (place) *gymnase* ⓜ zheem·naz
gymnastics *gymnastique* ①
zheem·na·steek
gynaecologist *gynécologue* ⓜ/①
zhee·nay·ko·log

H

habit *habitude* ① a·bee·tewd
hair *cheveux* ⓜ shver
hairbrush *brosse ① à cheveux*
bros a shver
haircut *coupe* ① koop
hairdresser *coiffeur/coiffeuse* ⓜ/①
kwa·fer/kwa·ferz
Halal *halal* a·lal
half *moitié* ① mwa·tyay
half a litre *demi-litre* ⓜ der·mee·lee·trer
hallucinate *avoir des hallucinations*
a·vwar day za·lew·see·na·syon
ham *jambon* ⓜ zhom·bon
hammer *marteau* ⓜ mar·to
hammock *hamac* ⓜ a·mak
hand *main* ① mun
handbag *sac* ⓜ *à main* sak a mun
handicrafts *objets* ⓜ *artisanaux* pl
ob·zhay ar·tee·za·no
handkerchief *mouchoir* ⓜ moo·shwar
handlebars *guidon* ⓜ gee·don
handmade *fait/faite à la main* ⓜ/①
fay/fet a la mun
handsome *beau/belle* ⓜ/① bo/bel
happy *heureux/heureuse* ⓜ/①
er·rer/er·rerz
harassment *harcèlement* ⓜ ar·sel·mon
harbour *port* ⓜ por
hard (not easy) *difficile* dee·fee·seel
hard (not soft) *dur(e)* ⓜ/① dewr
hardware store *quincaillerie* ①
kung·kay·ree
hare *lièvre* ⓜ lyev·rer
hash *teush* ⓜ tersh
hat *chapeau* ⓜ sha·po
hate *détester* day·tes·tay
have *avoir* a·vwar
have a cold *être enrhumé*
e·trer on·rew·may
have fun *s'amuser* sa·mew·zay
hay fever *rhume ⓜ des foins*
rewm day fwun
he *il* eel
head *tête* ① tet
headache *mal ⓜ à la tête* mal a la tet
headlights *phares* ⓜ far
health *santé* ① son·tay
hear *entendre* on·ton·drer

hearing aid *appareil ⓜ acoustique*
a·pa·ray a·koos·teek
heart *cœur* ⓜ ker
heart condition *maladie ① de cœur*
ma·la·dee der ker
heat *chaleur* ① sha·ler
heated *chauffé(e)* ⓜ/① sho·fay
heater *appareil ⓜ de chauffage*
a·pa·ray der sho·fazh
heavy *lourd(e)* ⓜ/① loor(d)
height *hauteur* ① o·ter
helmet *casque* ⓜ kask
help *aider* ay·day
help *aide* ① ed
hepatitis *hépatite* ① ay·pa·teet
her *son/sa/ses* ⓜ/①/pl son/sa/say
herbalist *herboriste* ⓜ/① air·bo·reest
herbs *fines herbes* ① feen zairb
here *ici* ee·see
heroin *héroïne* ① ay·ro·een
high *haut(e)* ⓜ/① o(t)
high school *établissement* ⓜ
d'enseignement secondaire
ay·ta·blees·mon don·say·nyer·mon
zgon·dair
highway *autoroute* ① o·to·root
hike *faire la randonnée*
fair la ron·do·nay
hiking *randonnée* ① ron·do·nay
hiking boots *chaussures ① pl de
marche* sho·sewr der marsh
hiking route *itinéraire ⓜ de randonnée*
ee·tee·nay·rair der ron·do·nay
hill *colline* ① ko·leen
Hindu *hindou(e)* ⓜ/① un·doo
hire *louer* loo·ay
his *son/sa/ses* ⓜ/①/pl son/sa/say
historical *historique* ees·to·reek
history *histoire* ① ees·twar
hitchhike *faire du stop* fair dew stop
HIV *VIH (virus immunodéficitaire
humain)* ⓜ vay·ee·ash (vee·rews
ee·mew·no·day·fee·see·tair ew·mun)
HIV positive *séropositif/séropositive*
ⓜ/① say·ro·po·zee·teef/
say·ro·po·zee·teev
hobby *passe-temps* ⓜ pas·ton
hockey *hockey* ⓜ o·kay
hole *trou* ⓜ troo
holidays *vacances* ① pl va·kons

home *à la maison* a la may·zon
homeless *sans-abri* son·za·bree
homemaker *femme* ① *au foyer*
fam o fwa·yay
homesick *nostalgique* nos·tal·zheek
homework *devoirs* ⓜ der·vwar
homosexual *homosexuel(le)* ⓜ/①
o·mo·sek·swel
honest *honnête* o·net
honeymoon *lune* ① *de miel*
lewn der myel
hope *espoir* ⓜ es·pwar
hope *espérer* es·pay·ray
horoscope *horoscope* ⓜ o·ro·skop
horse *cheval* ⓜ shval
horse riding *équitation* ①
ay·kee·ta·syon
hospital *hôpital* ⓜ o·pee·tal
hospitality *hospitalité* ①
os·pee·ta·lee·tay
hot *chaud(e)* ⓜ/① sho(d)
hotel *hôtel* ⓜ o·tel
hour *heure* ① er
house *maison* ① may·zon
housework *ménage* ⓜ may·nazh
how *comment* ko·mon
hug *serrer dans ses bras*
say·ray don say bra
huge *énorme* ay·norm
human *humain* ew·mun
human rights *droits* ⓜ pl *de l'homme*
drwa der lom
humanities *lettres* ① pl *classiques*
le·trer kla·seek
humour *humour* ⓜ ew·moor
hundred *cent* son
hungry (to be) *avoir faim* a·vwar fum
hunting *chasse* ① shas
hurt *blessé(e)* ⓜ/① blay·say
husband *mari* ⓜ ma·ree

I

I *je* zher
ice *glace* ① glas
ice cream *glace* ① glas
ice hockey *hockey* ⓜ *sur glace*
o·kay sewr glas
idea *idée* ① ee·day

identification *pièce* ① *d'identité*
pyes dee·don·tee·tay
identification card (ID) *carte* ① *d'identité*
kart dee·don·tee·tay
idiot *idiot(e)* ⓜ/① ee·dyo(t)
if *si* see
ignorant *ignorant(e)* ⓜ/① ee·nyo·ron(t)
ill *malade* ma·lad
illegal *illégal(e)* ⓜ/① ee·lay·gal
imagination *imagination* ①
ee·ma·zhee·na·syon
immediately/right now *immédiatement*
ee·may·dyat·mon
immigration *immigration* ①
ee·mee·gra·syon
impolite *impoli(e)* ⓜ/① um·po·lee
import *importer* um·por·tay
important *important(e)* ⓜ/①
um·por·ton(t)
impossible *impossible* um·po·see·bler
improve *améliorer* a·may·lyo·ray
in *dans* don
in a hurry *pressé(e)* ⓜ/① pray·say
in front of *devant* der·von
included *compris(e)* ⓜ/① kom·pree(z)
income *revenus* ⓜ pl rerv·new
income tax *impôt* ⓜ *sur le revenu*
um·po sewr ler rerv·new
inconvenient *inopportun(e)* ⓜ/①
ee·no·por·tun/ee·no·por·tewn
independent *indépendant(e)* ⓜ/①
un·day·pon·don(t)
India *Inde* ① und
indicator (on car) *clignotant* ⓜ
klee·nyo·ton
indigestion *indigestion* ①
un·dee·zhes·tyon
individual *individu* ⓜ un·dee·vee·dew
industrial *industriel/industrielle* ⓜ/①
un·dews·tree·el
industry *industrie* ① un·dews·tree
infection *infection* ① un·fek·syon
inflammation *inflammation* ①
un·fla·ma·syon
influence *influence* ① un·flew·ons
influenza *grippe* ① greep
information *renseignements* ⓜ pl
ron·sen·yer·mon
ingredient *ingrédient* ⓜ ung·gray·dyon

inject *injecter* un·zhek·tay
injection *piqûre* ① pee·kewr
injured *blessé(e)* ⓜ/① blay·say
injury *blessure* ① blay·sewr
innocent *innocent(e)* ⓜ/① ee·no·son(t)
insect *insecte* ⓜ un·sekt
inside *dedans* der·don
insurance *assurance* ① a·sew·rons
insure *assurer* a·sew·ray
intelligent *intelligent(e)* ⓜ/①
  un·tay·lee·zhon(t)
interesting *intéressant(e)* ⓜ/①
  un·tay·ray·son(t)
intermission *entracte* ⓜ on·trakt
international *international(e)* ⓜ/①
  un·tair·na·syo·nal
Internet *Internet* ⓜ un·tair·net
Internet cafe *cybercafé* ⓜ
  see·bair·ka·fay
interpreter *interprète* ⓜ/① un·tair·pret
intersection *carrefour* ⓜ kar·foor
interview *entrevue* ① on·trer·vew
intimate *intime* un·teem
into *dans* don
introduce (people) *présenter*
  pray·zon·tay
invite *inviter* un·vee·tay
Ireland *Irlande* ① eer·lond
iron (clothes) *repasser* rer·pa·say
iron (for clothes) *fer* ⓜ *à repasser*
  fair a rer·pa·say
island *île* ① eel
IT *informatique* ① un·for·ma·teek
Italy *Italie* ① ee·ta·lee
itch *démangeaison* ① day·mon·zhay·zon
itemised *détaillé(e)* ⓜ/① day·ta·yay
itinerary *itinéraire* ⓜ ee·tee·nay·rair
IUD *stérilet* ⓜ stay·ree·lay

J

jacket *veste* ① vest
jail *prison* ① pree·zon
January *janvier* ⓜ zhon·vyay
Japan *Japon* ⓜ zha·pon
jar (jam) *pot* ⓜ po
jaw *mâchoire* ① ma·shwar
jealous *jaloux/jalouse* ⓜ/①
  zha·loo/zha·looz

jeans *jean* ⓜ zheen
jeep *jeep* ① zheep
jet lag *fatigue* ① *due au décalage horaire*
  fa·teeg dew o day·ka·lazh o·rair
jewellery *bijoux* ⓜ pl bee·zhoo
Jewish *juif/juive* ⓜ/①
  zhweef/zhweev
job *travail* ⓜ tra·vai
jockey *jockey* ⓜ zho·kay
jogging *jogging* ⓜ zho·geeng
join *joindre* zhwun·drer
joke *plaisanterie* ① play·zon·tree
journalist *journaliste* ⓜ/①
  zhoor·na·leest
journey *voyage* ⓜ vwa·yazh
joy *joie* ① zhwa
judge *juge* ⓜ zhewzh
July *juillet* ⓜ zhwee·yay
jump *sauter* so·tay
jumper (sweater) *pull* ⓜ pewl
jumper leads ⓜ pl *câbles de démarrage*
  ka·bler der day·ma·razh
June *juin* ⓜ zhwun
justice *justice* ① zhew·stees

K

kerb *bord* ⓜ *du trottoir* bor dew tro·twar
key *clé* ① klay
keyboard *clavier* ⓜ kla·vyay
kick (person) *donner un coup de pied*
  à do·nay ung koo der pyay a
kick (football) *donner un coup de pied*
  dans do·nay ung koo der pyay don
kid (child) *gamin/gamine* ⓜ/①
  ga·mun/ga·meen
kill *tuer* tew·way
kilo *kilo* ⓜ kee·lo
kilogram *kilogramme* ⓜ kee·lo·gram
kilometre *kilomètre* ⓜ kee·lo·may·trer
kind (nice) *gentil/gentille* ⓜ/① zhon·tee
kind (type) *genre* ⓜ zhon·rer
kindergarten *jardin* ⓜ *d'enfants*
  zhar·dun don·fon
king *roi* ⓜ rwa
kingdom *royaume* ⓜ rwa·yom
kiosk *kiosque* ⓜ kyosk
kiss *baiser* ⓜ bay·zay

kiss *embrasser* om·bra·say
kitchen *cuisine* ① kwee·zeen
kitten *chaton* ⓜ sha·ton
knee *genou* ⓜ koo·to
kneel *se mettre à genoux*
  ser may·trer a zher·noo
knife *couteau* ⓜ koo·to
knitting *tricot* ⓜ tree·ko
know *savoir* sa·vwar
know (be familiar with) *connaître*
  ko·nay·trer
kosher *casher/kascher* ka·shair

L

labourer *manoeuvre* ⓜ ma·ner·vrer
lace *dentelle* ① don·tel
lake *lac* ⓜ lak
lamp *lampe* ① lomp
land *terre* ① tair
landlady *propriétaire* ① prop·ryay·tair
landlord *propriétaire* ① prop·ryay·tair
lane (city) *ruelle* ① rwel
lane (country) *chemin* ⓜ shmun
language *langue* ① long
laptop *ordinateur* ⓜ *portable*
  or·dee·na·ter por·ta·bler
large *grand(e)* ⓜ/① gron(d)
last (previous) *dernier/dernière* ⓜ/①
  dair·nyay/dair·nyair
late *en retard* on rer·tar
later *plus tard* plew·tar
laugh *rire* reer
launderette *laverie* ① lav·ree
laundry (place) *blanchisserie* ①
  blon·shees·ree
laundry (clothes) *linge* ⓜ lunzh
law *loi* ① lwa
law (study, professsion) *droit* ⓜ drwa
lawyer *avocat(e)* ⓜ/① a·vo·ka(t)
laxative *laxatif* ⓜ lak·sa·teef
lazy *paresseux/paresseuse* ⓜ/①
  pa·ray·ser/pa·ray·serz
leader *chef* ⓜ shef
leaf *feuille* ① fer·yee
learn *apprendre* a·pron·drer
lease *bail* ⓜ ba·yer
lease *louer à bail* loo·way a ba·yer
least *moins* ⓜ mwun

leather *cuir* ⓜ kweer
leave *partir* par·teer
leave (something) *laisser* lay·say
lecturer *professeur* ⓜ *(à l'université)*
  pro·fay·ser (a lew·nee·vair·see·tay)
ledge *rebord* ⓜ rer·bor
left (direction) *à gauche* a gosh
left luggage (office) *consigne* ①
  kon·see·nyer
left-wing *de gauche* der gosh
leg *jambe* ① zhomb
legal *légal(e)* ⓜ/① lay·gal
legislation *législation* ①
  lay·zhee·sla·syon
length *longueur* ① long·ger
lens *objectif* ⓜ ob·zhek·teef
lesbian *lesbienne* ① les·byen
less *moins* mwun
less *moins de* mwun der
letter *lettre* ① lay·trer
liar *menteur/menteuse* ⓜ/①
  mon·ter/mon·terz
library *bibliothèque* ① bee·blee·o·tek
lice *poux* ⓜ pl poo
license plate number
  plaque ① *d'immatriculation*
  plak dee·ma·tree·kew·la·syon
lie *mensonge* ⓜ mon·sonzh
lie (not stand) *s'allonger* sa·lon·zhay
lie (tell lies) *mentir* mon·teer
life *vie* ① vee
life jacket *gilet* ⓜ *de sauvetage*
  zhee·lay der sov·tazh
lift (something heavy) *soulever*
  sool·vay
lift (arm) *lever* ler·vay
lift (elevator) *ascenseur* ⓜ a·son·ser
light *lumière* ① lew·myair
light (on vehicle) *phare* ⓜ far
light (not heavy) *léger/légère* ⓜ/①
  lay·zhay/lay·zhair
light (of colour) *clair(e)* ⓜ/① klair
light bulb *ampoule* ① om·pool
light meter *posemètre* ⓜ poz·may·trer
lighter *briquet* ⓜ bree·kay
lights (on car) *phares* ⓜ pl far
like *comme* kom
like *aimer* ay·may

line *ligne* ① lee·nyer
linen (material) *lin* ⓜ lun
linen (sheets etc) *linge* ⓜ lunzh
lingerie *lingerie* ① lun·zhree
lip balm *pommade* ① *pour les lèvres*
    po·mad poor lay lay·vrer
lip *lèvre* ① lay·vrer
lipstick *rouge* ① *à lèvres* roozh a lay·vrer
liquor store
    magasin ⓜ *de vins et spiritueux*
    ma·ga·zun der vun ay spee·ree·twer
listen (to) *écouter* ay·koo·tay
little *petit(e)* ⓜ/① per·tee(t)
little bit *peu* ⓜ per
live *vivre* vee·vrer
live (in a place) *habiter* a·bee·tay
liver *foie* ① fwa
lizard *lézard* ⓜ lay·zar
local *local(e)* ⓜ/① lo·kal
lock *fermer à clé* fair·may a klay
lock *serrure* ① say·rewr
locked *fermé(e) à clé* ⓜ/①
    fair·may a klay
long *long/longue* ⓜ/① long(k)
long-distance (flight) *long-courrier*
    long·koo·ryay
look *regarder* rer·gar·day
look after *s'occuper de* so·kew·pay der
look at *regarder* rer·gar·day
look for *chercher* shair·shay
look out *faire attention* fair a·ton·syon
loose (clothes) *ample* om·pler
loose change *petite monnaie* ①
    per·teet mo·nay
lorry *camion* ⓜ ka·myon
lose *perdre* pair·drer
loser *perdant(e)* ⓜ/① pair·don(t)
loss *perte* ① pairt
lost *perdu(e)* ⓜ/① pair·dew
lost property office *bureau* ⓜ *des objets
    trouvés* bew·ro day zob·zhay troo·vay
loud *fort(e)* ⓜ/① for(t)
love *amour* ⓜ a·moor
love *aimer* ay·may
lover *amant(e)* ⓜ/① a·mon(t)
low *bas/basse* ⓜ/① ba(s)
loyal *loyal(e)* ⓜ/① lwa·yal
lubricant *lubrifiant* ⓜ lew·bree·fyon

luck *chance* ① shons
lucky (to be) *avoir de la chance*
    a·vwar der la shons
luggage *bagages* ⓜ pl ba·gazh
luggage lockers
    consigne ① *automatique*
    kon·see·nyer o·to·ma·teek
luggage tag *étiquette* ① ay·tee·ket
lump *grosseur* ① gro·ser
lunch *déjeuner* ⓜ day·zher·nay
lung *poumon* ⓜ poo·mon
luxury *luxe* ⓜ lewks
luxury *de luxe* der lewks

M

machine *machine* ① ma·sheen
mad (angry) *fâché(e)* ⓜ/① fa·shay
mad (crazy) *fou/folle* ⓜ/① foo/fol
made of (cotton, wood etc) *en* on
magazine *magazine* ⓜ ma·ga·zeen
magician *magicien/magicienne* ⓜ/①
    ma·zhee·syun/ma·zhees·yen
mail (letters) *courrier* ⓜ koo·ryay
mail (postal system) *poste* ① post
mailbox *boîte* ① *aux lettres*
    bwat o lay·trer
main *principal(e)* ⓜ/① prun·see·pal
main road *grande route* ① grond root
main square *place* ① *centrale*
    plas son·tral
majority *majorité* ① ma·zho·ree·tay
make *faire* fair
make-up *maquillage* ⓜ ma·kee·yazh
mammogram *mammographie* ①
    ma·mo·gra·fee
man *homme* ⓜ om
manage (business) *diriger* dee·ree·zhay
manager *directeur/directrice* ⓜ/①
    dee·rek·ter/dee·rek·trees
manager (restaurant, hotel) *gérant(e)*
    ⓜ/① zhay·ron(t)
manner *façon* ① fa·son
manual (le) ⓜ/① ma·nwel
manual worker *ouvrier/ouvrière* ⓜ/①
    oo·vree·yay/oo·vree·yair
many *beaucoup de* bo·koo der
map (of country) *carte* ① kart
map (of town) *plan* ⓜ plon
March *mars* ⓜ mars

marihuana *marihuana* ⓕ
ma·ree·wa·na

marital status *situation* ⓕ *familiale*
see·twa·syon fa·mee·lyal

market *marché* ⓜ mar·shay

marriage *mariage* ⓜ ma·ryazh

married *marié(e)* ⓜ/ⓕ ma·ryay

marry *épouser* ay·poo·zay

martial arts *arts* ⓜ pl *martiaux*
ar mar·syo

mass (Catholic) *messe* ⓕ mes

massage *massage* ⓜ ma·sazh

massage/masser ma·say

masseur/masseuse *masseur/masseuse*
ⓜ/ⓕ ma·ser/ma·serz

mat *petit tapis* ⓜ per·tee ta·pee

match (sports) *match* ⓜ matsh

matches (for lighting) *allumettes* ⓕ pl
a·lew·met

material *matériel* ⓜ ma·tay·ryel

mattress *matelas* ⓜ mat·la

May *mai* ⓜ may

maybe *peut-être* per·tay·trer

mayor *maire* ⓜ mair

me *moi* mwa

meal *repas* ⓜ rer·pa

measles *rougeole* ⓕ roo·zhol

meat *viande* ⓕ vyond

mechanic *mécanicien/mécanicienne*
ⓜ/ⓕ may·ka·nee·syun/
may·ka·nee·syen

media *médias* ⓜ pl may·dya

medicine *médecine* ⓕ med·seen

medicine (medication) *médicament* ⓜ
may·dee·ka·mon

meditation *méditation* ⓕ
may·dee·ta·syon

meet *rencontrer* ron·kon·tray

member *membre* ⓜ mom·brer

memory (ability to remember)
mémoire ⓕ may·mwar

memory (recollection) *souvenir* ⓜ
soov·neer

menstruation *menstruation* ⓕ
mon·strew·a·syon

menu *carte* kart

message *message* ⓜ may·sazh

messy *en désordre* on day·zor·drer

metal *métal* ⓜ may·tal

metre *mètre* ⓜ may·trer

metro station *station* ⓕ *de métro*
sta·syon der may·tro

microwave (oven) *four* ⓜ *à micro-ondes*
foor a mee·kro·ond

midday/noon *midi* mee·dee

midnight *minuit* mee·nwee

migraine *migraine* ⓕ mee·gren

military *militaire* mee·lee·tair

military service *service* ⓜ *militaire*
sair·vees mee·lee·tair

milk *lait* ⓜ lay

millennium *millénaire* ⓜ mee·lay·nair

millimetre *millimètre* ⓜ
mee·lee·may·trer

million *million* ⓜ mee·lyon

mineral water *eau* ⓕ *minérale*
o mee·nay·ral

minority *minorité* ⓕ mee·no·ree·tay

minute *minute* ⓕ mee·newt

mirror *miroir* ⓜ mee·rwar

miscarriage (to have a) *faire une*
fausse couche fair ewn fos koosh

miss *manquer* mong·kay

mistake *erreur* ⓕ ay·rer

mix *mélanger* may·lon·zhay

mix up (confuse) *confondre*
kon·fon·drer

mobile phone *téléphone* ⓜ *portable*
tay·lay·fon por·ta·bler

modem *modem* ⓜ mo·dem

modern *moderne* mo·dairn

moisturiser *crème* ⓕ *hydratante*
krem ee·dra·tont

mom *maman* ⓕ ma·mon

monarchy *monarchie* ⓕ mo·nar·shee

monastery *monastère* ⓜ mo·na·stair

Monday *lundi* ⓜ lun·dee

money *argent* ⓜ ar·zhon

monkey *singe* ⓜ sunzh

month *mois* ⓜ mwa

monument *monument* ⓜ mo·new·mon

more *plus de* plews der

more *plus* plew

morning *matin* ⓜ ma·tun

morning sickness *nausées* ⓕ pl
matinales no·zay ma·tee·nal

mosque *mosquée* ① mo·skay
mosquito *moustique* ⓜ moo·steek
mosquito coil
  allume-feu ⓜ *anti-moustiques*
  a·lewm·fer on·tee·moo·steek
mosquito net *moustiquaire* ①
  moo·stee·kair
most *plus* ⓜ plews
motel *motel* ⓜ mo·tel
mother *mère* ① mair
mother-in-law *belle-mère* ① bel·mair
motorboat *canot* ⓜ *automobile*
  ka·no o·to·mo·beel
motorcycle *moto* ① mo·to
motorway (tollway) *autoroute* ①
  o·to·root
mountain *montagne* ① mon·ta·nyer
mountain bike *vélo* ⓜ *tout terrain (VTT)*
  vay·lo too tay·run (vay·tay·tay)
mountain path *chemin* ⓜ *de montagne*
  shmun der mon·ta·nyer
mountain range *chaîne* ① *de montagnes*
  shen der mon·ta·nyer
mountaineering *alpinisme* ⓜ
  al·pee·nee·smer
mouse *souris* ① soo·ree
mouth *bouche* ① boosh
move *bouger* boo·zhay
movie *film* ⓜ feelm
Mr *Monsieur* mer·syer
Mrs *Madame* ma·dam
Ms; Miss *Mademoiselle* mad·mwa·zel
mud *boue* ① boo
multimedia *multimédia* ⓜ
  mewl·tee·may·dya
mum *maman* ① ma·mon
muscle *muscle* ⓜ mews·kler
museum *musée* ⓜ mew·zay
music *musique* ① mew·zeek
music shop *disquaire* ⓜ dee·skair
musician *musicien/musicienne* ⓜ/①
  mew·zees·yun/mew·zees·yen
Muslim *musulman(e)* ⓜ/①
  mew·zewl·mon/mew·zewl·man
my *mon/ma/mes* ⓜ/①/pl mon/ma/may

N

nail clippers *coupe-ongles* ⓜ
  koop·ong·gler

name *nom* ⓜ nom
napkin *serviette* ① sair·vyet
nappy *couche* ① koosh
narcotic *stupéfiant* ⓜ stew·pay·fyon
national park *parc* ⓜ *national*
  park na·syo·nal
nationality *nationalité* ①
  na·syo·na·lee·tay
nature *nature* ① na·tewr
naturopath *naturopathe* ⓜ/①
  na·tew·ro·pat
nausea *nausée* ① no·zay
near *près de* pray der
nearby *tout près* too pray
nearest *le/la plus proche* ⓜ/①
  ler/la plew prosh
necessary *nécessaire* nay·say·sair
necklace *collier* ⓜ ko·lyay
need *avoir besoin de* a·vwar ber·zwun de
needle *aiguille* ① ay·gwee·yer
neither *ni* nee
net *filet* ⓜ fee·lay
Netherlands *Pays-Bas* ⓜ pl pay·ee·ba
network *réseau* ⓜ ray·zo
never *jamais* zha·may
new *nouveau/nouvelle* ⓜ/①
  noo·vo/noo·vel
New Year's Day *jour* ⓜ *de l'An*
  zhoor der lon
New Year's Eve *Saint-Sylvestre* ①
  sun·seel·ves·trer
New Zealand *Nouvelle-Zélande* ①
  noo·vel·zay·lond
news *les nouvelles* lay noo·vel
news (on TV etc) *les actualités*
  lay zak·twa·lee·tay
newsagent *marchand* ⓜ *de journaux*
  mar·shon der zhoor·no
newspaper *journal* ⓜ zhoor·nal
next (month) *prochain(e)* ⓜ/①
  pro·shun/pro·shen
**next to ... ** *à côté de ...* a ko·tay der
nice (pleasant) *agréable* a·gray·a·bler
nice (kind) *gentil/gentille* ⓜ/①
  zhon·tee/zhon·tee·yer
nickname *surnom* ⓜ sewr·nom
night *nuit* ① nwee
night out *soirée* ① swa·ray
nightclub *boîte* ① bwat
nine *neuf* nerf

no vacancy *complet* kom·play
no *non* non
noisy *bruyant(e)* ⓜ/ⓕ brew·yon(t)
non-direct *non-direct* non·dee·rekt
none *aucun(e)* ⓜ/ⓕ o·kun/o·kewn
non-smoking *non-fumeur* non·few·mer
noon *midi* mee·dee
north *nord* ⓜ nor
northern hemisphere *hémisphère* ⓜ
  nord ay·mees·fair nor
nose *nez* ⓜ nay
not bad *pas mal* pa mal
not yet *pas encore* pa zong·kor
notebook *carnet* ⓜ kar·nay
nothing *rien* ryun
novel *roman* ⓜ ro·mon
now *maintenant* mun·ter·non
nuclear energy *énergie* ⓕ *nucléaire*
  ay·nair·zhee new·klay·air
nuclear power *puissance* ⓕ *nucléaire*
  pwee·sons new·klay·air
nuclear test *essai* ⓜ *nucléaire*
  ay·say new·klay·air
nuclear waste *déchets* ⓜ *nucléaires*
  day·shay new·klay·air
number *numéro* ⓜ new·may·ro
nun *religieuse* ⓕ rer·lee·zhyerz
nurse *infirmier/infirmière* ⓜ/ⓕ
  un·feer·myay/un·feer·myair

O

obtain *obtenir* op·ter·neer
obvious *évident(e)* ⓜ/ⓕ ay·vee·don(t)
occupation *occupation* ⓕ
  o·kew·pa·syon
ocean *océan* ⓜ o·say·on
off (meat) *mauvais(e)* ⓜ/ⓕ mo·vay(z)
offence *délit* ⓜ day·lee
office *bureau* ⓜ bew·ro
office worker *employé(e)* ⓜ/ⓕ
  de bureau om·plwa·yay der bew·ro
officer *officier* ⓜ o·fees·yay
officer (police) *agent* ⓜ *de police*
  a·zhon der po·lees
offside (sport) *hors jeu* or·zher
often *souvent* soo·von
oil *huile* ⓕ weel
oil (petrol) *pétrole* ⓜ pay·trol
old *vieux/vieille* ⓜ/ⓕ vyer/vyay

Olympic Games *Les Jeux Olympiques*
  lay zher zo·lum·peek
on *sur* sewr
on strike *en grève* ong grev
on the corner *au coin* o kwun
on time *à l'heure* a ler
once *une fois* ewn fwa
one *un(e)* ⓜ/ⓕ un/ewn
one-way (ticket) *(billet) simple*
  (bee·yay) sum·pler
only *seule(e)* ⓜ/ⓕ serl
open *ouvert(e)* ⓜ/ⓕ oo·vair(t)
open *ouvrir* oo·vreer
opening hours *heures* ⓕ pl *d'ouverture*
  lay zer doo·vair·tewr
opera *opéra* ⓜ o·pay·ra
operation *opération* ⓕ o·pay·ra·syon
operator *opérateur/opératrice* ⓜ/ⓕ
  o·pay·ra·ter/o·pay·ra·trees
opinion *avis* ⓜ a·vee
opponent *adversaire* ⓜ/ⓕ ad·vair·sair
opportunity *occasion* ⓕ o·ka·zyon
opposite *en face de* on fas der
or *ou* oo
orange (colour) *orange* o·ronzh
order *ordre* ⓜ or·drer
order *ordonner* or·do·nay
ordinary *ordinaire* or·dee·nair
organisation *organisation* ⓕ
  or·ga·nee·za·syon
organise *organiser* or·ga·nee·zay
orgasm *orgasme* ⓜ or·gas·mer
original *original(e)* ⓜ/ⓕ o·ree·zhee·nal
other *autre* o·trer
our *notre* no·trer
out of order *hors service* or sair·vees
outside *dehors* der·or
oven *four* ⓜ foor
over (above) *par-dessus* par·der·sew
over (finished) *fini(e)* ⓜ/ⓕ fee·nee
overdose *overdose* ⓕ o·vair·doz
overnight *pendant la nuit*
  pon·don la nwee
overseas *outre-mer* oo·trer·mair
owe *devoir* der·vwar
owner *propriétaire* ⓜ/ⓕ pro·pree·ay·tair
ox *bœuf* ⓜ berf
oxygen *oxygène* ⓜ ok·see·zhen
ozone layer *couche* ⓕ *d'ozone*
  koosh do·zon

P

pacemaker *pacemaker* ⓜ pes·may·ker
pacifier (dummy) *tétine* ① tay·teen
package *paquet* ⓜ pa·kay
packet (general) *paquet* ⓜ pa·kay
padlock *cadenas* ⓜ kad·na
page *page* ① pazh
pain *douleur* ① doo·ler
painful *douloureux/douloureuse* ⓜ/①
doo·loo·rer/doo·loo·rerz
painkiller *analgésique* ⓜ
a·nal·zhay·zeek
painter *peintre* ⓜ pun·trer
painting (a work) *tableau* ⓜ ta·blo
painting (the art) *peinture* ① pun·tewr
pair (couple) *paire* ① pair
palace *palais* ⓜ pa·lay
panties *slip* ⓜ sleep
pan *casserole* ① kas·rol
pants *pantalon* ⓜ pon·ta·lon
pants (underpants) *slip* ⓜ sleep
panty liners *protège-slips* ⓜ pl
pro·tezh·sleep
pantyhose *collant* ⓜ ko·lon
pap smear *frottis* ⓜ fro·tee
paper *papier* ⓜ pa·pyay
paperwork *paperasserie* ① pa·pras·ree
parade (ceremony) *parade* ① pa·rad
paraplegic *paraplégique* pa·ra·play·zheek
parcel *colis* ⓜ ko·lee
parents *parents* ⓜ pl pa·ron
park *parc* ⓜ park
park (a car) *garer (une voiture)*
ga·ray (ewn vwa·tewr)
part *partie* ① par·tee
participate *participer* par·tee·see·pay
particular *particulier/particulière* ⓜ/①
par·tee·kew·lyay/par·tee·kew·lyair
part-time *à temps partiel* a tom par·syel
party (night out) *soirée* ① swa·ray
party (politics) *parti* ⓜ par·tee
pass *passer* pa·say
pass (football) *pas* ⓜ pas
passenger *voyageur/voyageuse* ⓜ/①
vwa·ya·zher/vwa·ya·zherz
passport *passeport* ⓜ pas·por
passport number *numéro* ⓜ *de
passeport* new·may·ro der pas·por

past *passé* ⓜ pa·say
path *chemin* ⓜ shmun
pay *payer* pay·yay
payment *paiement* ⓜ pay·mon
peace *paix* ① pay
peak *cime* ① seem
pedal *pédale* ① pay·dal
pedestrian *piéton* ① pyay·ton
pen (ballpoint) *stylo* ⓜ stee·lo
pencil *crayon* ⓜ kray·yon
penicillin *pénicilline* ① pay·nee·see·leen
penis *pénis* ⓜ pay·nees
penknife *canif* ⓜ ka·neef
pensioner *retraité(e)* ⓜ/① rer·tray·tay
people *gens* ⓜ pl zhon
per (day) *par* par
percent *pour cent* poor son
perfect *parfait(e)* ⓜ/① par·fay(t)
performance *spectacle* ⓜ spek·ta·kler
perfume *parfum* ⓜ par·fum
period pain *règles* ① pl *douloureuses*
ray·gler doo·loo·rerz
permanent *permanent(e)* ⓜ/①
pair·ma·non(t)
permission *permission* ①
pair·mee·syon
permit *permis* ⓜ pair·mee
permit *permettre* pair·may·trer
person *personne* ① pair·son
personal *personnel(le)* ⓜ/① pair·so·nel
personality *personnalité* ①
pair·so·na·lee·tay
pet *animal* ⓜ *familier*
a·nee·mal fa·mee·lyay
petition *pétition* ① pay·tees·yon
petrol *essence* ① ay·sons
petrol station *station-service* ①
sta·syon·sair·vees
pharmacy *pharmacie* ① far·ma·see
phone book *annuaire* ⓜ an·wair
phone box *cabine* ① *téléphonique*
ka·been tay·lay·fo·neek
phone card *télécarte* ① tay·lay·kart
photo *photo* ① fo·to
photographer *photographe* ⓜ/①
fo·to·graf
photography *photographie* ①
fo·to·gra·fee
phrase *expression* ① ek·spray·syon

phrasebook *recueil* ⓜ *d'expressions*
rer·ker·yer dek·spray·syon
physiotherapist *kinésithérapeute* ⓜ/①
kee·nay·zee·tay·ra·pert
physiotherapy *kinésithérapie* ①
kee·nay·zee·tay·ra·pee
pick (choose) *choisir* shwa·zeer
pick up (something) *ramasser* ra·ma·say
picnic *pique-nique* ⓜ peek·neek
picture *image* ① ee·mazh
piece *morceau* ⓜ mor·so
pig *cochon* ⓜ ko·shon
pill *pilule* ① pee·lewl
pillow *oreiller* ⓜ o·ray·yay
pillowcase *taie* ① *d'oreiller*
tay do·ray·yay
pin *épingle* ① ay·pung·gler
pink *rose* roz
pipe *pipe* ① peep
place *lieu* ⓜ lyer
place of birth *lieu* ⓜ *de naissance*
lyer der nay·sons
plane *avion* ⓜ a·vyon
planet *planète* ① pla·net
plastic *plastique* ⓜ plas·teek
plate *assiette* ① a·syet
platform *quai* ⓜ kay
play (cards etc) *jouer* zhoo·ay
play (guitar etc) *jouer de* zhoo·ay der
play (football etc) *jouer au* zhoo·ay o
play (theatre) *pièce* ① *de théâtre*
pyes der tay·a·trer
playground *terrain* ⓜ *de jeux*
tay·run der zher
plenty *abondance* ① a·bon·dons
plenty *beaucoup de* bo·koo der
plug (bath) *bonde* ① bond
plug (electricity) *prise* ① preez
pocket *poche* ① posh
poetry *poésie* ① po·ay·zee
point *pointe* ① pwunt
point *indiquer* un·dee·kay
poisonous *venimeux/venimeuse* ⓜ/①
ver·nee·mer/ver·nee·merz
police *police* ① po·lees
police car *voiture* ① *de police*
vwa·tewr der po·lees
police officer (in city) *policier* ⓜ
po·lee·syay

police officer (in country) *gendarme* ⓜ
zhon·darm
police station *commissariat* ⓜ
ko·mee·sar·ya
policy *politique* ① po·lee·teek
politician *homme/femme* ⓜ/①
politique om/fam po·lee·teek
politics *politique* ① po·lee·teek
pollen *pollen* ⓜ po·len
pollution *pollution* ① po·lew·syon
pond *étang* ⓜ ay·tong
pool (game) *billard* ⓜ *américain*
bee·yar a·may·ree·kun
pool (swimming) *piscine* ① pee·seen
poor *pauvre* po·vrer
popular *populaire* po·pew·lair
port *port* ⓜ por
positive *positif/positive* ⓜ/①
po·zee·teef/po·zee·teev
possible *possible* po·see·bler
post code *code* ⓜ *postal* kod pos·tal
post office *bureau* ⓜ *de poste*
bew·ro der post
postage *tarifs* ⓜ pl *postaux*
ta·reef pos·to
postcard *carte postale* ① kart pos·tal
postman *facteur* ⓜ fak·ter
pot (ceramics) *pot* ⓜ po
pot (dope) *marie-jeanne* ① ma·ree·zhan
pottery *poterie* ① po·tree
pound (money, weight) *livre* ① leev·rer
poverty *pauvreté* ① po·vrer·tay
power *pouvoir* ⓜ poo·vwar
practical *pratique* pra·teek
practise *pratiquer* pra·tee·kay
prayer *prière* ① pree·yair
prefer *préférer* pray·fay·ray
pregnancy test kit *test* ⓜ *de grossesse*
test der gro·ses
pregnant *enceinte* on·sunt
premenstrual tension
syndrome ⓜ *prémenstruel*
sun·drom pray·mon·strwel
prepare *préparer* pray·pa·ray
prescription *ordonnance* ① or·do·nons
present (gift) *cadeau* ⓜ ka·do
present (time) *présent* ⓜ pray·zon
president *président* ⓜ pray·zee·don
pressure *pression* ① pray·syon

pretend *faire semblant* fair som·blon
pretty *joli(e)* ⓜ/ⓕ zho·lee
prevent *empêcher* om·pay·shay
previous *précédent(e)* ⓜ/ⓕ
  pray·say·don(t)
price *prix* ⓜ pree
priest *prêtre* ⓜ pray·trer
prime minister *premier ministre* ⓜ
  prer·myay mee·nee·strer
printer (computer) *imprimante* ⓕ
  um·pree·mont
prison *prison* ⓕ pree·zon
prisoner *prisonnier/prisonnière* ⓜ/ⓕ
  pree·zo·nyay/pree·zo·nyair
private *privé(e)* ⓜ/ⓕ pree·vay
private hospital *clinique* ⓕ *privée*
  klee·neek pree·vay
probable *probable* pro·ba·bler
problem *problème* ⓜ pro·blem
produce *produire* pro·dweer
professional *professionnel(le)* ⓜ/ⓕ
  pro·fay·syo·nel
profit *bénéfice* ⓜ bay·nay·fees
programme *programme* ⓜ pro·gram
projector *projecteur* ⓜ pro·zhek·ter
promise *promesse* ⓕ pro·mes
promise *promettre* pro·may·trer
promote *promouvoir* pro·moo·vwar
prostitute *prostituée* ⓕ pro·stee·tway
protect *protéger* pro·tay·zhay
protected (species) *protégé(e)* ⓜ/ⓕ
  pro·tay·zhay
protection *protection* ⓕ pro·tek·syon
protest *manif(estation)* ⓕ
  ma·neef(ay·sta·syon)
protest *manifester* ma·nee·fay·stay
provisions *provisions* ⓕ pl
  pro·vee·zyon
psychotherapy *psychothérapie* ⓕ
  psee·ko·tay·ra·pee
pub (bar) *bar* ⓜ bar
public *public* ⓜ pewb·leek
public telephone *téléphone* ⓜ *public*
  tay·lay·fon pewb·leek
public toilet *toilettes* ⓕ pl twa·let
pull *tirer* tee·ray
pump *pompe* ⓕ pomp
puncture *crevaison* ⓕ krer·vay·zon

punish *punir* pew·neer
puppy *chiot* ⓜ shyo
pure *pur(e)* ⓜ/ⓕ pewr
purple *violet(te)* ⓜ/ⓕ vyo·lay(·let)
purpose *objet* ⓜ ob·zhay
purse *porte-monnaie* ⓜ port·mo·nay
push *pousser* poo·say
push chair *poussette* ⓕ poo·set
put *mettre* may·trer

Q

qualification *qualification* ⓕ
  ka·lee·fee·ka·syon
quality *qualité* ⓕ ka·lee·tay
quantity *quantité* ⓕ kon·tee·tay
quarantine *quarantaine* ⓕ ka·ron·ten
quarrel *dispute* ⓕ dees·pewt
quarter *quart* ⓜ kar
queen *reine* ⓕ ren
question *question* ⓕ kay·styon
queue *queue* ⓕ ker
quick *rapide* ra·peed
quiet *tranquille* trong·keel
quit *quitter* kee·tay

R

rabbit *lapin* ⓜ la·pun
race *race* ⓕ ras
race (sport) *course* ⓕ koors
racetrack *champ* ⓜ *de courses*
  shon der koors
racism *racisme* ⓜ ra·sees·mer
racquet *raquette* ⓕ ra·ket
radiator *radiateur* ⓜ ra·dya·ter
radical *radical(e)* ra·dee·kal
radio *radio* ⓕ ra·dyo
rail *garde-fou* ⓜ gard·foo
railway *chemin* ⓜ *de fer*
  shmun der fair
railway station *gare* ⓕ gar
rain *pluie* ⓕ plwee
rain *pleuvoir* pler·vwar
raincoat *imperméable* um·pair·may·abler
raise (lift) *soulever* sool·vay
rape *violer* vyo·lay
rare *rare* rar

rash *rougeur* ① roo·zher
rat *rat* ⓜ ra
rave *rave* ① raiv
raw *cru(e)* ⓜ/① krew
razor *rasoir* ⓜ ra·zwar
razor blade *lame* ① *de rasoir*
lam der ra·zwar
reach *atteindre* a·tun·drer
read *lire* leer
ready *prêt(e)* ⓜ/① pray/pret
real *vrai(e)* ⓜ/① vray
real estate agent *agent* ⓜ *immobilier*
a·zhon ee·mo·bee·lyay
realise *se rendre compte de*
ser ron·drer kont der
realistic *réaliste* ray·a·leest
reality *réalité* ① ray·a·lee·tay
really *vraiment* vray·mon
rear (seat etc) *arrière* a·ryair
reason *raison* ① ray·zon
receipt *reçu* ⓜ rer·sew
receive *recevoir* rer·ser·vwar
recently *récemment* ray·sa·mon
recognise *reconnaître* rer·ko·nay·trer
recommend *recommander*
rer·ko·mon·day
record *enregistrer* on·rer·zhees·tray
record (music) *disque* ⓜ deesk
recording *enregistrement* ⓜ
on·rer·zhees·trer·mon
recyclable *recyclable* rer·see·kla·bler
recycle *recycler* rer·see·klay
recycling *recyclage* ⓜ rer·see·klazh
red *rouge* roozh
reduce *réduire* ray·dweer
referee *arbitre* ⓜ ar·bee·trer
reference *référence* ① ray·fay·rons
reflexology *réflexologie* ①
ray·flek·so·lo·zhee
refrigerator *réfrigérateur* ⓜ
ray·free·zhay·ra·ter
refugee *réfugié(e)* ⓜ/① ray·few·zhyay
refund *remboursement* ⓜ
rom·boor·ser·mon
refuse *refuser* rer·few·zay
region *région* ① ray·zhyon
registered mail/post (by) *en*
recommandé on rer·ko·mon·day
regular *normal(e)* ⓜ/① nor·mal

relationship *relation* ① rer·la·syon
relax (rest) *se reposer* ser rer·po·zay
relevant *pertinent(e)* ⓜ/① pair·tee·non(t)
religion *religion* ① rer·lee·zhyon
religious *religieux/religieuse* ⓜ/①
rer·lee·zhyer/rer·lee·zhyerz
remember *se souvenir* ser soo·ver·neer
remote *éloigné(e)* ⓜ/① ay·lwa·nyay
remote control *télécommande* ①
tay·lay·ko·mond
rent *louer* loo·ay
repair *réparer* ray·pa·ray
reply *répondre* ray·pon·drer
represent *représenter* rer·pray·zon·tay
republic *république* ① ray·pewb·leek
research *recherches* ① pl rer·shairsh
reservation *réservation* ①
ray·zair·va·syon
response *réponse* ① ray·pons
rest *repos* ⓜ rer·po
restaurant *restaurant* ⓜ res·to·ron
resumé *CV* ⓜ say·vay
retired *retraité(e)* ⓜ/① rer·tray·tay
return *revenir* rerv·neer
return (ticket) *aller retour* ⓜ
a·lay rer·toor
review (article) *critique* ① kree·teek
revolution *révolution* ① ray·vo·lew·syon
rhythm *rythme* ⓜ reet·mer
rice *riz* ⓜ ree
rich (wealthy) *riche* reesh
ride *promenade* ① prom·nad
ride (horse) *monter à (cheval)*
mon·tay a (shval)
right (to be right) *avoir raison*
a·vwar ray·zon
right (direction) *à droite* a drwat
right (entitlement) *droite* ⓜ drwa
right-wing *de droite* der drwat
ring (shape) *anneau* ⓜ a·no
ring (on finger) *bague* ① bag
ring (of phone) *sonner* so·nay
ring road (boulevard) *périphérique (BP)*
ⓜ (bool·var) pay·ree·fay·reek (bay pay)
rip-off *arnaque* ① ar·nak
risk *risque* ⓜ reesk
river *rivière* ① ree·vyair
road *route* ① root
road map *carte* ① *routière* kart roo·tyair

rob (person) *voler* vo·lay
robbery *vol* ⓜ vol
rock *rocher* ⓜ ro·shay
rock (music) *rock* ⓜ rok
rock climbing *varappe* ① va·rap
rock group *groupe* ⓜ *de rock*
  groop der rok
rollerblading *roller* ① ro·lair
romantic *romantique* ro·mon·teek
roof *toit* ⓜ twa
room *chambre* ① shom·brer
room number *numéro* ⓜ *de chambre*
  new·may·ro der shom·brer
rooster *coq* ⓜ kok
rope *corde* ① kord
round *rond(e)* ⓜ/① ron(d)
roundabout (traffic) *rond-point* ⓜ
  rom·pwun
route *itinéraire* ① ee·tee·nay·rair
rowing *aviron* ⓜ a·vee·ron
rubbish *ordures* ① or·dewr
rubbish bin *poubelle* ① poo·bel
rubbish dump *décharge* ① day·sharzh
rude *impoli(e)* ⓜ/① um·po·lee
rug *tapis* ⓜ ta·pee
rugby *rugby* ⓜ rewg·bee
ruins *ruines* ① pl rween
rules *règles* ① ray·gler
run *courir* koo·reer
run out of *manquer de* mong·kay der

S

Sabbath *sabbat* ⓜ sa·ba
sad *triste* treest
saddle *selle* ① sel
safe *sans danger* son don·zhay
safe *coffre-fort* ⓜ kof·rer·for
safe sex *rapports* ⓜ pl *sexuels protégés*
  ra·por seks·wel pro·tay·zhay
safety *sécurité* ① say·kew·ree·tay
sail *voile* ① vwal
sailing *voile* ① vwal
saint *saint(e)* ⓜ/① sun(t)
salary *salaire* ⓜ sa·lair
sale *vente* ① vont
sales tax *taxe* ⓐ *à la vente*
  taks a la vont

salt *sel* ⓜ sel
same *même* mem
sand *sable* ⓜ sa·bler
sandals *sandales* ① son·dal
sanitary napkin *serviette* ① *hygiénique*
  sair·vyet ee·zhyay·neek
satisfied *satisfait(e)* ⓜ/①
  sa·tees·fay/sa·tees·fet
Saturday *samedi* ⓜ sam·dee
sauna *sauna* ⓜ so·na
save *sauver* so·vay
say *dire* deer
scared *effrayé(e)* ⓜ/① ay·fray·yay
scarf *écharpe* ① ay·sharp
scenery *paysage* ⓜ pay·yee·zazh
school *école* ① ay·kol
science *science* ① syons
science fiction *science-fiction* ①
  syons·feek·syon
scientist *scientifique* ⓜ/① syon·tee·feek
scissors *ciseaux* ① pl see·zo
score *score* ⓜ skor
scoreboard *tableau* ⓜ *d'affichage*
  ta·blo da·fee·shazh
Scotland *Ecosse* ① ay·kos
screen *écran* ⓜ ay·kron
script *scénario* ⓜ say·na·ryo
scriptwriter *scénariste* ⓜ/① say·na·reest
sculpture *sculpture* ① skewl·tewr
sea *mer* ① mair
seashell *coquillage* ⓜ ko·kee·yazh
seasick (to be) *avoir le mal de mer*
  a·vwar ler mal der mair
seaside *bord* ⓜ *de la mer* bor der la mair
season *saison* ① say·zon
seat (place) *place* ① plas
seatbelt *ceinture* ① *de sécurité*
  sun·tewr der say·kew·ree·tay
second (clock) *seconde* ① skond
second *second(e)* ⓜ/① skon/skond
second class *de seconde classe*
  der skond klas
secondhand *d'occasion* do·ka·zyon
secret *secret* ⓜ ser·kray
secretary *secrétaire* ⓜ/① ser·kray·tair
security *sécurité* ① say·kew·ree·tay
see *voir* vwar

self-employed *indépendant(e)* ⓜ/ⓕ
un·day·pon·don(t)
selfish *égoïste* ay·go·eest
self service *libre-service* ⓜ
lee·brer·sair·vees
sell *vendre* von·drer
seminar *séminaire* ⓜ say·mee·nair
send *envoyer* on·vwa·yay
sensible *raisonnable* ray·zo·na·bler
sensual *sensuel(le)* ⓜ/ⓕ son·swel
separate *séparé(e)* ⓜ/ⓕ say·pa·ray
September *septembre* ⓜ sep·tom·brer
series *série* ⓕ say·ree
serious *sérieux/sérieuse* ⓜ/ⓕ
say·ree·yer/say·ree·yerz
service *service* ⓜ sair·vees
service station *station-service* ⓕ
sta·syon·sair·vees
service charge *service* ⓜ sair·vees
seven *sept* set
several *plusieurs* plew·zyer
sew *coudre* koo·drer
sex *sexe* ⓜ seks
sexism *sexisme* ⓜ sek·see·smer
sexist *sexiste* sek·seest
sexy *sexy* sek·see
shade *ombre* ⓕ om·brer
shadow *ombre* ⓕ om·brer
shake (something) *agiter* a·zhee·tay
shallow *peu profond* ⓜ per pro·fon(d)
shampoo *shampooing* ⓜ shom·pwung
shape *forme* ⓕ form
shape *façonner* fa·so·nay
share (a dorm etc) *partager* par·ta·zhay
share (with) *partager (avec)*
par·ta·zhay (a·vek)
sharp (blade etc) *tranchant(e)* ⓜ/ⓕ
tron·shon(t)
shave *se raser* ser ra·zay
shaving cream *mousse* ⓕ *à raser*
moos a ra·zay
she *elle* el
sheep *mouton* ⓜ moo·ton
sheet (of paper) *feuille* ⓕ fer·yee
sheet (bed) *drap* ⓜ dra
shelf *étagère* ⓕ ay·ta·zhair
shelter *abri* ⓜ a·bree
ship *navire* ⓜ na·veer

shirt *chemise* ⓕ sher·meez
shoe *chaussure* ⓕ sho·sewr
shoe shop *magasin* ⓜ *de chaussures*
ma·ga·zun der sho·sewr
shoot *tirer* tee·ray
shoot (and kill someone)
tuer d'un coup de pistolet
tew·way dung koo der pee·sto·lay
shop *magasin* ⓜ ma·ga·zun
shop *faire des courses* fair day koors
shopping centre *centre* ⓜ *commercial*
son·trer ko·mair·syal
short (height) *court(e)* ⓜ/ⓕ koor(t)
shortage *manque* ⓜ mongk
shorts *short* ⓜ short
shoulder *épaule* ⓕ ay·pol
shout *crier* kree·yay
show *montrer* mon·tray
show *spectacle* ⓜ spek·ta·kler
shower *douche* ⓕ doosh
shrine *lieu* ⓜ *saint* lyer sun
shut *fermé(e)* ⓜ/ⓕ fair·may
shy *timide* tee·meed
sick *malade* ma·lad
sickness *maladie* ⓕ ma·la·dee
side *côté* ⓜ ko·tay
sign *signe* ⓜ see·nyer
signature *signature* ⓕ see·nya·tewr
silk *soie* ⓕ swa
silver *argent* ⓜ ar·zhon
similar *semblable* som·bla·bler
simple *simple* sum·pler
since (May etc) *depuis* der·pwee
sing *chanter* shon·tay
Singapore *Singapour* sung·ga·poor
singer *chanteur/chanteuse* ⓜ/ⓕ
shon·ter/shon·terz
single (person) *célibataire* say·lee·ba·tair
single room *chambre* ⓕ *pour une
personne* shom·brer poor ewn pair·son
singlet *maillot* ⓜ *de corps* ma·yo der kor
sister *sœur* ⓕ ser
sit *s'asseoir* sa·swar
situation *situation* ⓕ see·twa·syon
six *six* sees
size (general) *taille* ⓕ tai
skateboarding *skateboard* ⓜ sket·bord
ski *skier* skee·yay

skiing *ski* ⓜ skee
skis *skis* ⓜ skee
skill *compétence* ⓕ kom·pay·tons
skin *peau* ⓕ po
skirt *jupe* ⓕ zhewp
sky *ciel* ⓜ syel
sleep *sommeil* ⓜ so·may
sleep *dormir* dor·meer
sleeping bag *sac* ⓜ *de couchage*
  sak der koo·shazh
sleeping car *wagon-lit* ⓜ va·gon·lee
sleeping pill *somnifère* ⓜ som·nee·fair
sleepy (to be sleepy) *avoir sommeil*
  a·vwar so·may
slice *tranche* ⓕ tronsh
slide (film) *diapositive* ⓕ dya·po·zee·teev
slow *lent(e)* ⓜ/ⓕ lon(t)
slowly *lentement* lon·ter·mon
small *petit(e)* ⓜ/ⓕ per·tee/·teet
smaller *plus petit(e)* ⓜ/ⓕ
  plew per·tee/·teet
smallest *le plus petit/la plus petite* ⓜ/ⓕ
  ler plew per·tee/la plew per·teet
smell *odeur* ⓕ o·der
smell *sentir* son·teer
smile *sourire* ⓜ soo·reer
smile *sourire* soo·reer
smoke *fumée* ⓕ few·may
smoke *fumer* few·may
snack *casse-croûte* ⓜ kas·kroot
snail *escargot* ⓜ es·kar·go
snake *serpent* ⓜ sair·pon
snorkel *nager avec un tuba*
  na·zhay a·vek un tew·ba
snow *neige* ⓕ nezh
snow *neiger* nay·zhay
snowboarding *surf (des neiges)*
  ⓜ serf (day nezh)
soap *savon* ⓜ sa·von
soccer (football) *foot(ball)* ⓜ foot(bol)
social welfare *sécurité* ⓕ *sociale*
  say·kew·ree·tay so·syal
socialism *socialisme* ⓜ so·sya·lees·mer
socialist *socialiste* so·sya·leest
society *société* ⓕ so·syay·tay
socks *chaussettes* ⓕ sho·set
soft *doux/douce* ⓜ/ⓕ doo/doos
software *logiciel* ⓜ lo·zhee·syel
soldier *soldat* ⓜ sol·da
solid *solide* so·leed

some *quelques* kel·ker
some *du/de la/des* ⓜ/ⓕ/pl
  dew/der la/day
someone *quelqu'un* kel·kun
something *quelque chose* kel·ker shoz
sometimes *quelquefois* kel·ker·fwa
son *fils* ⓜ fees
song *chanson* ⓕ shon·son
soon *bientôt* byun·to
sore *douloureux/douloureuse* ⓜ/ⓕ
  doo·loo·rer/doo·loo·rerz
south *sud* ⓜ sewd
southern hemisphere *hémisphère* ⓜ *sud*
  ay·mees·fair sewd
souvenir *souvenir* ⓜ soov·neer
souvenir shop *magasin* ⓜ *de souvenirs*
  ma·ga·zun der soov·neer
space *espace* ⓜ es·pas
Spain *Espagne* ⓕ es·pa·nyer
speak *parler* par·lay
special *spécial(e)* ⓜ/ⓕ spay·syal
specialist *spécialiste* ⓜ/ⓕ spay·sya·leest
speech *discours* ⓜ dees·koor
speed *vitesse* ⓕ vee·tes
speed limit *limitation* ⓕ *de vitesse*
  lee·mee·ta·syon der vee·tes
speedometer *compteur* ⓜ *(de vitesse)*
  kon·ter (der vee·tes)
spend (money) *dépenser* day·pon·say
spend (time) *passer* pa·say
spicy *épicé(e)* ⓜ/ⓕ ay·pee·say
spider *araignée* ⓕ a·ray·nyay
spine *colonne* ⓕ *vertébrale*
  ko·lon vair·tay·bral
spirit *esprit* ⓜ es·pree
spoon *cuillère* ⓕ kwee·yair
sport *sport* ⓜ spor
sports ground *terrain* ⓜ *de sport*
  tay·run der spor
sports store/shop *magasin* ⓜ *de sports*
  ma·ga·zun der spor
sportsperson *sportif/sportive* ⓜ/ⓕ
  spor·teef/spor·teev
spot (place) *endroit* ⓜ on·drwa
sprain *entorse* ⓕ on·tors
spring (coil) *ressort* ⓜ rer·sor
spring (season) *printemps* ⓜ prun·tom
square (town) *place* ⓕ plas
stadium *stade* ⓜ stad

216

stage *scène* ① sen
stairway *escalier* ⑩ es·ka·lyay
stale *pas frais/fraîche* ⑩/① pa fray/fresh
stale (bread) *rassis(e)* ⑩/① ra·see(z)
stamp *timbre* ⑩ tum·brer
stand-by ticket *billet* ⑩ *stand-by*
  bee·yay stond·bai
stars *étoiles* ① ay·twal
start *commencement* ⑩ ko·mons·mon
start *commencer* ko·mon·say
station *gare* ① gar
stationer's (shop) *papeterie* ① pa·pet·ree
stay *rester* res·tay
steal *voler* vo·lay
steep *raide* red
step *marche* ① marsh
stereo (system) *chaîne* ① *hi-fi*
  shen ee·fee
stockings *bas* ⑩ ba
stolen *volé(e)* ⑩/① vo·lay
stomach *estomac* ⑩ es·to·ma
stomachache (to have a) *avoir mal au*
  ventre a·vwar mal o von·trer
stone *pierre* ① pyair
stop (something, someone) *arrêter*
  a·ray·tay
stop (doing) *s'arrêter* sa·ray·tay
stop *arrêt* ⑩ a·ray
storm *orage* ⑩ o·razh
story *histoire* ① ees·twar
stove *réchaud* ⑩ ray·sho
straight *droit(e)* ⑩/① drwa(t)
straight ahead *tout droit* too drwa
strange *étrange* ay·tronzh
stranger *étranger/étrangère* ⑩/①
  ay·tron·zhay/ay·tron·zhair
stream *ruisseau* ⑩ rwee·so
street *rue* ① rew
street market *braderie* ① bra·dree
strike (go on strike) *se mettre en grève*
  ser may·trer ong grev
string *ficelle* ① fee·sel
stroller *poussette* ① poo·set
strong *fort(e)* ⑩/① for(t)
student *étudiant(e)* ⑩/① ay·tew·dyon(t)
studio *atelier* ⑩ a·ter·lyay
study *étudier* ay·tew·dyay
stupid *stupide* stew·peed

style *style* ⑩ steel
subtitles *sous-titres* ⑩ soo·tee·trer
suburb *banlieue* ① bon·lyer
subway *métro* ⑩ may·tro
suffer *souffrir* soo·freer
suitcase *valise* ① va·leez
summer *été* ⑩ ay·tay
sun *soleil* ⑩ so·lay
sunblock *écran* ⑩ *solaire total*
  ay·kron so·lair to·tal
sunburn *coup* ⑩ *de soleil* koo der so·lay
Sunday *dimanche* ① dee·monsh
sunglasses *lunettes* ① *de soleil*
  lew·net der so·lay
sunny *ensoleillé(e)* ⑩/① on·so·lay·yay
sunrise *lever* ⑩ *du soleil*
  ler·vay dew so·lay
sunscreen *écran* ⑩ *solaire*
  ay·kron so·lair
sunset *coucher* ⑩ *du soleil*
  koo·shay dew so·lay
supermarket *supermarché* ⑩
  sew·pair·mar·shay
superstition *superstition* ①
  sew·pair·stee·syon
support *supporter* sew·por·tay
sure *sûr(e)* ⑩/① sewr
surf *surfer* ser·fay
surface mail (land) *voie de terre*
  vwa der tair
surface mail (sea) *voie maritime*
  vwa ma·ree·teem
surfboard *planche* ① *de surf*
  plonsh der serf
surname *nom* ⑩ *de famille*
  nom der fa·mee·yer
surprise *surprise* ① sewr·preez
survive *survivre* sewr·vee·vrer
sweater *pull* ⑩ pewl
Sweden *Suède* ① swayd
sweet *sucré(e)* ⑩/① sew·kray
swim *nager* na·zhay
swimming pool *piscine* ① pee·seen
swimsuit *maillot* ⑩ *de bain*
  ma·yo der bun
Switzerland *Suisse* ① swees
synagogue *synagogue* ① see·na·gog
synthetic *synthétique* sun·tay·teek
syringe *seringue* ① ser·rung*

T

table *table* ① ta·bler
table tennis *tennis* ⓜ *de table*
  tay·nees der ta·bler
tablecloth *nappe* ① nap
tail *queue* ① ker
tailor *tailleur* ⓜ ta·yer
take *prendre* pron·drer
take a photo *prendre en photo*
  pron·drer on fo·to
talk *parler* par·lay
talk *conversation* ① kon·vair·sa·syon
talk (lecture) *exposé* ⓜ eks·po·zay
tall *grand(e)* ⓜ/① gron(d)
tampon *tampon* ⓜ *hygiénique*
  tom·pon ee·zhyay·neek
tanning lotion *crème* ① *de bronzage*
  krem der bron·zazh
tap *robinet* ⓜ ro·bee·nay
tasty *délicieux/délicieuse* ⓜ/①
  day·lees·yer/day·lees·yerz
tax *taxe* ① taks
taxi *taxi* ⓜ tak·see
taxi stand *station* ① *de taxi*
  sta·syon der tak·see
teacher *professeur* ⓜ pro·fay·ser
team *équipe* ① ay·keep
teaspoon *petite cuillère* ①
  per·teet kwee·yair
technique *technique* ① tek·neek
teeth *dents* ① don
telegram *télégramme* ⓜ tay·lay·gram
telephone *téléphone* ⓜ tay·lay·fon
telephone *téléphoner* tay·lay·fo·nay
telephone box *cabine* ① *téléphonique*
  ka·been tay·lay·fo·neek
telescope *télescope* ⓜ tay·lay·skop
television *télé(vision)* ① tay·lay(vee·zyon)
tell *dire* deer
tell (a story) *raconter* ra·kon·tay
teller *caissier/caissière* ⓜ/①
  kay·syay/kay·syair
temperature (fever) *température* ①
  tom·pay·ra·tewr
temperature (weather) *température* ①
  tom·pay·ra·tewr
temple *temple* ⓜ tom·pler

ten *dix* dee(s)
tenant *locataire* ⓜ/① lo·ka·tair
tennis *tennis* ⓜ tay·nees
tennis court *court* ⓜ *de tennis*
  koor der tay·nees
tent *tente* ① tont
tent pegs *piquets* ⓜ *de tente*
  pee·kay der tont
terrible *affreux/affreuse* ⓜ/①
  a·frer/a·frerz
terrorism *terrorisme* ⓜ tay·ro·rees·mer
test *essai* ⓜ ay·say
thank *remercier* rer·mair·syay
that (month, etc) *ce/cette* ⓜ/① ser/set
that (one) *cela* ser·la
theatre *théâtre* ⓜ tay·a·trer
their *leur/leurs* sg/pl ler
then (next) *puis* pwee
then (at the time) *alors* a·lor
there *là* la
therefore *donc* dongk
they *ils/elles* ⓜ/① eel/el
thick *épais/épaisse* ⓜ/① ay·pay/ay·pes
thief *voleur/voleuse* ⓜ/① vo·ler/vo·lerz
thin *maigre* may·grer
thing *chose* ① shoz
think *penser* pon·say
third *troisième* trwa·zyem
thirsty (to be) *avoir soif* a·vwar swaf
this (month etc) *ce/cette* ⓜ/① ser/set
this (one) *ceci* ser·see
three *trois* trwa
throat *gorge* ① gorzh
throw *jeter* zher·tay
thrush (illness) *muguet* ⓜ mew·gay
Thursday *jeudi* ⓜ zher·dee
ticket *billet* ⓜ bee·yay
ticket collector *contrôleur* ⓜ kon·tro·ler
ticket machine *distributeur* ⓜ *de tickets*
  dee·stree·bew·ter der tee·kay
ticket office *guichet* ⓜ gee·shay
tide *marée* ① ma·ray
tie (draw) *match* ⓜ *nul* matsh newl
tight *étroit(e)* ⓜ/① ay·trwa(t)
time *heure* ① er
time (general) *temps* ⓜ tom
time difference *décalage* ⓜ *horaire*
  day·ka·lazh o·rair
timetable *horaire* ⓜ o·rair

tin (can) *boîte* ① bwat
tin opener *ouvre-boîte* ⑩ oo·vrer·bwat
tiny *minuscule* mee·new·skewl
tip (gratuity) *pourboire* ⑩ poor·bwar
tire *pneu* ⑩ pner
tired *fatigué(e)* ⑩/① fa·tee·gay
tissues *mouchoirs* ⑩ pl *en papier*|
moo·shwar om pa·pyay
to *à* a
toast *pain grillé* ⑩ pung gree·yay
toaster *grille-pain* ⑩ greey·pun
tobacco *tabac* ⑩ ta·ba
tobacconist *bureau* ⑩ *de tabac*
bew·ro der ta·ba
today *aujourd'hui* o·zhoor·dwee
toe *orteil* ⑩ or·tay
together *ensemble* on·som·bler
toilet *toilettes* ① pl twa·let
toilet paper *papier* ⑩ *hygiénique*
pa·pyay ee·zhyay·neek
tomorrow *demain* der·mun
tomorrow afternoon *demain
après-midi* der·mun a·pray·mee·dee
tomorrow evening *demain soir*
der·mun swar
tomorrow morning *demain matin*
der·mum ma·tun
tonight *ce soir* ser swar
too (expensive etc) *trop* tro
too much/many *trop* tro
**too much (rain etc)/too many (people
etc)** *trop de* tro der
tooth *dent* ① don
toothache *mal* ⑩ *de dents*
a·vwar mal o don
toothbrush *brosse* ① *à dents* bros a don
toothpaste *dentifrice* ⑩ don·tee·frees
toothpick *cure-dent* ⑩ kewr·don
torch (flashlight) *lampe* ① *de poche*
lomp der posh
touch *toucher* too·shay
touch (sense) *toucher* ⑩ too·shay
tour *voyage* ⑩ vwa·yazh
tourist *touriste* ⑩/① too·reest
tourist office *office de tourisme* ⑩
o·fees·der too·rees·mer
tournament *tournoi* ⑩ toor·nwa
tow truck *dépanneuse* ① day·pa·nerz
toward (direction) *vers* vair

toward (feelings) *envers* on·vair
towel *serviette* ① sair·vyet
tower *tour* ① toor
town *ville* ① veel
toxic waste *déchets* ⑩ pl *toxiques*
day·shay tok·seek
toy *jouet* ⑩ zhway
track (path) *chemin* ⑩ *(de randonnée)*
sher·mun (der ron·do·nay)
track (sports) *piste* ① peest
trade *commerce* ⑩ ko·mairs
traffic *circulation* ① seer·kew·la·syon
traffic jam *bouchon* ⑩ boo·shon
traffic lights *feux* ⑩ fer
trail *piste* ① peest
train *train* ⑩ trun
train station *gare* ① gar
transfer *transfert* ⑩ trons·fair
transit lounge *salle* ① *de transit*
sal der tron·zeet
translate *traduire* tra·dweer
transport *transport* ⑩ trons·por
travel *voyager* vwa·ya·zhay
travel agency *agence* ① *de voyage*
a·zhons der vwa·yazh
travel sickness *mal* ⑩ *des transports*
mal day trons·por
travellers cheque *chèque* ⑩ *de voyage*
shek der vwa·yazh
treatment *traitement* ⑩ tret·mon
tree *arbre* ⑩ ar·brer
trek *randonnée* ⑩ ran·do·nay
trick *ruse* ① rewz
trick *tromper* trom·pay
trip *voyage* ⑩ vwa·yazh
trolley *chariot* ⑩ shar·yo
trouble *peine* ① pen
trousers *pantalon* ⑩ pon·ta·lon
truck *camion* ⑩ ka·myon
true *vrai(e)* ⑩/① vray
trust *faire confiance à* fair kon·fyons a
trust *confiance* ① kon·fyons
truth *vérité* ① vay·ree·tay
try *essayer* ay·say·yay
T-shirt *T-shirt* ⑩ tee·shert
tube (tyre) *chambre* ① *à air*
shom·brer a air
Tuesday *mardi* ⑩ mar·dee
tune *air* ⑩ air

turn *tourner* toor·nay
TV *télé* ① tay·lay
TV series *série* ① say·ree
tweezers *pince* ① *à épiler*
puns a ay·pee·lay
twice *deux fois* der fwa
twin beds *lits* ⓜ pl *jumeaux*
day lee zhew·mo
twins *jumeaux/jumelles* ⓜ/①
zhew·mo/zhew·mel
two *deux* der
type *type* ⓜ teep
typical *typique* tee·peek
tyre *pneu* ⓜ pner

U

ugly *laid(e)* ⓜ/① lay/led
ultrasound *ultrason* ⓜ ewl·tra·son
umbrella *parapluie* ⓜ pa·ra·plwee
uncertain *incertain(e)* ⓜ/①
un·sair·tun/un·sair·ten
uncomfortable *inconfortable*
ung·kon·for·ta·bler
under *sous* soo
understand *comprendre* kom·pron·drer
underwear *sous-vêtements* ⓜ
soo·vet·mon
unemployed *chômeur/chômeuse* ⓜ/①
sho·mer/sho·merz
unemployment *chômage* ⓜ sho·mazh
unfair *injuste* un·zhewst
unfurnished *non-meublé(e)* ⓜ/①
no·mer·blay
uniform *uniforme* ⓜ ew·nee·form
union *union* ① ew·nyon
union (trade) *syndicat* ⓜ sun·dee·ka
universe *univers* ⓜ ew·nee·vair
university *université* ①
ew·nee·vair·see·tay
unleaded *sans plomb* son plom
unsafe *dangereux/dangereuse* ⓜ/①
don·zhrer/don·zhrerz
until (Friday, etc) *jusqu'à* zhew·ska
unusual *peu commun(e)* ⓜ/①
per ko·mun/ko·mewn
up *en haut* on o
upstairs *en haut* on o

uphill (to go) *monter* mon·tay
urgent *urgent(e)* ⓜ/① ewr·zhon(t)
us *nous* noo
USA *les USA* ⓜ lay zew·es·a
use *utiliser* ew·tee·lee·zay
useful *utile* ew·teel
usually *habituellement* a·bee·twel·mon

V

vacancy *chambre* ① *libre*
shom·brer lee·brer
vacant *libre* lee·brer
vacation *vacances* ① pl va·kons
vaccination *vaccination* ①
vak·see·na·syon
vagina *vagin* ⓜ va·zhun
validate *valider* va·lee·day
valley *vallée* ① va·lay
valuable *de valeur* der va·ler
value (price) *valeur* ① va·ler
van *camionnette* ① ka·myo·net
vegetable *légume* ⓜ lay·gewm
vegetarian *végétarien/végétarienne* ⓜ/①
vay·zhay·ta·ryun/vay·zhay·ta·ryen
vehicle *véhicule* ⓜ vay·ee·kewl
vein *veine* ① ven
venereal disease *maladie* ① *vénérienne*
ma·la·dee vay·nay·ryen
very *très* tray
vest *maillot* ⓜ *de corps* ma·yo der kor
via *via* vee·a
video recorder *magnétoscope* ⓜ
ma·nyay·to·skop
video tape *bande* ① *vidéo*
bond vee·day·o
view *vue* ① vew
village *village* ⓜ vee·lazh
vine *vigne* ① vee·nyer
vineyard *vignoble* ⓜ vee·nyo·bler
virus *virus* ⓜ vee·rews
visa *visa* ⓜ vee·za
visit (museum etc) *visiter* vee·zee·tay
visit (person) *aller voir* a·lay vwar
visitor *visiteur/visiteuse* ⓜ/①
vee·zee·ter/vee·zee·terz
visitor (guest) *invité(e)* ⓜ/① un·vee·tay
vitamin *vitamine* ① vee·ta·meen

volume *volume* ⑩ vo·lewm
voluntary (not paid) *bénévole*
  bay·nay·vol
volunteer *bénévole* ⑩/① bay·nay·vol
vomit *vomir* vo·meer
vote *voter* vo·tay

W

wage *salaire* ⑩ sa·lair
wait (for) *attendre* a·ton·drer
waiter *serveur/serveuse* ⑩/①
  sair·ver/sair·verz
waiting room *salle* ① *d'attente*
  sal da·tont
wake up *se réveiller* ser ray·vay·yay
wake (someone) up *réveiller* ray·vay·yay
walk *marcher* mar·shay
wall (outer) *mur* ⑩ mewr
want *vouloir* voo·lwar
war *guerre* ① gair
wardrobe *penderie* ① pon·dree
warm *chaud(e)* ⑩/① sho(d)
warn *prévenir* prayv·neer
warning *avertissement* ⑩ a·vair·tees·mon
wash (oneself) *se laver* ser la·vay
wash (something) *laver* la·vay
washing machine *machine* ① *à laver*
  ma·sheen a la·vay
wasp *guêpe* ① gep
watch *regarder* rer·gar·day
watch *montre* ① mon·trer
water *eau* ① o
water bottle (hot) *bouillotte* ① boo·yot
waterfall *cascade* ① kas·kad
waterproof *imperméable*
  um·pair·may·abler
waterskiing *ski* ⑩ *nautique* skee no·teek
wave *vague* ① vag
way *direction* ① dee·rek·syon
way (manner) *façon* ① fa·son
way (road) *chemin* ⑩ sher·mun
we *nous* noo
weak *faible* fay·bler
wealthy *riche* reesh
wear *porter* por·tay
weather *temps* ⑩ tom
weather forecast *météo* ① may·tay·o

wedding *mariage* ⑩ ma·ree·azh
Wednesday *mercredi* ⑩ mair·krer·dee
week *semaine* ① ser·men
weekend *week-end* ⑩ week·end
weigh *peser* per·zay
weight *poids* ⑩ pwa
welcome *accueillir* a·ker·yeer
welfare (aid) *assistance* ① *publique*
  a·sees·tons pewb·leek
well *bien* byun
west *ouest* ⑩ west
wet *mouillé(e)* ⑩/① moo·yay
what *quel(le)* ⑩/① kel
wheel *roue* ① roo
wheelchair *fauteuil* ⑩ *roulant*
  fo·ter·yee roo·lon
when *quand* kon
where *où* oo
which *quel(le)* ⑩/① kel
which *lequel/laquelle* ⑩/①
  ler·kel/la·kel
which *qui* kee
whistle *siffler* see·flay
white *blanc/blanche* ⑩/① blong/blonsh
who *qui* kee
whole *tout entier/toute entière* ⑩/①
  too ton·tyay/too ton·tyair
why *pourquoi* poor·kwa
wide *large* larzh
widow *veuve* ① verv
widower *veuf* ⑩ verf
wife *femme* ① fam
wild *sauvage* so·vazh
win *gagner* ga·nyay
wind *vent* ⑩ von
window *fenêtre* ① fer·nay·trer
windscreen/windshield *pare-brise* ⑩
  par·breez
windsurfer *planche* ① *à voile*
  plonsh a vwal
windsurfing (to go) *faire de la planche*
  à voile fair der la plonsh a vwal
wine *vin* ⑩ vun
winery *cave viticole* ① kaav vee·tee·kol
wings *ailes* ① el
winner *gagnant(e)* ⑩/① ga·nyon(t)
winter *hiver* ⑩ ee·vair
wire *fil* ⑩ *de fer* feel der fair

Y

wish *souhaiter* sway·tay
with *avec* a·vek
withdrawal *retrait* Ⓜ rer·tray
within (an hour etc) *avant* a·von
without *sans* son
witness *témoin* Ⓜ tay·mwun
woman *femme* Ⓕ fam
wonderful *merveilleux/merveilleuse*
 Ⓜ/Ⓕ mair·vay·yer/mair·vay·yerz
wood *bois* Ⓜ bwa
wool *laine* Ⓕ len
word *mot* Ⓜ mo
work *travail* Ⓜ tra·vai
work *travailler* tra·va·yay
work experience *stage* Ⓜ *en entreprise*
 stazh on on·trer·preez
work permit *permis* Ⓜ *de travail*
 pair·mee der tra·vai
world *monde* Ⓜ mond
World Cup *la Coupe du Monde*
 la koop dew mond
worms *vers* Ⓜ vair
worried *inquiet/inquiète* Ⓜ/Ⓕ
 ung·kyay/ung·kyet
worry *s'inquiéter* sung·kyay·tay
worse *pire* peer
worship *faire ses dévotions*
 fair say day·vo·syon
worship (someone) *adorer* a·do·ray
wrist *poignet* Ⓜ pwa·nyay
write *écrire* ay·kreer

writer *écrivain* Ⓜ ay·kree·vun
wrong *faux/fausse* Ⓜ/Ⓕ fo/fos
wrong (direction) *mauvais(e)* Ⓜ/Ⓕ
 mo·vay(z)
(to be) wrong *avoir tort* a·vwar tor

Y

year *année* Ⓕ a·nay
yellow *jaune* zhon
yes *oui* wee
yesterday *hier* ee·yair
yet *encore* ong·kor
yoga *yoga* Ⓜ yo·ga
you *vous* pl pol voo
you *tu* inf tew
young *jeune* zhern
your pol *votre/vos* sg/pl
 vo·trer/vo
your sg&inf *ton/ta/tes* Ⓜ/Ⓕ/pl
 ton/ta/tay
youth hostel *auberge* Ⓕ *de jeunesse*
 o·bairzh der zher·nes

Z

zero *zéro* zay·ro
zip/zipper *fermeture* Ⓕ *éclair*
 fair·mer·tewr ay·klair
zoo *zoo* Ⓜ zo

DICTIONARY

222

french–english

français–anglais

A

Nouns in this dictionary have their gender indicated by ⑩ or ①. If it's a plural noun, you'll also see pl. Where a word that could be either a noun or a verb has no gender indicated, it's a verb.

A

à a *at • to*
à bord a bor *aboard*
à côté de a ko·tay der *beside*
à côté de a ko·tay der *next to*
à droite a drwat *right (direction)*
à gauche a gosh *left (direction)*
à l'étranger a lay·tron·zhay *abroad*
à l'heure a ler *on time*
à la maison a la may·zon *home*
à peu près a per pray *approximately*
à plein temps a plun ton *full-time*
à temps partiel a tom par·syel *part-time*
abeille ① a·bay *bee*
abondance ① a·bon·dons *plenty*
abri ⑩ a·bree *shelter*
accepter ak·sep·tay *accept*
accident ⑩ ak·see·don *accident*
accident ⑩ ak·see·don *crash*
accueillir a·ker·yeer *welcome*
accumulation ① a·kew·mew·la·syon *collection*
acheter ash·tay *buy*
acide ⑩ a·seed *acid (drug)*
acte ⑩ de naissance akt der nay·sons *birth certificate*
acteur/actrice ⑩/① ak·ter/ak·trees *actor*
actualités ak·twa·lee·tay *news (on TV etc)*
actuel(le) ⑩/① ak·twel *current*
acupuncture ① a·kew·pongk·tewr *acupuncture*
adaptateur ⑩ a·dap·ta·ter *adaptor*
addition ① a·dee·syon *bill • check*
admettre ad·me·trer *admit*
administration ① ad·mee·nee·stra·syon *administration*
admirer ad·mee·ray *admire*
adorer a·do·ray *worship (someone)*
adresse ① a·dres *address*

adulte ⑩/① a·dewlt *adult*
adversaire ⑩/① ad·vair·sair *opponent*
aérobic ⑩ a·ay·ro·beek *aerobics*
aérogramme ⑩ a·ay·ro·gram *aerogram*
aéroport ⑩ a·ay·ro·por *airport*
affaires ① a·fair *business*
affreux/affreuse ⑩/① a·frer/a·frerz *awful • terrible*
Afrique ① a·freek *Africa*
âge ⑩ azh *age*
âgé(e) ⑩/① a·zhay *elderly*
agence ① de voyage a·zhons der vwa·yazh *travel agency*
agence ① immobilière a·zhons ee·mo·bee·lyair *estate agency*
agenda ⑩ a·zhun·da *diary*
agent ⑩ de police a·zhon der po·lees *officer (police)*
agent ⑩ immobilier a·zhon ee·mo·bee·lyay *real estate agent*
agiter a·zhee·tay *shake (something)*
agréable a·gray·a·bler *nice (pleasant)*
agressif/agressive ⑩/① a·gray·seef/a·gray·seev *aggressive*
agriculteur/agricultrice ⑩/① a·gree·kewl·ter/a·gree·kewl·trees *farmer*
agriculture ① a·gree·kewl·tewr *agriculture*
aide ① ed *help*
aider ay·day *help*
aiguille ① ay·gwee·yer *needle*
ailes ① el *wings*
aimant(e) ⑩/① ay·mon(t) *caring*
aimer ay·may *like • love*
air ⑩ air air *• tune*
alcool ⑩ al·kol *alcohol*
Allemagne ① al·ma·nyer *Germany*
aller a·lay *go*
aller retour ⑩ a·lay rer·toor *return (ticket)*

french–english

223

aller voir a·lay vwar *visit (person)*
allergie ① a·lair·zhee *allergy*
allocation ① **de chômage** a·lo·ka·syon der sho·mazh *dole*
allume-feu ⑩ **anti-moustiques** a·lewm·fer on·tee·moo·steek *mosquito coil*
allumettes ① pl a·lew·met *matches (for lighting)*
alors a·lor *then (at the time)*
alpinisme ⑩ al·pee·nee·smer *mountaineering*
alternative ① al·tair·na·teev *alternative*
altitude ① al·tee·tewd *altitude*
amant(e) ⑩/① a·mon(t) *lover*
amateur ⑩ a·ma·ter *amateur*
ambassade ① om·ba·sad *embassy*
ambassadeur/ambassadrice ⑩/① om·ba·sa·der/om·ba·sa·drees *ambassador*
ambulance ① om·bew·lons *ambulance*
améliorer a·may·lyo·ray *improve*
amende ① a·mond *fine (penalty)*
amener am·nay *bring (a person)*
amer/amère ⑩/① a·mair *bitter*
ami/amie ⑩/① a·mee *friend*
amical(e) ⑩/① a·mee·kal *friendly*
amitié ① a·mee·tyay *friendship*
amour a·moor *love*
ample om·pler *loose (clothes)*
ampoule ① om·pool *blister • light bulb*
analgésique ⑩ a·nal·zhay·zeek *painkiller*
analyse ① **de sang** a·na·leez der son *blood test*
anglais(e) ⑩/① ong·glay(z) *English*
Angleterre ① ong·gler·tair *England*
animal ⑩ a·nee·mal *animal*
animal familier a·nee·mal fa·mee·lyay *pet*
anneau ⑩ a·no *ring (shape)*
année ① a·nay *year*
anniversaire ⑩ a·nee·vair·sair *birthday*
annuaire ⑩ an·wair *phone book*
annuel(le) ⑩/① a·nwel *annual*
annuler a·new·lay *cancel*
antibiotiques ⑩ on·tee·byo·teek *antibiotics*

anti-nucléaire on·tee·new·klay·air *antinuclear*
antique on·teek *ancient*
antiquité ① on·tee·kee·tay *antique*
antiseptique ⑩ on·tee·sep·teek *antiseptic*
août ⑩ oot *August*
appareil acoustique a·pa·ray a·koos·teek *hearing aid*
appareil de chauffage a·pa·ray der sho·fazh *heater*
appareil photo a·pa·ray fo·to *camera*
appel en PCV a·pel on pay·say·vay *collect call*
appeler a·play *call*
appendice ⑩ a·pun·dees *appendix*
apporter a·por·tay *bring (a thing)*
apprendre a·pron·drer *learn*
après a·pray *after*
après-demain a·pray·der·mun *day after tomorrow (the)*
après-midi ⑩ a·pray·mee·dee *afternoon*
après-rasage ⑩ a·pray·ra·zazh *aftershave*
après-shampooing a·pray·shom·pwung *conditioner (hair)*
araignée ① a·ray·nyay *spider*
arbitre ⑩ ar·bee·trer *referee*
arbre ⑩ ar·brer *tree*
archéologie ① ar·kay·o·lo·zhee *archaeology*
architecte(e) ⑩/① ar·shee·tekt *architect*
architecture ar·shee·tek·tewr *architecture*
argent ⑩ ar·zhon *cash • money • silver*
arnaque ① ar·nak *rip-off*
arrêt ⑩ a·ray *stop*
arrêt d'autobus a·ray do·to·bews *bus stop*
arrêter a·ray·tay *stop (something, someone)*
arrêter a·ray·tay *arrest*
arrière a·ryair *rear (seat etc)*
arrivées ① a·ree·vay *arrivals*
arriver a·ree·vay *arrive*
art ⑩ ar *art*
artisanat ⑩ ar·tee·za·na *crafts*
artiste ⑩/① ar·teest *artist*

arts ⓜ pl **martiaux** ar mar·syo *martial arts*
ascenseur ⓜ a·son·ser *elevator • lift*
Asie ⓕ a·zee *Asia*
aspirine ⓕ as·pee·reen *aspirin*
assez a·say *enough*
assiette ⓕ a·syet *plate*
assistance ⓕ **publique** a·sees·tons pewb·leek *welfare (aid)*
assurance ⓕ a·sew·rons *insurance*
assurer a·sew·ray *insure*
asthme ⓜ as·mer *asthma*
atelier ⓜ a·ter·lyay *studio*
athlétisme ⓜ at·lay·tees·mer *athletics*
atmosphère ⓕ at·mos·fair *atmosphere*
attaché(e) ⓜ/ⓕ a·ta·shay *attached*
atteindre a·tun·drer *reach • wait (for)*
Attention! a·ton·syon *Careful!*
attraper a·tra·pay *catch*
au coin o kwun *on the corner*
au revoir o rer·vwar *goodbye*
aube ob *dawn*
auberge ⓕ **de jeunesse** o·bairzh der zher·nes *youth hostel*
aucun(e) ⓜ/ⓕ o·kun/o·kewn *none*
au-dessus o·der·sew *above*
aujourd'hui o·zhoor·dwee *today*
aussi o·see *also*
Australie ⓕ o·stra·lee *Australia*
autel ⓜ o·tel *altar*
autobus ⓜ o·to·bews *bus (city)*
autocar ⓜ o·to·kar *bus (intercity)*
automatique o·to·ma·teek *automatic*
automne ⓜ o·ton *autumn • fall*
autoroute ⓕ o·to·root *highway • motorway*
autour o·toor *around*
autre o·trer *other*
avant a·von *before*
avant-hier a·von·tyair *day before yesterday*
avec a·vek *with*
avenir av·neer *future*
avenue ⓕ av·new *avenue*
avertissement ⓜ a·vair·tees·mon *warning*
aveugle a·ver·gler *blind*
avide a·veed *greedy (money)*
avion ⓜ a·vyon *aeroplane*

aviron ⓜ a·vee·ron *rowing*
avis ⓜ a·vee *opinion*
avocat(e) ⓜ/ⓕ a·vo·ka(t) *lawyer*
avoir a·vwar *have*
— **besoin de** ber·zwun de *need*
— **de la chance** der la shons *lucky (to be)*
— **des hallucinations** day za·lew·see·na·syon *hallucinate*
— **faim** fum *hungry (to be)*
— **la tête qui tourne** la tet kee toorn *dizzy (to be dizzy)*
— **le mal de mer** ler mal der mair *seasick (to be)*
— **mal au ventre** mal o von·trer *stomachache (to have a)*
— **mal aux dents** mal o don *toothache*
— **raison** ray·zon *right (to be right)*
— **soif** swaf *thirsty (to be)*
— **sommeil** so·may *sleepy (to be sleepy)*
— **tort** tor *wrong (to be)*
avortement ⓜ a·vor·ter·mon *abortion*
avril ⓜ a·vreel *April*

B

baby-sitter ⓜ&ⓕ ba·bee·see·ter *babysitter*
bac ⓜ bak *ferry*
bagages ⓜ pl ba·gazh *baggage • luggage*
bagarre ⓕ ba·gar *fight*
bague ⓕ bag *ring (on finger)*
baignoire ⓕ be·nywar *bath*
bail ⓜ ba·yer *lease*
bain ⓜ bun *bath (have a)*
baiser bay·zay *fuck*
baiser ⓜ bay·zay *kiss*
balcon ⓜ bal·kon *balcony*
balle ⓕ **(de tennis)** bal (der tay·nees) *(tennis) ball*
ballet ⓜ ba·lay *ballet*
ballon ⓜ **(de football)** ba·lon (der foot·bol) *football • soccer ball*
bande dessinée ⓕ bond day·see·nay *comic (magazine)*
bande ⓕ bond *band (music)*

bande ⓕ **vidéo** bond vee·day·o *video tape*

banlieue ⓕ bon·lyer *suburb*

banque ⓕ bonk *bank*

baptême ⓜ ba·tem *baptism*

bar ⓜ bar *bar • pub*

barrière ⓕ bar·yair *fence • gate*

bas ⓜ ba *stockings*

bas/basse ⓜ/ⓕ ba(s) *low*

baseball ⓜ bez·bol *baseball*

basket(ball) ⓜ bas·ket(bol) *basketball*

bateau ⓜ ba·to *boat*

bâtiment ⓜ ba·tee·mon *building*

batterie ⓕ bat·ree *battery (car) • drums*

bavarder ba·var·day *chat*

bavoir ⓜ ba·vwar *bib*

beau/belle ⓜ/ⓕ bo/bel *beautiful • handsome*

beaucoup (de) bo·koo (der) *a lot (of)*

beaucoup de bo·koo der *many • plenty*

beau-père ⓜ bo·pair *father-in-law*

bébé ⓜ bay·bay *baby*

belle-mère ⓕ bel·mair *mother-in-law*

bénéfice ⓜ bay·nay·fees *profit*

bénévole ⓜ/ⓕ bay·nay·vol *voluntary (not paid) • volunteer*

bible ⓕ bee·bler *bible*

bibliothèque ⓕ bee·blee·o·tek *library*

bien byun *well*

bien déterminé byun day·tair·mee·nay *definite*

bientôt byun·to *soon*

bière ⓕ byair *beer*

bijoux ⓜ pl bee·zhoo *jewellery*

billard ⓜ **américain** bee·yar a·may·ree·kun *pool (game)*

billet ⓜ bee·yay *ticket*

— **de banque** der bonk *banknote*

— **stand-by** stond·bai *stand-by ticket*

blanc/blanche ⓜ/ⓕ blong/blonsh *white*

blanchisserie ⓕ blon·shees·ree *laundry (place)*

blessé(e) ⓜ/ⓕ blay·say *hurt • injured*

blessure ⓕ blay·sewr *injury*

bleu ⓜ bler *bruise*

bleu(e) ⓜ/ⓕ bler *blue*

bloqué(e) ⓜ/ⓕ blo·kay *blocked*

bœuf ⓜ berf *ox*

bohémien/bohémienne ⓜ/ⓕ bo·ay·myun/bo·ay·myen *gipsy*

boire bwar *drink*

bois ⓜ bwa *wood*

bois ⓜ **de chauffage** bwa der sho·fazh *firewood*

boisson ⓕ bwa·son *drink*

boîte ⓕ bwat *box • can (tin) • carton (for ice cream) • nightclub*

boîte ⓕ **aux lettres** bwat o lay·trer *mailbox*

bol ⓜ bol *bowl*

bon/bonne ⓜ/ⓕ bon/bon *good*

bon marché ⓜ bon mar·shay *cheap*

bonde ⓕ bond *plug (bath)*

bondé(e) ⓜ/ⓕ bon·day *crowded*

bord ⓜ bor *edge*

— **de la mer** der la mair *seaside*

— **du trottoir** dew tro·twar *kerb*

botte ⓕ bot *boot (footwear)*

bouche ⓕ boosh *mouth*

boucherie ⓕ boosh·ree *butcher's shop*

bouchon ⓜ boo·shon *traffic jam*

boucles ⓕ **d'oreille** boo·kler do·ray *earrings*

bouddhiste boo·deest *Buddhist*

boue ⓕ boo *mud*

bouger boo·zhay *move*

bougie ⓕ boo·zhee *candle*

bouillie ⓕ boo·yee *baby food*

bouillotte ⓕ boo·yot *water bottle (hot)*

boulangerie ⓕ boo·lon·zhree *bakery*

boulevard ⓜ bool·var *boulevard*

boussole ⓕ boo·sol *compass*

bout ⓜ boo *end*

bouteille ⓕ boo·tay *bottle*

bouton ⓜ boo·ton *button*

boxe ⓕ boks *boxing*

boxer-short ⓜ bok·sair·short *boxer shorts*

braderie ⓕ bra·dree *street market*

braille ⓜ bra·yer *Braille*

bras ⓜ bra *arm*

briquet ⓜ bree·kay *cigarette lighter*

brochure ⓕ bro·shewr *brochure*

broderie ⓕ bro·dree *embroidery*

bronchite ⓕ bron·sheet *bronchitis*

brosse ① bros *brush*
— **à dents** a don *toothbrush*
— **à cheveux** a shver *hairbrush*
brûler brew·lay *burn*
brûlure ① brew·lewr *burn*
brumeux/brumeuse ⑩/① brew·mer/
brew·merz *foggy*
brun/brune ⑩/① brun/brewn *brown*
bruyant(e) ⑩/① brew·yon(t) *noisy*
budget ⑩ bewd·zhay *budget*
buffet ⑩ bew·fay *buffet*
bureau ⑩ bew·ro *office*
— **de poste** der post *post office*
— **de tabac** der ta·ba *tobacconist*
— **des objets trouvés** day zob·zhay
troo·vay *lost property office*
bus ⑩ bews *bus (city)*
but ⑩ bewt *goal*

C

cabine ① **téléphonique** ka·been
tay·lay·fo·neek *phone box*
cabine ① **téléphonique** ka·been
tay·lay·fo·neek *telephone box*
câble ⑩ ka·bler *cable*
cache-sexe ⑩ kash·seks *g-string*
cadeau ⑩ ka·do *gift • present*
cadenas ⑩ kad·na *padlock*
cafard ⑩ ka·far *cockroach*
café ⑩ ka·fay *cafe • coffee*
caisse ① **(enregistreuse)** kes
(on·rer·zhee·strerz) *cash register*
caissier/caissière ⑩/① kay·syay/
kay·syair *cashier • teller*
calculatrice ① kal·kew·la·trees *calculator*
calendrier ⑩ ka·lon·dree·yay *calendar*
camion ⑩ ka·myon *lorry • truck*
camionnette ① ka·myo·net *van*
camp ⑩ kon *camp*
campagne ① kom·pa·nyer *countryside*
camping ⑩ kom·peeng *camping ground*
Canada ⑩ ka·na·da *Canada*
canard ⑩ ka·nar *duck*
cancer ⑩ kon·sair *cancer*
canif ⑩ ka·neef *penknife*
canot ⑩ **automobile** ka·no
o·to·mo·beel *motorboat*
cape ① kap *cloak*

capitalisme ⑩ ka·pee·ta·lees·mer
capitalism
car ⑩ kar *bus (intercity)*
caravane ① ka·ra·van *caravan*
carnet ⑩ kar·nay *notebook*
carrefour ⑩ kar·foor *intersection*
carrière ① kar·ryair *career*
carte ⑩ kart *menu*
carte ① kart *map (of country)*
— **de crédit** kart der kray·dee
credit card
— **d'embarquement** kart
dom·bar·ker·mon *boarding pass*
— **d'identité** kart dee·don·tee·tay
identification card (ID)
— **grise** kart greez *car owner's title*
— **postale** kart pos·tal *postcard*
— **routière** kart roo·tyair *road map*
cartouche ① **de gaz** kar·toosh der gaz
gas cartridge
cas urgent ⑩ ka ewr·zhon *emergency*
cascade ① kas·kad *waterfall*
casher ka·shair *kosher*
casque ⑩ kask *helmet*
cassé(e) ⑩/① ka·say *broken*
casse-croûte ⑩ kas·kroot *snack*
casser ka·say *break*
casserole ① kas·rol *pan*
cassette ① ka·set *cassette*
cathédrale ① ka·tay·dral *cathedral*
catholique ka·to·leek *Catholic*
cause ① koz *cause*
CD ⑩ say·day *CD*
ce soir ser swar *tonight*
ce ⑩ ser *that • this*
ceci ser·see *this (one)*
ceinture ① **de sécurité** sun·tewr der
say·kew·ree·tay *seatbelt*
cela ser·la *that (one)*
célèbre say·leb·rer *famous*
célibataire say·lee·ba·tair *single (person)*
cendrier ⑩ son·dree·yay *ashtray*
cent ⑩ son *hundred*
cent ⑩ sent *cent*
centimètre ⑩ son·tee·me·trer *centimetre*
centre ⑩ son·trer *centre*
centre ⑩ **commercial** son·trer
ko·mair·syal *shopping centre*
centre-ville ⑩ son·trer·veel *city centre*

C

céramique ① say·ra·meek *ceramic*
cercle ⑩ sair·kler *circle*
certain(e) ⑩/① sair·tun/·ten *certain*
certificat ⑩ sair·tee·fee·ka *certificate*
cette ① set *that* • *this*
chaîne ① shen *chain* • *channel*
— **de bicyclette** der bee·see·klet *bike chain*
— **de montagnes** der mon·ta·nyer *mountain range*
— **hi-fi** ee·fee *stereo (system)*
chaise ① shez *chair*
chaleur ① sha·ler *heat*
chambre ① shom·brer *room*
— **à air** a air *tube (tyre)*
— **à coucher** a koo·shay *bedroom*
— **libre** lee·brer *vacancy*
— **pour deux personnes** poor der pair·son *double room*
— **pour une personne** poor ewn pair·son *single room*
champ ⑩ shom *field*
champ ⑩ **de courses** shon der koors *racetrack*
champagne ⑩ shom·pa·nyer *champagne*
championnat ⑩ shom·pyo·na *championship*
chance ① shons *luck*
changer shon·zhay *change*
chanson ① shon·son *song*
chanter shon·tay *sing*
chanteur/chanteuse ⑩/① shon·ter/shon·terz *singer*
chapeau ⑩ sha·po *hat*
chaque shak *each* • *every*
charcuterie ① shar·kew·tree *delicatessen*
chariot ⑩ shar·yo *trolley*
charmant(e) ⑩/① shar·mon(t) *charming*
chasse ① shas *hunting*
chat ⑩ sha *cat*
château ⑩ sha·to *castle*
chaton ⑩ sha·ton *kitten*
chaud(e) ⑩/① sho(d) *hot* • *warm*
chauffé(e) ⑩/① sho·fay *heated*
chaussettes ① sho·set *socks*
chaussure ① sho·sewr *shoe*

chaussures ① pl **de marche** sho·sewr der marsh *hiking boots*
chef de cuisine ⑩ shef der kwee·zeen *chef*
chef ⑩ shef *leader*
chemin ⑩ shmun *path* • *lane* • *way*
— **de fer** der fair *railway*
— **de montagne** der mon·ta·nyer *mountain path*
chemise ① sher·meez *shirt*
chèque ⑩ shek *check (banking)* • *cheque*
chèque ⑩ **de voyage** shek der vwa·yazh *travellers cheque*
cher/chère ⑩/① shair *expensive*
chercher shair·shay *look for*
cheval ⑩ shval *horse*
cheveux ⑩ shver *hair*
cheville ① sher·vee·yer *ankle*
chèvre ① shev·rer *goat*
chien ⑩ shyun *dog*
chien ⑩ **d'aveugle** shyun da·ver·gler *guide dog*
chiot ⑩ shyo *puppy*
chocolat ⑩ sho·ko·la *chocolate*
choisir shwa·zeer *choose*
choix ⑩ shwa *choice*
chômage ⑩ sho·mazh *unemployment*
chômeur/chômeuse ⑩/① sho·mer/sho·merz *unemployed*
chose ① shoz *thing*
chrétien(ne) ⑩/① kray·tyun/kray·tyen *Christian*
ciel ⑩ syel *sky*
cigare ⑩ see·gar *cigar*
cigarette ① see·ga·ret *cigarette*
cime ① seem *peak*
cimetière ⑩ seem·tyair *cemetery*
cinéma ⑩ see·nay·ma *cinema*
cinq sungk *five*
circulation ① seer·kew·la·syon *traffic*
cirque ⑩ seerk *circus*
ciseaux ⑩ pl see·zo *scissors*
citoyen(ne) ⑩/① see·twa·yun/see·twa·yen *citizen*
citoyenneté ① see·twa·yen·tay *citizenship*
clair(e) ⑩/① klair *clear* • *light (of colour)*

classe ① klas *class*
— **affaires** klas a·fair *business class*
— **touriste** klas too·reest
economy class
classique kla·seek *classical*
clavier ⓜ kla·vyay *keyboard*
clé ① klay *key*
client(e) ⓜ/① klee·on(t)
client • customer
clignotant ⓜ klee·nyo·ton
indicator (on car)
climatisé kee·ma·tee·zay
air-conditioned
clinique ① **privée** klee·neek pree·vay
private hospital
cocaïne ① ko·ka·een *cocaine*
cochon ⓜ ko·shon *pig*
cocktail ⓜ kok·tel *cocktail*
code ⓜ **postal** kod pos·tal *post code*
cœur ⓜ ker *heart*
coffre-fort ⓜ kof·rer·for *safe*
coiffeur/coiffeuse ⓜ/① kwa·fer/
kwa·ferz *hairdresser*
coin ⓜ kwun *corner*
colis ⓜ ko·lee *parcel*
collant ⓜ ko·lon *pantyhose*
colle ① kol *glue*
collectionner ko·lek·syo·nay
collect (stamps etc)
collègue ⓜ/① ko·leg *colleague*
collier ⓜ ko·lyay *necklace*
colline ① ko·leen *hill*
colloque ⓜ ko·lok *conference (small)*
colonne ① **vertébrale** ko·lon
vair·tay·bral *spine*
combinaison ① kom·bee·nay·zon
combination
comédie ① ko·may·dee *comedy*
comme kom *as • like*
commencement ⓜ ko·mons·mon *start*
commencer ko·mon·say *begin • start*
comment ko·mon *how*
commerce ⓜ ko·mairs *trade*
commissariat ⓜ ko·mee·sar·ya
police station
commission ① ko·mee·syon *commission*
commotion ① **cérébrale** ko·mo·syon
say·ray·bral *concussion*

commun(e) ⓜ/① ko·mun/ko·mewn
common
communauté ① ko·mew·no·tay
community
communisme ⓜ ko·mew·nees·mer
communism
communiste ko·mew·neest *communist*
compagnon/compagne ⓜ/①
kom·pa·nyon/kom·pa·nyer
companion
compétence ① kom·pay·tons *skill*
compétition ① kom·pay·tees·yon
competition
complet/complète ⓜ/① kom·play/
kom·plet *booked up • no vacancy*
composition ① **directe**
kom·po·zees·yon dee·rekt *direct-dial*
comprendre kom·pron·drer *understand*
compris(e) ⓜ/① kom·pree(z) *included*
compte ⓜ kont *account*
compte ⓜ **bancaire** kont bong·kair
bank account
compter kon·tay *count*
compteur ⓜ **(de vitesse)** kon·ter (der
vee·tes) *speedometer*
comptoir ⓜ kon·twar *counter (at bar)*
concert ⓜ kon·sair *concert*
concessionnaire ⓜ kon·say·syo·nair
distributor
concevoir kon·ser·vwar *design*
conduire kon·dweer *drive*
confession ① kon·fay·syon
confession (religious)
confiance ① kon·fyons *trust*
confirmer kon·feer·may
confirm (a booking)
confondre kon·fon·drer
mix up (confuse)
confortable kon·for·ta·bler *comfortable*
congrès ⓜ kong·gray *conference (big)*
connaître ko·nay·trer
know (be familiar with)
conseil ⓜ kon·say *advice*
conservateur/conservatrice ⓜ/①
kon·sair·va·ter/kon·sair·va·trees
conservative
consigne ① kon·see·nyer
left luggage (office)

consigne ⓕ automatique kon·see·nyer o·to·ma·teek *luggage lockers*
constiptation ⓕ kon·stee·pa·syon *constipation*
construire kon·strweer *build*
consulat ⓜ kon·so·la *consulate*
contraceptif ⓜ kon·trer·sep·teef *contraceptive*
contrat ⓜ kon·tra *contract*
contre kon·trer *against*
contrôle ⓜ kon·trol *checkpoint*
contrôleur ⓜ kon·tro·ler *ticket collector*
conversation ⓕ kon·vair·sa·syon *conversation*
coopérer ko·o·pay·ray *cooperate*
coq ⓜ kok *rooster*
coquillage ⓜ ko·kee·yazh *seashell*
corde à linge ⓕ kord a lunzh *clothes line*
corde ⓕ kord *rope*
corps ⓜ kor *body*
correct(e) ⓜ/ⓕ ko·rekt *correct*
corrompu(e) ⓜ/ⓕ ko·rom·pew *corrupt*
côté ⓜ ko·tay *side*
côte ⓕ kot *coast*
coton ⓜ ko·ton *cotton*
couche ⓕ koosh *diaper • nappy*
couche ⓕ d'ozone koosh do·zon *ozone layer*
coucher ⓜ du soleil koo·shay dew so·lay *sunset*
coudre koo·drer *sew*
couleur ⓕ koo·ler *colour*
couloir ⓜ koo·lwar *aisle (on plane)*
coup ⓜ de soleil koo der so·lay *sunburn*
coupable koo·pa·bler *guilty*
coupe ⓕ koop *haircut*
coupe-ongles ⓜ koop·ong·gler *nail clippers*
couper koo·pay *cut*
coupon ⓜ koo·pon *coupon*
courageux/courageuse ⓜ/ⓕ koo·ra·zher/koo·ra·zherz *brave*
courant ⓜ koo·ron *current (electricity)*
courir koo·reer *run*
courrier ⓜ koo·ryay *mail (letters)*
courroie ⓕ de ventilateur koor·wa der von·tee·la·ter *fanbelt*
course ⓕ koors *race (sport)*

court ⓜ koor *court (tennis)*
court(e) ⓜ/ⓕ koor(t) *short (height)*
court ⓜ de tennis koor der tay·nees *tennis court*
coût ⓜ koo *cost*
couteau ⓜ koo·to *knife*
coutume ⓕ koo·tewm *custom*
couvent ⓜ koo·von *convent*
couvert ⓜ koo·vair *cover charge*
couverts ⓜ koo·vair *cutlery*
couverture ⓕ koo·vair·tewr *blanket*
crayon ⓜ kray·yon *pencil*
crèche ⓕ kresh *creche*
crédit ⓜ kray·dee *credit*
crème ⓕ krem *cream*
 — de bronzage der bron·zazh *tanning lotion*
 — hydratante ee·dra·tont *moisturiser*
crevaison ⓕ krer·vay·zon *puncture*
crier kree·yay *shout*
crique ⓕ kreek *creek*
critique ⓕ kree·teek *review (article)*
croire krwar *believe*
croix ⓕ krwa *cross (religious)*
croyance ⓕ krwa·yons *belief*
cru(e) ⓜ/ⓕ krew *raw*
cueillette ⓕ de fruits ker·yet der frwee *fruit picking*
cuillère ⓕ kwee·yair *spoon*
cuir ⓜ kweer *leather*
cuire kweer *cook*
cuisine ⓕ kwee·zeen *kitchen*
cuisinier/cuisinière ⓜ/ⓕ kwee·zee·nyay/kwee·zee·nyair *cook*
cul ⓜ kew *ass (bum)*
cul ⓜ kew *bum*
culture ⓕ kewl·tewr *crop (grown)*
cure-dent ⓜ kewr·don *toothpick*
CV ⓜ say·vay *CV • resumé*
cybercafé ⓜ see·bair·ka·fay *Internet cafe*
cyclisme ⓜ see·klee·smer *cycling*
cycliste ⓜ/ⓕ see·kleest *cyclist*

D

dangereux/dangereuse ⓜ/ⓕ don·zhrer/don·zhrerz *dangerous*
dans don *in • into*

danse ① dons *dancing*
danser don·say *dance*
date ① dat *date (day)*
date ① **de naissance** dat der nay·sons *date of birth*
de der *from*
— **droite** drwat *right-wing*
— **gauche** gosh *left-wing*
— **la** la *some*
— **l'autre côté de** lo·trer ko·tay der *across*
— **luxe** lewks *luxury*
— **seconde classe** skond klas *second class*
— **valeur** va·ler *valuable*
débat ⓜ day·ba *argument*
déboisement ⓜ day·bwaz·mon *deforestation*
décalage ⓜ **horaire** day·ka·lazh o·rair *time difference*
décembre ⓜ day·som·brer *December*
décharge ① day·sharzh *rubbish dump*
déchets ⓜ **nucléaires** day·shay new·klay·air *nuclear waste*
déchets ⓜ pl **toxiques** day·shay tok·seek *toxic waste*
décision ① day·see·zyon *decision*
découvrir day·koov·reer *discover*
déçu(e) ⓜ/① day·sew *disappointed*
dedans der·don *inside*
défectueux/défectueuse ⓜ/① day·fek·twer/day·fek·twerz *faulty*
dégâts ⓜ day·ga *damage*
dehors der·or *outside*
déjà day·zha *already*
déjeuner ⓜ day·zher·nay *lunch*
délicieux/délicieuse ⓜ/① day·lees·yer/day·lees·yerz *tasty*
délit ⓜ day·lee *crime*
demain der·mun *tomorrow*
— **après-midi** a·pray·mee·dee *tomorrow afternoon*
— **matin** ma·tun *tomorrow morning*
— **soir** swar *tomorrow evening*
demander der·mon·day *ask for (something)*
démangeaison ① day·mon·zhay·zon *itch*
demi-litre ⓜ der·mee·lee·trer *half a litre*

démocratie ① day·mo·kra·see *democracy*
dent ① don *tooth*
dentelle ① don·tel *lace*
dentifrice ⓜ don·tee·frees *toothpaste*
dentiste ⓜ don·teest *dentist*
dents ① don *teeth*
déodorant ⓜ day·o·do·ron *deodorant*
dépanneuse ① day·pa·nerz *tow truck*
départ ⓜ day·par *departure*
dépendance ① day·pon·dons *addiction*
dépenser day·pon·say *spend (money)*
dépôt ⓜ day·po *deposit*
depuis der·pwee *since (May etc)*
déranger day·ron·zhay *disturb*
dernier/dernière ⓜ/① dair·nyay/dair·nyair *last (previous)*
derrière dair·yair *behind*
des pl day *some*
désastre ⓜ day·zas·trer *disaster*
descendant(e) ⓜ/① day·son·don(t) *descendent*
descendre day·son·drer *get off (a train, etc) • go down (stairs, etc)*
désert ⓜ day·zair *desert*
désinfectant ⓜ day·zun·fek·ton *disinfectant*
dessert ⓜ day·sair *dessert*
dessin ⓜ day·sun a·nee·may *cartoon*
dessiner day·see·nay *draw (picture)*
destin ⓜ des·tun *fate*
destination ① des·tee·na·syon *destination*
détail ⓜ day·tai *detail*
détaillé(e) ⓜ/① day·ta·yay *itemised*
détester day·tes·tay *hate*
détruire day·trweer *destroy*
deux der *two*
deux fois der fwa *twice*
devant der·von *in front of*
développement ⓜ day·vlop·mon *development*
devenir derv·neer *become*
deviner der·vee·nay *guess*
devoir ⓜ der·vwar *owe*
devoir ⓜ der·vwar *duty*
devoirs ⓜ der·vwar *homework*
diabète ⓜ dya·bet *diabetes*

diaphragme ⓜ dya·frag·mer *diaphragm*
diapositive ⓕ dya·po·zee·teev *slide (film)*
diarrhée ⓕ dya·ray *diarrhoea*
dictionnaire ⓜ deek·syo·nair *dictionary*
dieu ⓜ dyer *god*
différent(e) ⓜ/ⓕ dee·fay·ron(t) *different*
difficile dee·fee·seel *difficult*
dimanche ⓜ dee·monsh *Sunday*
dîner ⓜ dee·nay *dinner*
diplôme ⓜ dee·plom *degree • diploma*
dire deer *say • tell*
direct(e) ⓜ/ⓕ dee·rekt *direct*
directeur/directrice ⓜ/ⓕ dee·rek·ter/
dee·rek·trees *manager*
direction ⓕ dee·rek·syon *direction*
diriger dee·ree·zhay *manage (business)*
discours ⓜ dees·koor *speech*
discriminationⓕ
dee·skree·mee·na·syon *discrimination*
discuter dee·skew·tay *discuss*
diseuse ⓕ **de bonne aventure** deez·zerz
der bon a·von·tewr *fortune teller*
disponible dees·po·nee·bler
free (available)
dispute ⓕ dees·pewt *quarrel*
disquaire ⓜ dee·skair *music shop*
disquette ⓕ dees·ket *disk (floppy)*
distance ⓕ dees·tons *distance*
distributeur ⓜ **de tickets**
dee·stree·bew·ter der tee·kay
ticket machine
divorcé(e) ⓜ/ⓕ dee·vor·say *divorced*
dix dee(s) *ten*
doigt ⓜ dwa *finger*
dollar ⓜ do·lar *dollar*
donc dongk *therefore*
donner do·nay *deal (cards) • give*
dormir dor·meer *sleep*
dos ⓜ do *back (body)*
dose ⓕ doz *dose*
douane ⓕ dwan *customs*
double doo·bler *double*
douche ⓕ doosh *shower*
douleur ⓕ doo·ler *ache • pain*
douloureux/douloureuse ⓜ/ⓕ
doo·loo·rer/doo·loo·rerz *painful*
douloureux/douloureuse ⓜ/ⓕ
doo·loo·rer/doo·loo·rerz *sore*
doux/douce ⓜ/ⓕ doo/doos *soft*

douzaine ⓕ doo·zen *dozen*
draguer dra·gay *chat up*
drap ⓜ dra *sheet (bed)*
drapeau ⓜ dra·po *flag*
draps ⓜ dra *bed linen*
drogué dro·gay *addicted (to drugs)*
drogue ⓕ drog *drug • drugs*
droit ⓜ drwa *law (study, professsion)*
droit(e) ⓜ/ⓕ drwa(t) *straight*
droite ⓕ drwa *right (entitlement)*
droits ⓜ pl **civils** drwa see·veel
civil rights
droits ⓜ pl **de l'homme** drwa der lom
human rights
drôle drol *funny*
du ⓜ dew *some*
dur(e) ⓜ/ⓕ dewr *hard (not soft)*

E

eau ⓕ o *water*
eau ⓕ **minérale** o mee·nay·ral
mineral water
échange ⓜ ay·shonzh *exchange*
échanger ay·shon·zhay
change (money) • exchange
échapper ay·sha·pay *escape*
écharpe ⓕ ay·sharp *scarf*
échec ⓜ ay·shek *failure*
échecs ⓜ ay·shek *chess*
échiquier ⓜ ay·shee·kyay *chess board*
école ⓕ ay·kol *school*
école professionnelleⓕ ay·kol
pro·fay·syo·nel *college (vocational)*
économie ⓕ ay·ko·no·mee *economy*
Ecosse ⓕ ay·kos *Scotland*
écouter ay·koo·tay *listen (to)*
écran ⓜ ay·kron *screen*
— **solaire** so·lair *sunscreen*
— **solaire total** so·lair to·tal *sunblock*
écrire ay·kreer *write*
écrivain ⓜ ay·kree·vun *writer*
ecstasy ⓕ ek·sta·zee *ecstasy (drug)*
eczéma ⓜ eg·zay·ma *eczema*
éducation ⓕ ay·dew·ka·syon *education*
effet ⓜ ay·fay *effect*
effrayé(e) ⓜ/ⓕ ay·fray·yay *scared*
égale ay·gal *equal*
égalité ⓕ ay·ga·lee *equality*

égalité ① des chances ay·ga·lee·tay day shons *equal opportunity*
église ① ay·gleez *church*
égoïste ⑩/① ay·go·eest *selfish*
élection ① ay·lek·syon *election*
électricité ① ay·lek·tree·see·tay *electricity*
elle el *she*
elles ① el *they (women)*
éloigné(e) ⑩/① ay·lwa·nyay *remote*
e-mail ⑩ ay·mel *email*
embrasser om·bra·say *kiss*
embrayage om·bray·yazh *clutch*
empêcher om·pay·shay *prevent*
employé(e) ⑩/① de bureau om·plwa·yay der bew·ro *office worker*
employé/employée ⑩/① om·plwa·yay/om·plwa·yer *employee*
employeur ⑩ om·plwa·yer *employer*
emprunter om·prun·tay *borrow*
en on *made of (cotton, wood etc)*
— avant a·von *ahead*
— bas ba *down*
— désordre day·zor·drer *messy*
— face de der *opposite*
— grève grev *on strike*
— haut o *up • upstairs*
— panne *broken down*
— recommandé rer·ko·mon·day *registered mail/post (by)*
— retard rer·tar *late*
encaisser ong·kay·say *cash (a cheque)*
enceinte on·sunt *pregnant*
encore ong·kor *again • yet*
endroit ⑩ on·drwa *spot (place)*
énergie ① ay·nair·zhee *energy*
énergie ① nucléaire ay·nair·zhee new·klay·air *nuclear energy*
enfant ⑩&① on·fon *child*
enfants ⑩&① pl on·fon *children*
ennuyeux/ennuyeuse ⑩/① on·nwee·yer/on·nwee·yerz *boring*
énorme ay·norm *huge*
enregistrement on·rer·zhee·strer·mon *check-in (desk)*
enregistrer on·rer·zhees·tray *record*
ensemble on·som·bler *together*
ensoleillé(e) ⑩/① on·so·lay·yay *sunny*

entendre on·ton·drer *hear*
enterrement ⑩ on·tair·mon *funeral*
enthousiaste on·tooz·yast *enthusiastic*
entorse ① on·tors *sprain*
entracte ⑩ on·trakt *intermission*
entraîneur ⑩ on·tray·ner *coach*
entre on·trer *between*
entrée ① on·tray *entry*
entreprise ① on·trer·preez *company*
entrer on·tray *enter*
entrevue ① on·trer·vew *interview*
enveloppe ① on·vlop *envelope*
envers on·vair *toward (feelings)*
environ on·vee·ron *about*
environnement ⑩ on·vee·ron·mon *environment*
envoyer on·vwa·yay *send*
épais/épaisse ⑩/① ay·pay/ay·pes *thick*
épaule ① ay·pol *shoulder*
épicé(e) ⑩/① ay·pee·say *spicy*
épicerie ① ay·pee·sree *grocery*
épilepsie ① ay·pee·lep·see *epilepsy*
épingle ① ay·pung·gler *pin*
épouser ay·poo·zay *marry*
épuisé(e) ⑩/① ay·pwee·zay *exhausted*
équipe ① ay·keep *team*
équipement ⑩ ay·keep·mon *equipment*
équipement ⑩ de plongée ay·keep·mon der plon·zhay *diving equipment*
équitation ① ay·kee·ta·syon *horse riding*
erreur ① ay·rer *mistake*
escalier ⑩ es·ka·lyay *stairway*
escalier ⑩ roulant es·ka·lyay roo·lon *escalator*
escargot ⑩ es·kar·go *snail*
escrime ① es·kreem *fencing*
espace ⑩ es·pas *space*
Espagne ① es·pa·nyer *Spain*
espèce ① menacée de disparition es·pes mer·na·say der dees·pa·ree·syon *endangered species*
espérer es·pay·ray *hope*
espoir ⑩ es·pwar *hope*
esprit ⑩ ay·spree *mind*
esprit ⑩ es·pree *spirit*
essai ⑩ ay·say *test*

E

french-english

233

essayer ay·say·yay *try*
essence ① ay·sons *gas • petrol*
est ⓜ est *east*
estomac ⓜ es·to·ma *stomach*
et ay *and*
établissement ⓜ **d'enseignement secondaire** ay·ta·blees·mon don·say·nyer·mon zgon·dair *high school*
étage ⓜ ay·tazh *floor (storey)*
étagère ① ay·ta·zhair *shelf*
étang ⓜ ay·tong *pond*
été ⓜ ay·tay *summer*
étiquette ① ay·tee·ket *luggage tag*
étoiles ① ay·twal *stars*
étrange ay·tronzh *strange*
étranger/étrangère ⓜ/① ay·tron·zhay/ ay·tron·zhair *foreign • stranger*
être e·trer *be*
être d'accord e·trer da·kor *agree*
être enrhumé e·trer on·rew·may *have a cold*
étroit(e) ⓜ/① ay·trwa(t) *tight*
étudiant(e) ⓜ/① ay·tew·dyon(t) *student*
étudier ay·tew·dyay *study*
euro ⓜ er·ro *euro*
Europe ① er·rop *Europe*
euthanasie ① er·ta·na·zee *euthanasia*
événement ⓜ ay·ven·mon *event*
évident(e) ⓜ/① ay·vee·don(t) *obvious*
exactement eg·zak·ter·mon *exactly*
examen ⓜ eg·za·mun *exam*
excédent ek·say·don *excess (baggage)*
excellent(e) ⓜ/① ek·say·lon *excellent*
exemple ⓜ eg·zom·pler *example*
exercice ⓜ eg·zair·sees *exercise*
exiger eg·zee·zhay *demand*
expérience ① eks·pair·yons *experience*
expliquer eks·plee·kay *explain*
exploitation ① eks·plwa·ta·syon *exploitation*
exporter eks·por·tay *export*
exposé ⓜ eks·po·zay *talk (lecture)*
exposition ① ek·spo·zee·syon *exhibition*
exprès eks·pres *express (mail)*
expression ① ek·spray·syon *phrase*
extraordinaire eks·tra·or·dee·nair *extraordinary*

F

fâché(e) ⓜ/① fa·shay *angry*
facile fa·seel *easy*
facilement ému fa·seel·mon ay·mew *emotional (person)*
façon ① fa·son *manner*
façon ① fa·son *way (manner)*
facteur ⓜ fak·ter *postman*
faible fay·bler *weak*
faire fair *do • make*
— **attention** a·ton·syon *look out*
— **confiance à** kon·fyons a *trust*
— **de la planche à voile** der la plonsh a vwal *windsurfing (to go)*
— **des courses** day koors *shop*
— **du lèche-vitrines** dew lesh·vee·treen *go window-shopping*
— **du stop** dew stop *hitchhike*
— **du vélo** dew vay·lo *cycle*
— **frire** freer *fry*
— **la randonnée** la ron·do·nay *hike*
— **les courses** lay koors *go shopping*
— **semblant** som·blon *pretend*
— **ses dévotions** say day·vo·syon *worship*
— **une fausse couche** ewn fos koosh *miscarriage (to have a)*
fait ⓜ fet *fact*
fait/faite à la main ⓜ/① fay/fet a la mun *handmade*
falaise ① fa·lez *cliff*
famille ① fa·mee·yer *family*
fan ⓜ/① fan *fan (of person)*
fasciste fa·sheest *fascist*
fatigué(e) fa·tee·gay *tired*
faute ① fot *foul (football) • fault*
fauteuil ⓜ fo·ter·yee *armchair*
fauteuil ⓜ **roulant** fo·ter·yee roo·lon *wheelchair*
faux/fausse ⓜ/① fo/fos *false • wrong*
fax ⓜ faks *fax machine*
félicitations fay·lee·see·ta·syon *congratulations*
femelle fer·mel *female*
femme ① fam *wife • woman*
— **au foyer** o fwa·yay *homemaker*
— **d'affaires** da·fair *business woman*

fenêtre ① fer·nay·trer *window*
fer ⓜ à repasser fair a rer·pa·say *iron (for clothes)*
ferme ① ferm *farm*
fermé(e) ⓜ/① fair·may *closed*
fermé(e) à clé ⓜ/① fair·may a klay *locked*
fermer fair·may *close*
fermer à clé fair·may a klay *lock*
fermeture ① éclair fair·mer·tewr ay·klair *zip • zipper*
fête ① fet *celebration • festival*
feu ⓜ fer *fire*
feuille ① fer·yee *leaf • sheet (of paper)*
feux ⓜ fer *traffic lights*
février ⓜ fayv·ree·yay *February*
fiançailles ① fyon·sai *engagement*
fiancé ⓜ fyon·say *fiance*
fiancé(e) ⓜ/① fyon·say *engaged*
fiancée ① fyon·say *fiancee*
ficelle ① fee·sel *string*
fiction ① feek·syon *fiction*
fièvre ① fyev·rer *fever*
fil ⓜ de fer feel der fair *wire*
fil ⓜ dentaire feel don·tair *dental floss*
filet ⓜ fee·lay *net*
fille ① fee·yer *daughter • girl*
film ⓜ feelm *film (cinema) • movie*
fils ⓜ fees *son*
fines herbes ① feen zairb *herbs*
fini(e) ⓜ/① fee·nee *over (finished)*
finir fee·neer *end • finish*
fleur ① fler *flower*
fleuriste ⓜ&① fler·reest *florist*
flic ⓜ fleek *cop*
foi ① fwa *faith*
foie ⓜ fwa *liver*
foncé(e) ⓜ/① fon·say *dark (of colour)*
fondamental fon·da·mon·tal *basic*
foot(ball) ⓜ foot(bol) *football • soccer*
forêt ① fo·ray *forest*
forme ① form *shape*
fort(e) ⓜ/① for(t) *loud • strong*
fortune ① for·tewn *fortune (money)*
fou/folle ⓜ/① foo/fol *crazy*
foule ① fool *crowd*
four ⓜ foor *oven*
four ⓜ à micro-ondes foor a mee·kro·ond *microwave (oven)*

fourchette ① foor·shet *fork*
fourmi ① foor·mee *ant*
fragile fra·zheel *fragile*
frais/fraîche ⓜ/① fray/fresh *cool • fresh*
franchise ① fron·sheez *baggage allowance*
freins ⓜ frun *brakes*
fréquent(e) ⓜ/① fray·kon(t) *frequent*
frère ⓜ frair *brother*
froid(e) ⓜ/① frwa(d) *cold*
frontière ① fron·tyair *border*
frottis ⓜ fro·tee *pap smear*
fruit ⓜ frwee *fruit*
fumée ① few·may *smoke*
fumer few·may *smoke*

G

gagnant(e) ⓜ/① ga·nyon(t) *winner*
gagner ga·nyay *earn • win*
galerie ① gal·ree *art gallery (private)*
gamin/gamine ⓜ/① ga·mun/ga·meen *kid (boy or girl)*
gant ⓜ de toilette gon der twa·let *face cloth*
gants ⓜ pl gon *gloves*
garage ⓜ ga·razh *garage*
garanti(e) ⓜ/① ga·ron·tee *guaranteed*
garçon ⓜ gar·son *boy*
garde-fou ⓜ gard·foo *rail*
garderie ① gard·ree *childminding*
gardien ⓜ de but gar·dyun der bewt *goalkeeper*
gare ① gar *train station*
gare ① routière gar roo·tyair *bus station*
garer (une voiture) ga·ray (ewn vwa·tewr) *park (a car)*
gas-oil ⓜ gaz·wal *diesel*
gastro-entérite ① gastro·on·tay·reet *gastroenteritis*
gaz ⓜ gaz *gas (for cooking)*
gazon ⓜ ga·zon *grass (lawn)*
gel ⓜ zhel *frost*
gelé(e) ⓜ/① zher·lay *frozen*
geler zher·lay *freeze*
gênant(e) ⓜ/① zhay·non(t) *embarrassing*

gendarme ⓜ zhon·darm
police officer (in country)
gêné(e) ⓜ/ⓕ zhay·nay *embarrassed*
gêner zhay·nay *embarrass*
général(e) ⓜ/ⓕ zhay·nay·ral *general*
généreux/généreuse ⓜ/ⓕ
zhay·nay·rer/zhay·nay·rerz *generous*
génial(e) ⓜ/ⓕ zhay·nyal *brilliant*
genou ⓜ zhnoo *knee*
genre ⓜ zhon·rer *kind (type)*
gens ⓜ pl zhon *people*
gentil/gentile ⓜ/ⓕ zhon·tee
kind • nice
gérant(e) ⓜ/ⓕ zhay·ron(t)
manager (restaurant, hotel)
gilet ⓜ **de sauvetage** zhee·lay der
sov·tazh *life jacket*
glace ⓕ glas *ice • ice cream*
gorge ⓕ gorzh *throat*
gourmand(e) ⓜ/ⓕ goor·mon(d)
greedy (food)
goût ⓜ goo *flavour*
gouvernement ⓜ goo·vair·ner·mon
government
grâce ⓕ gras *blessing*
gramme ⓜ gram *gram*
grand lit ⓜ gron lee *double bed*
grand magasin ⓜ gron ma·ga·zun
department store
grand(e) ⓜ/ⓕ gron(d) *big • large • tall*
grande route ⓕ grond root *main road*
grand-mère ⓕ grom·mair *grandmother*
grand-père ⓜ grom·pair *grandfather*
grands-parents ⓜ grom·pa·ron
grandparents
gras/grasse ⓜ/ⓕ gra/gras *fat*
gratuit(e) ⓜ/ⓕ gra·twee(t) *free (gratis)*
grenouille ⓕ grer·noo·yer *frog*
grille-pain ⓜ greey·pun *toaster*
grippe ⓕ greep *flu*
gris(e) ⓜ/ⓕ gree(z) *gray • grey*
grosseur ⓜ gro·ser *lump*
grotte ⓕ grot *cave*
groupe ⓜ **de rock** groop der rok
rock group
groupe ⓜ **sanguin** groop song·gun
blood group
guêpe ⓕ gep *wasp*
guerre ⓕ gair *war*

guichet ⓜ gee·shay *ticket office*
guichet ⓜ **automatique de banque**
(GAB) gee·shay o·to·ma·teek der
bonk *automatic teller machine (ATM)*
guide ⓜ geed
guide (person) • guidebook
guidon ⓜ gee·don *handlebars*
guitare ⓕ gee·tar *guitar*
gym(nastique) ⓕ zheem(na·steek)
gymnastics
gym ⓕ zheem *gym (activity)*
gymnase ⓜ zheem·naz *gym (place)*
gynécologue ⓜ/ⓕ zhee·nay·ko·log
gynaecologist

H

habiter a·bee·tay *live (in a place)*
habitude ⓕ a·bee·tewd *habit*
habituellement a·bee·twel·mon *usually*
halal a·lal *Halal*
hall ⓜ ol *foyer (of cinema)*
hamac ⓜ a·mak *hammock*
handicapé(e) ⓜ/ⓕ on·dee·ka·pay
disabled
harcèlement ⓜ ar·sel·mon *harassment*
hasard ⓜ a·zar *chance*
haut(e) ⓜ/ⓕ o(t) *high*
hauteur ⓕ o·ter *height*
hémisphère ⓜ **sud** ay·mees·fair sewd
southern hemisphere
hémisphère ⓜ **nord** ay·mees·fair nor
northern hemisphere
hépatite ⓕ ay·pa·teet *hepatitis*
herbe ⓕ airb *grass (marijuana)*
herboriste ⓜ/ⓕ air·bo·reest *herbalist*
héroïne ⓕ ay·ro·een *heroin*
heure ⓕ er *hour • time*
heures ⓕ pl **d'ouverture** lay zer
doo·vair·tewr *opening hours*
heureux/heureuse ⓜ/ⓕ
er·rer/er·rerz *happy*
hier ee·yair *yesterday*
hindou(e) ⓜ/ⓕ un·doo *Hindu*
histoire ⓕ ees·twar *history • story*
historique ees·to·reek *historical*
hiver ⓜ ee·vair *winter*
hockey ⓜ o·kay *hockey*
hockey ⓜ **sur glace** o·kay sewr glas
ice hockey

homme ⓜ om *man*

homme d'affaires ⓜ/ⓕ om da·fair
business man

homme/femme ⓜ/ⓕ om/
fam po·lee·teek *politician*

homosexuel(le) ⓜ/ⓕ o·mo·sek·swel
gay • *homosexual*

honnête o·net *honest*

hôpital ⓜ o·pee·tal *hospital*

horaire ⓜ o·rair *timetable*

horoscope ⓜ o·ro·skop *horoscope*

hors jeu or·zher *offside (sport)*

hors service or sair·vees *out of order*

hospitalité ⓕ os·pee·ta·lee·tay
hospitality

hôtel ⓜ o·tel *hotel*

huile ⓕ weel *oil*

huit weet *eight*

humain ⓜ ew·mun *human*

humour ⓜ ew·moor *humour*

I

ici ee·see *here*

idée ⓕ ee·day *idea*

idiot(e) ⓜ/ⓕ ee·dyo(t) *idiot*

ignorant(e) ⓜ/ⓕ ee·nyo·ron(t) *ignorant*

il eel *he*

île ⓕ eel *island*

illégal(e) ⓜ/ⓕ ee·lay·gal *illegal*

ils eel *they (men)*

image ⓕ ee·mazh *picture*

imagination ⓕ ee·ma·zhee·na·syon
imagination

immatriculation ee·ma·tree·kew·la·syon
car registration

immédiatement ee·may·dyat·mon
immediately/right now

immigration ⓕ ee·mee·gra·syon
immigration

imperméable um·pair·may·abler
raincoat • *waterproof*

impoli(e) ⓜ/ⓕ um·po·lee
rude • *impolite*

important(e) ⓜ/ⓕ um·por·ton(t)
important

importer um·por·tay *import*

impossible um·po·see·bler *impossible*

impôt ⓜ **sur le revenu** um·po sewr ler
rerv·new *income tax*

imprimante ⓕ um·pree·mont
printer (computer)

incertain(e) ⓜ/ⓕ un·sair·tun/
un·sair·ten *uncertain*

inconfortable ung·kon·for·ta·bler
uncomfortable

Inde ⓕ und *India*

indépendant(e) ⓜ/ⓕ
un·day·pon·don(t)
independent • *self-employed*

indigestion ⓕ un·dee·zhes·tyon
indigestion

indiquer un·dee·kay *point*

individu ⓜ un·dee·vee·dew *individual*

industrie ⓕ un·dews·tree *industry*

industriel/industrielle ⓜ/ⓕ
un·dews·tree·el *industrial*

infection ⓕ un·fek·syon *infection*

infirmier/infirmière ⓜ/ⓕ
un·feer·myay/un·feer·myair *nurse*

inflammation ⓕ un·fla·ma·syon
inflammation

influence ⓕ un·flew·ons *influence*

informatique ⓕ un·for·ma·teek *IT*

ingénierie un·zhay·nee·ree *engineering*

ingénieur ⓜ un·zhay·nyer *engineer*

ingrédient ⓜ ung·gray·dyon *ingredient*

injecter un·zhek·tay *inject*

injuste un·zhewst *unfair*

innocent(e) ⓜ/ⓕ ee·no·son(t) *innocent*

inondation ⓕ ee·non·da·syon *flood*

inopportun(e) ⓜ/ⓕ ee·no·por·tun/
ee·no·po·tewn *inconvenient*

inquiet/inquiète ⓜ/ⓕ ung·kyay/
ung·kyet *worried*

insecte ⓜ un·sekt *bug* • *insect*

institut universitaire ⓜ un·stee·tew
ew·nee·vair·see·tair *college*

intelligent(e) ⓜ/ⓕ un·tay·lee·zhon(t)
intelligent

intéressant(e) ⓜ/ⓕ un·tay·ray·son(t)
interesting

international(e) ⓜ/ⓕ un·tair·na·syo·nal
international

Internet ⓜ un·tair·net *Internet*

interprète ⓜ un·tair·pret *interpreter*

intime un·teem *intimate*

invité(e) ⓜ/ⓕ un·vee·tay *visitor (guest)*

inviter un·vee·tay *invite*
Irlande ① eer·lond *Ireland*
itinéraire ⓜ ee·tee·nay·rair *itinerary • route*
itinéraire ⓜ **de randonnée** ee·tee·nay·rair der ron·do·nay *hiking route*
ivre ee·vrer *drunk*

J

jaloux/jalouse ⓜ/① zha·loo/zha·looz *jealous*
jamais zha·may *never*
jambe ① zhomb *leg*
jambon ⓜ zhom·bon *ham*
janvier ⓜ zhon·vyay *January*
Japon ⓜ zha·pon *Japan*
jardin ⓜ zhar·dun *garden*
   — **botanique** bo·ta·neek *botanic garden*
   — **d'enfants** don·fon *kindergarten*
jardinage ⓜ zhar·dee·nazh *gardening*
jaune zhon *yellow*
je zher *I*
jean ⓜ zheen *jeans*
jeep ① zheep *jeep*
jeter zher·tay *throw*
jeu ⓜ zher *game*
jeu ⓜ **électronique** zher ay·lek·tro·neek *computer game*
jeudi ⓜ zher·dee *Thursday*
jeune zhern *young*
jockey ⓜ zho·kay *jockey*
jogging ⓜ zho·geeng *jogging*
joie ① zhwa *joy*
joindre zhwun·drer *join*
joli(e) ⓜ/① zho·lee *pretty*
jouer zhoo·ay *act • play*
jouet ⓜ zhway *toy*
jour ⓜ zhoor *day*
   — **de l'An** der lon *New Year's Day*
   — **de Noël** der no·el *Christmas Day*
journal ⓜ zhoor·nal *newspaper*
journaliste ⓜ/① zhoor·na·leest *journalist*
juge ⓜ zhewzh *judge*
juif/juive ⓜ/① zhweef/zhweev *Jewish*
juillet ⓜ zhwee·yay *July*

juin ⓜ zhwun *June*
jumeaux/jumelles ⓜ/① zhew·mo/ zhew·mel *twins*
jupe ① zhewp *skirt*
jusqu'à zhew·ska *until (Friday, etc)*
justice ① zhew·stees *justice*

K

kascher ka·shair *kosher*
kilo ⓜ kee·lo *kilo*
kilogramme ⓜ kee·lo·gram *kilogram*
kilomètre ⓜ kee·lo·may·trer *kilometre*
kinésithérapeute ⓜ/① kee·nay·zee·tay·ra·pert *physiotherapist*
kinésithérapie ① kee·nay·zee·tay·ra·pee *physiotherapy*
kiosque ⓜ kyosk *kiosk*

L

là la *there*
lac ⓜ lak *lake*
laid(e) ⓜ/① lay/led *ugly*
laine ① len *wool*
laisser lay·say *leave (something)*
laisser tomber lay·say tom·bay *drop*
lait ⓜ lay *milk*
lame ① **de rasoir** lam der ra·zwar *razor blade*
lampe ① lomp *lamp*
   — **de poche** der posh *flashlight*
   — **de poche** der posh *torch (flashlight)*
langue ① long *language*
lapin ⓜ la·pun *rabbit*
large larzh *wide*
laver la·vay *wash (something)*
laverie ① lav·ree *launderette*
laxatif ⓜ lak·sa·teef *laxative*
le plus petit/la plus petite ⓜ/① ler plew per·tee/la plew per·teet *smallest*
le/la plus grand(e) ⓜ/① ler/la plew gron(d) *biggest*
le/la plus proche ⓜ/① ler/la plew prosh *nearest*
le/la meilleur(e) ⓜ/① ler/la may·yer *best*

légal(e) ⓜ/ⓕ lay·gal *legal*
léger/légère ⓜ/ⓕ lay·zhay/lay·zhair *light (not heavy)*
législation ⓕ lay·zhee·sla·syon *legislation*
légume ⓜ lay·gewm *vegetable*
lent(e) ⓜ/ⓕ lon(t) *slow*
lentement lon·ter·mon *slowly*
lequel/laquelle ⓜ/ⓕ ler·kel/la·kel *which*
Les Jeux Olympiques lay zher zo·lum·peek *Olympic Games*
lesbienne ⓕ les·byen *lesbian*
lettre ⓕ lay·trer *letter*
lettres ⓕ pl **classiques** le·trer kla·seek *humanities*
leur/leurs sg/pl ler *their*
lever ler·vay *lift (arm)*
lever ⓜ **du soleil** ler·vay dew so·lay *sunrise*
lèvre ⓕ lay·vrer *lip*
lézard ⓜ lay·zar *lizard*
liaison ⓕ lyay·zon *affair*
liberté ⓕ lee·bair·tay *freedom*
librairie ⓕ lee·bray·ree *bookshop*
libre lee·brer *free (at liberty)* • *vacant*
libre-service ⓜ lee·brer·sair·vees *self service*
lieu ⓜ lyer *place*
— **de naissance** der nay·sons *place of birth*
— **saint** sun *shrine*
lièvre ⓜ lyev·rer *hare*
ligne ⓕ **aérienne** lee·nyer a·ay·ryen *airline*
ligne ⓕ lee·nyer *line*
limitation ⓕ **de vitesse** lee·mee·ta·syon der vee·tes *speed limit*
lin ⓜ lun *linen (material)*
linge ⓜ lunzh *laundry (clothes)* • *linen*
lingerie ⓕ lun·zhree *lingerie*
lire leer *read*
lit ⓜ lee *bed*
literie ⓕ leet·ree *bedding*
lits ⓜ pl **jumeaux** day lee zhew·mo *twin beds*
livre ⓜ leev·rer *book*
livre ⓕ leev·rer *pound (money, weight)*

livrer leev·ray *deliver*
local(e) ⓜ/ⓕ lo·kal *local*
locataire ⓜ/ⓕ lo·ka·tair *tenant*
location ⓕ **de voitures** lo·ka·syon der vwa·tewr *car hire*
logement ⓜ lozh·mon *accommodation*
logiciel ⓜ lo·zhee·syel *software*
loi ⓕ lwa *law*
lointain(e) ⓜ/ⓕ lwun·tun/·ten *far*
long ⓜ long *long*
long-courrier long·koo·ryay *long-distance (flight)*
longue ⓕ longk *long*
longueur ⓕ long·ger *length*
louer loo·ay *hire* • *rent*
louer à bail loo·way a ba·yer *lease*
lourd(e) ⓜ/ⓕ loor(d) *heavy*
loyal(e) ⓜ/ⓕ lwa·yal *loyal*
lubrifiant ⓜ lew·bree·fyon *lubricant*
lumière ⓕ lew·myair *light*
lundi ⓜ lun·dee *Monday*
lune ⓕ **de miel** lewn der myel *honeymoon*
lunettes ⓕ pl lew·net *glasses (spectacles)*
lunettes ⓕ pl lew·net *goggles (skiing)*
lunettes ⓕ **de soleil** lew·net der so·lay *sunglasses*
luxe ⓜ lewks *luxury*

M

ma ⓕ ma *my*
machine ⓕ ma·sheen *machine*
machine ⓕ **à laver** ma·sheen a la·vay *washing machine*
mâchoire ⓕ ma·shwar *jaw*
Madame ma·dam *Mrs*
Mademoiselle mad·mwa·zel *Ms; Miss*
magasin ⓜ ma·ga·zun *shop*
— **de chaussures** der sho·sewr *shoe shop*
— **de souvenirs** der soov·neer *souvenir shop*
— **de sports** der spor *sports store/shop*
— **de vêtements** der vet·mon *clothing store*

M

— **de vins et spiritueux** der vun ay spee·ree·twer *liquor store*

— **pour équipement de camping** poor ay·keep·mon der kom·peeng *camping store*

— **qui vend des appareils électriques** kee von day za·pa·ray ay·lek·treek *electrical store*

magazine ⓜ ma·ga·zeen *magazine*

magicien/magicienne ⓜ/ⓕ ma·zhee·syun/ma·zhees·yen *magician*

magnétoscope ⓜ ma·nyay·to·skop *video recorder*

mai ⓜ may *May*

maigre may·grer *thin*

maillot ⓜ **de corps** ma·yo der kor *singlet • vest*

maillot ⓜ **de bain** may·yo der bun *bathing suit*

main ⓕ mun *hand*

maintenant mun·ter·non *now*

maire ⓜ mair *mayor*

mairie ⓕ may·ree *city hall*

mais may *but*

maison ⓕ may·zon *house*

majorité ⓕ ma·zho·ree·tay *majority*

mal ⓜ **à la tête** mal a la tet *headache*

mal ⓜ **des transports** mal day trons·por *travel sickness*

malade ma·lad *ill • sick*

maladie ⓕ ma·la·dee *disease • sickness*

— **vénérienne** vay·nay·ryen *venereal disease*

— **de cœur** der ker *heart condition*

malhonnête mal·o·net *dishonest*

maman ⓕ ma·mon *mum*

mammographie ⓕ ma·mo·gra·fee *mammogram*

manger mon·zhay *eat*

manif(estation) ⓕ ma·neef(·ay·sta·syon) *protest*

manifester ma·nee·fay·stay *protest*

manoeuvre ⓜ ma·ner·vrer *labourer*

manque ⓜ mongk *shortage*

manquer mong·kay *miss*

manquer de mong·kay der *run out of*

manteau ⓜ mon·to *coat*

maquillage ⓜ ma·kee·yazh *make-up*

marchand ⓜ mar·shon *shopkeeper*

— **de journaux** mar·shon der zhoor·no *newsagent*

— **de légumes** mar·shon der lay·gewm *greengrocer*

marche ⓕ marsh *step*

marché ⓜ mar·shay *market*

marché ⓜ **aux puces** mar·shay o pews *fleamarket*

marcher mar·shay *walk*

mardi ⓜ mar·dee *Tuesday*

marée ⓕ ma·ray *tide*

mari ⓜ ma·ree *husband*

mariage ⓜ ma·ryazh *marriage*

mariage ⓜ ma·ree·azh *wedding*

marié(e) ⓜ/ⓕ ma·ryay *married*

marihuana ⓕ ma·ree·wa·na *marihuana*

mars ⓜ mars *March*

marteau ⓜ mar·to *hammer*

massage ⓜ ma·sazh *massage*

masser ma·say *massage*

masseur/masseuse ⓜ/ⓕ ma·ser/ma·serz *masseur/masseuse*

match ⓜ matsh *game (sports)*

match ⓜ **nul** matsh newl *tie (draw)*

matelas ⓜ mat·la *mattress*

matériel ⓜ ma·tay·ryel *material*

matin ⓜ ma·tun *morning*

mauvais(e) ⓜ/ⓕ mo·vay(z) *bad • off (meat) • wrong (direction)*

mécanicien/mécanicienne ⓜ/ⓕ may·ka·nee·syun/ may·ka·nee·syen *mechanic*

médecin ⓜ mayd·sun *doctor*

médecine ⓕ med·seen *medicine*

médias ⓜ pl may·dya *media*

médicament ⓜ may·dee·ka·mon *medicine (medication)*

méditation ⓕ may·dee·ta·syon *meditation*

meilleur(e) ⓜ/ⓕ may·yer *better*

mélanger may·lon·zhay *mix*

membre ⓜ mom·brer *member*

même mem *same*

mémoire ⓕ may·mwar *memory (ability to remember)*

ménage ⓜ may·nazh *housework*

mensonge ⓜ mon-sonzh *lie*

menstruation ⓕ mon-strew-a-syon *menstruation*

menteur/menteuse ⓜ/ⓕ mon-ter/mon-terz *liar*

mentir mon-teer *lie (tell lies)*

menuisier ⓜ mer-nwee-zyay *carpenter*

mer ⓕ mair *sea*

mercredi ⓜ mair-krer-dee *Wednesday*

mère ⓕ mair *mother*

merveilleux/merveilleuse ⓜ/ⓕ mair-vay-yer/mair-vay-yerz *wonderful*

mes pl may *my*

message ⓜ may-sazh *message*

messe ⓕ mes *mass (Catholic)*

métal ⓜ may-tal *metal*

météo ⓕ may-tay-o *weather forecast*

mètre ⓜ may-trer *metre*

métro ⓜ may-tro *subway*

mettre may-trer *put*

meublé(e) ⓜ/ⓕ mer-blay *furnished*

meubles ⓜ mer-bler *furniture*

midi mee-dee *midday • noon*

mignon/mignonne ⓜ/ⓕ mee-nyon/mee-nyon *cute*

migraine ⓕ mee-gren *migraine*

militaire mee-lee-tair *military*

militant/militante ⓜ/ⓕ mee-lee-ton(t) *activist*

millénaire ⓜ mee-lay-nair *millennium*

millimètre ⓜ mee-lee-may-trer *millimetre*

million ⓜ mee-lyon *million*

minorité ⓕ mee-no-ree-tay *minority*

minuit mee-nwee *midnight*

minuscule mee-new-skewl *tiny*

minute ⓕ mee-newt *minute*

miroir ⓜ mee-rwar *mirror*

mode ⓕ mod *fashion*

modem ⓜ mo-dem *modem*

moderne mo-dairn *modern*

moi mwa *me*

moins de mwun der *less*

moins ⓜ mwun *least*

mois ⓜ mwa *month*

moitié ⓕ mwa-tyay *half*

mon ⓜ mon *my*

monarchie ⓕ mo-nar-shee *monarchy*

monastère ⓜ mo-na-stair *monastery*

monde ⓜ mond *world*

monnaie ⓕ mo-nay *change (coins)*

mononucléose ⓕ infectieuse mo-no-new-klay-oz un-fek-syerz *glandular fever*

Monsieur mer-syer *Mr*

montagne ⓕ mon-ta-nyer *mountain*

monter mon-tay *climb*
— à (cheval) a (shval) *ride (horse)*
— à bord de a bor der *board (a plane, ship)*

montre ⓕ mon-trer *watch*

montrer mon-tray *show*

monument ⓜ mo-new-mon *monument*

morceau ⓜ mor-so *piece*

mordre mor-drer *bite*

morsure ⓕ mor-sewr *bite (dog)*

mort ⓕ mor *death*

mort(e) ⓜ/ⓕ mor(t) *dead*

mosquée ⓕ mo-skay *mosque*

mot ⓜ mo *word*

motel ⓜ mo-tel *motel*

moteur ⓜ mo-ter *engine*

moto ⓕ mo-to *motorcycle*

mouche ⓕ moosh *fly*

mouchoir ⓜ moo-shwar *handkerchief*

mouchoirs ⓜ pl en papier moo-shwar om pa-pyay *tissues*

mouillé(e) ⓜ/ⓕ moo-yay *wet*

mourir moo-reer *die*

mousse ⓕ à raser moos a ra-zay *shaving cream*

moustiquaire ⓕ moo-stee-kair *mosquito net*

moustique ⓜ moo-steek *mosquito*

mouton ⓜ moo-ton *sheep*

muguet ⓜ mew-gay *thrush (illness)*

multimédia ⓜ mewl-tee-may-dya *multimedia*

mur ⓜ mewr *wall (outer)*

muscle ⓜ mews-kler *muscle*

musée ⓜ mew-zay *museum*

musée ⓜ mew-zay *art gallery (state)*

musicien(ne) ⓜ/ⓕ des rues mew-zee-syun/mew-zee-syen day rew *busker*

musicien/musicienne ⓜ/ⓕ mew-zees-yun/mew-zees-yen *musician*

musique ⓕ mew-zeek *music*

musulman(e) ⓜ/ⓕ mew-zewl-mon/mew-zewl-man *Muslim*

N

N

n'importe où num·port oo *anywhere*
n'importe quel/quelle ⑩/① num·port kel *any*
n'importe qui num·port kee *anyone*
n'importe quoi num·port kwa *anything*
nager na·zhay *swim*
nager avec un tuba na·zhay a·vek un tew·ba *snorkel*
nappe ① nap *tablecloth*
nationalité ① na·syo·na·lee·tay *nationality*
nature ① na·tewr *nature*
naturopathe ⑩/① na·tew·ro·pat *naturopath*
nausée ① no·zay *nausea*
nausées ① pl **matinales** no·zay ma·tee·nal *morning sickness*
navire ⑩ na·veer *ship*
né(e) ⑩/① nay *born*
nécessaire nay·say·sair *necessary*
neige ① nezh *snow*
neiger nay·zhay *snow*
nettoyage ⑩ net·wa·yazh *cleaning*
nettoyer net·wa·yay *clean*
neuf nerf *nine*
nez ⑩ nay *nose*
ni nee *neither*
nier nee·ay *deny*
niveau ⑩ nee·vo *level (tier, height)*
Noël ⑩ no·el *Christmas*
noir(e) ⑩/① nwar *black*
noir et blanc nwar ay blong *B&W (film)*
nom ⑩ nom *name*
  — de famille der fa·mee·yer *family name*
  — de famille der fa·mee·yer *surname*
non non *no*
non-direct non·dee·rekt *non-direct*
non-fumeur non·few·mer *non-smoking*
non-meublé(e) ⑩/① no·mer·blay *unfurnished*
nord ⑩ nor *north*
normal(e) ⑩/① nor·mal *regular*
nostalgique nos·tal·zheek *homesick*
notre no·trer *our*
nourrir noo·reer *feed*

nourriture ① noo·ree·tewr *food*
nous noo *us • we*
nouveau/nouvelle ⑩/① noo·vo/ noo·vel *new*
Nouvelle-Zélande ① noo·vel·zay·lond *New Zealand*
nuage ⑩ nwazh *cloud*
nuageux/nuageuse ⑩/① nwa·zher/ nwa·zherz *cloudy*
nuit ① nwee *night*
numéro ⑩ new·may·ro *number*
  — de chambre der shom·brer *room number*
  — de passeport der pas·por *passport number*

O

objectif ⑩ ob·zhek·teef *lens*
objet ⑩ ob·zhay *purpose*
objets ⑩ pl **artisanaux** ob·zhay ar·tee·za·no *handicrafts*
obscur(e) ⑩/① ob·skewr *dark*
obtenir op·ter·neer *obtain*
occasion ① o·ka·zyon *opportunity*
occupation ① o·kew·pa·syon *occupation*
occupé(e) ⑩/① o·kew·pay *busy*
océan ⑩ o·say·on *ocean*
odeur ① o·der *smell*
œil ⑩ er·yee *eye*
office de tourisme ⑩ o·fees·der too·rees·mer *tourist office*
officier ⑩ o·fees·yay *officer*
oiseau ⑩ wa·zo *bird*
ombre ① om·brer *shade • shadow*
opéra ⑩ o·pay·ra *opera*
opérateur/opératrice ⑩/① o·pay·ra·ter/o·pay·ra·trees *operator*
opération ① o·pay·ra·syon *operation*
or ⑩ or *gold*
orage ⑩ o·razh *storm*
orange o·ronzh *orange (colour)*
ordinaire or·dee·nair *ordinary*
ordinateur ⑩ or·dee·na·ter *computer*
ordinateur ⑩ **portable** or·dee·na·ter por·ta·bler *laptop*
ordonnance ① or·do·nons *prescription*
ordonner or·do·nay *order*

ordre ⓜ or·drer *order*
ordures ⓕ pl or·dewr
  garbage • rubbish
oreille ⓕ o·ray *ear*
oreiller ⓜ o·ray·yay *pillow*
organisation ⓕ or·ga·nee·za·syon
  organisation
organiser or·ga·nee·zay *organise*
orgasme ⓜ or·gas·mer *orgasm*
original(e) ⓜ/ⓕ o·ree·zhee·nal *original*
orteil ⓜ or·tay *toe*
os ⓜ os *bone*
ou oo *or*
où oo *where*
ouate ⓕ **de coton** wat der ko·ton
  cotton balls
oublier oo·blee·yay *forget*
ouest ⓜ west *west*
oui wee *yes*
outre-mer oo·trer·mair *overseas*
ouvert(e) ⓜ/ⓕ oo·vair(t) *open*
ouvre-boîte ⓜ oo·vrer·bwat
  can/tin opener
ouvre-bouteille ⓜ oo·vrer·boo·tay
  bottle opener
ouvrier/ouvrière ⓜ/ⓕ oo·vree·yay/
  oo·vree·yair *manual worker*
ouvrier ⓜ **d'usine** oo·vree·yay
  dew·zeen *factory worker*
ouvrière ⓕ **d'usine** oo·vree·yair
  dew·zeen *factory worker*
ouvrir oo·vreer *open*
overdose ⓕ o·vair·doz *overdose*
oxygène ⓜ ok·see·zhen *oxygen*

P

pacemaker ⓜ pes·may·ker *pacemaker*
page ⓕ pazh *page*
paiement ⓜ pay·mon *payment*
pain ⓜ pun *bread*
pain grillé ⓜ pung gree·yay *toast*
paire ⓕ pair *pair (couple)*
paix ⓕ pay *peace*
palais ⓜ pa·lay *palace*
panier ⓜ pan·yay *basket*
panne pan *break down*
pansement ⓜ pons·mon *bandage*
pantalon ⓜ pon·ta·lon *pants • trousers*

papa ⓜ pa·pa *dad*
paperasserie ⓕ pa·pras·ree *paperwork*
papeterie ⓕ pa·pet·ree *stationer's (shop)*
papier ⓜ pa·pyay *paper*
papier ⓜ **hygiénique** pa·pyay
  ee·zhyay·neek *toilet paper*
papillon ⓜ pa·pee·yon *butterfly*
Pâques pak *Easter*
paquet ⓜ pa·kay *package • packet*
par par *by • per (day)*
  — **avion** a·vyon *airmail*
  — **exprès** eks·pres *express mail (by)*
  — **voie de terre** vwa der tair
    surface mail (by) (land)
  — **voie maritime** vwa ma·ree·teem
    surface mail (by) (sea)
parade ⓕ pa·rad *parade (ceremony)*
paraplégique pa·ra·play·zheek *paraplegic*
parapluie ⓜ pa·ra·plwee *umbrella*
parc ⓜ park *park*
parc ⓜ **national** park na·syo·nal
  national park
parce que pars ker *because*
par-dessus par·der·sew *over (above)*
pardonner par·do·nay *forgive*
pare-brise ⓜ par·breez
  windscreen • windshield
parents ⓜ pl pa·ron *parents*
paresseux/paresseuse ⓜ/ⓕ
  pa·ray·ser/pa·ray·serz *lazy*
parfait(e) ⓜ/ⓕ par·fay(t) *perfect*
parfum ⓜ par·fum *perfume*
pari ⓜ pa·ree *bet*
parier par·yay *bet*
parking ⓜ par·keeng *carpark*
parler par·lay *speak • talk*
parmi par·mee *among*
partager par·ta·zhay *share*
parti ⓜ par·tee *party (politics)*
participer par·tee·see·pay *participate*
particulier/particulière ⓜ/ⓕ
  par·tee·kew·lyay/par·tee·kew·lyair
  particular
partie ⓕ par·tee *part*
partir par·teer *depart • leave*
pas compris pa kom·pree *excluded*
pas encore pa zong·kor *not yet*
pas frais/fraîche ⓜ/ⓕ pa fray/fresh
  stale

pas mal pa mal *not bad*
passe ① pas *pass (football)*
passé ⓜ pa·say *past*
passeport ⓜ pas·por *passport*
passer pa·say *pass • spend (time)*
passe-temps ⓜ pas·ton *hobby*
pâtisserie ① pa·tees·ree *cake shop*
pauvre po·vrer *poor*
pauvreté ① po·vrer·tay *poverty*
payer pay·yay *pay*
pays ⓜ pay·ee *country*
paysage ⓜ pay·yee·zazh *scenery*
Pays-Bas ⓜ pl pay·ee·ba *Netherlands*
peau ① po *skin*
pêche ① pesh *fishing*
pédale ① pay·dal *pedal*
peigne ⓜ pe·nyer *comb*
peine ① pen *trouble*
peintre ⓜ pun·trer *painter*
peinture ① pun·tewr *painting (the art)*
pellicule ① pay·lee·kewl
   film (for camera)
pendant pon·don *during*
pendant la nuit pon·don la nwee
   overnight
penderie ① pon·dree *wardrobe*
pendule ① pon·dewl *clock*
pénicilline ① pay·nee·see·leen *penicillin*
pénis ⓜ pay·nees *penis*
penser pon·say *think*
pension ① pon·syon *boarding house*
pension ① **(de famille)** pon·syon (der
   fa·mee·yer) *guesthouse*
perdant(e) ⓜ/① pair·don(t) *loser*
perdre pair·drer *lose*
perdu(e) ⓜ/① pair·dew *lost*
père ⓜ pair *father*
permanent(e) ⓜ/① pair·ma·non(t)
   permanent
permettre pair·me·trer *allow*
permis ⓜ pair·mee *permit*
   — de travail der tra·vai *work permit*
   — de conduire der kon·dweer
   drivers licence
permission ① pair·mee·syon
   permission
personnalité ① pair·so·na·lee·tay
   personality
personne ① pair·son *person*

personnel(le) ⓜ/① pair·so·nel *personal*
perte ① pairt *loss*
pertinent(e) ⓜ/① pair·tee·non(t)
   relevant
peser per·zay *weigh*
petit(e) ⓜ/① per·tee(t) *little • small*
   — ami ⓜ per·tee ta·mee *boyfriend*
   — déjeuner ⓜ per·tee day·zher·nay
   breakfast
   — tapis ⓜ per·tee ta·pee *mat*
   — amie ① per·teet a·mee *girlfriend*
   — cuillère ① per·teet kwee·yair
   teaspoon
   — monnaie ① per·teet mo·nay
   loose change
petite-fille ① per·teet fee·yer
   granddaughter
petit-fils ⓜ per·tee fees *grandson*
pétition ① pay·tees·yon *petition*
pétrole ⓜ pay·trol *oil (petrol)*
peu ⓜ per *little bit*
   — commun(e) ⓜ/① ko·mun/
   ko·mewn *unusual*
   — profond(e) ⓜ/① pro·fon(d) *shallow*
peur ① per *fear*
peut-être per·tay·trer *maybe*
phares ⓜ pl far *headlights*
pharmacie ① far·ma·see
   chemist • pharmacy
pharmacien(ne) ⓜ/① far·ma·syun/
   far·ma·syen *chemist (person)*
photo ① fo·to *photo*
photographe ⓜ/① fo·to·graf
   photographer
photographie ① fo·to·gra·fee
   photography
pièce ① **(de théâtre)** pyes (der
   tay·a·trer) *play (theatre)*
pièce ① **d'identité** pyes
   dee·don·tee·tay *identification*
pièces ① pyes *coins*
pied ⓜ pyay *foot*
pierre ① pyair *stone*
piéton ⓜ pyay·ton *pedestrian*
pile ① peel *battery*
pilule ① pee·lewl *pill*
pince ① **à épiler** puns a ay·pee·lay
   tweezers
pipe ① peep *pipe*

pique-nique ⓜ peek·neek *picnic*
piquets ⓜ **de tente** pee·kay der tont
  tent pegs
piqûre ① pee·kewr
  bite (insect) • *injection*
pire peer *worse*
piscine ① pee·seen *swimming pool*
piste ① peest *track (sports)* • *trail*
piste ① **cyclable** peest see·kla·bler
  bike path
pistolet ⓜ pees·to·lay *gun*
placard ⓜ pla·kar *cupboard*
place ① plas
  seat (place) • *square (town)*
place ① **centrale** plas son·tral
  main square
plage ① plazh *beach*
plainte ① plunt *complaint*
plaisanterie ① play·zon·tree *joke*
plan ⓜ plon *map (of town)*
planche ① **à voile** plonsh a vwal
  windsurfer
planche ① **de surf** plonsh der serf
  surfboard
plancher ⓜ plon·shay *floor*
planète ① pla·net *planet*
plaque ① **d'immatriculation**
  plak dee·ma· tree·kew·la·syon
  license plate number
plastique ⓜ plas·teek *plastic*
plat ⓜ pla *dish*
plat(e) ⓜ/① pla(t) *flat*
plein(e) ⓜ/① plun/plen *full*
pleurer pler·ray *cry*
pleuvoir pler·vwar *rain*
plongée (sous-marine) ① plon·zhay
  (soo·ma·reen) *diving*
plonger plon·zhay *dive*
pluie ① plwee *rain*
plus ⓜ plews *most*
plus de plews der *more*
plus grand(e) ⓜ/① plew gron(d)
  bigger
plus petit(e) ⓜ/① plew per·tee/·teet
  smaller
plus tard plew·tar *later*
plusieurs plew·zyer *several*
pneu ⓜ pner *tyre*
poche ① posh *pocket*

poêle ① pwal *frying pan*
poésie ① po·ay·zee *poetry*
poids ⓜ pwa *weight*
poignet ⓜ pwa·nyay *wrist*
pointe ① pwunt *point*
poisson ⓜ pwa·son *fish*
poissonnerie ① pwa·son·ree *fish shop*
poitrine ① pwa·treen *chest*
police ① po·lees *police*
policier ⓜ po·lee·syay
  police officer (in city)
politique ① po·lee·teek
  policy • *politics*
pollen ⓜ po·len *pollen*
pollution ① po·lew·syon *pollution*
pommade ① **pour les lèvres** po·mad
  poor lay lay·vrer *lip balm*
pompe ① pomp *pump*
pont ⓜ pon *bridge*
populaire po·pew·lair *popular*
port ⓜ por *harbour* • *port*
porte ① port *door*
porte-monnaie ⓜ port·mo·nay *purse*
porter por·tay *carry* • *wear*
posemètre ⓜ poz·may·trer *light meter*
poser po·zay *ask (a question)*
positif/positive ⓜ/① po·zee·teef/
  po·zee·teev *positive*
possible po·see·bler *possible*
poste ① post *mail (postal system)*
pot ⓜ po *carton* • *jar* • *pot*
pot ⓜ **d'échappement** po
  day·shap·mon *exhaust (car)*
pot-de-vin ⓜ po·der·vun *bribe*
poterie ① po·tree *pottery*
poubelle ① poo·bel
  garbage/rubbish can
poulet ⓜ poo·lay *chicken*
poumon ⓜ poo·mon *lung*
poupée ① poo·pay *doll*
pour poor *for*
  — **cent** son *percent*
pourboire ⓜ poor·bwar *tip (gratuity)*
pourquoi poor·kwa *why*
pousser poo·say *grow* • *push*
poussette ① poo·set *push chair* • *stroller*
poussière ① poo·syair *dust*
pouvoir poo·vwar
  can (be able or have permission)

pouvoir ⓜ poo·vwar *power*

poux ⓜ pl poo *lice*

pratique pra·teek *practical*

pratiquer pra·tee·kay *practise*

précédent(e) ⓜ/ⓕ pray·say·don(t) *previous*

préférer pray·fay·ray *prefer*

premier/première ⓜ/ⓕ prer·myay/ prer·myair *first*

premier ministre ⓜ prer·myay mee·nee·strer *prime minister*

première classe ⓕ prer·myair klas *first class*

prendre pron·drer *take*

prendre en photo pron·drer on fo·to *take a photo of (someone)*

prénom ⓜ pray·non *Christian name*

préparer pray·pa·ray *prepare*

près de pray der *near*

présent ⓜ pray·zon *present (time)*

présenter pray·zon·tay *introduce (people)*

préservatif ⓜ pray·zair·va·teef *condom*

président ⓜ pray·zee·don *president*

presque pres·ker *almost*

pressé(e) ⓜ/ⓕ pray·say *in a hurry*

pression ⓕ pray·syon *pressure*

prêt(e) ⓜ/ⓕ pray/pret *ready*

prêtre ⓜ pray·trer *priest*

prévenir prayv·neer *warn*

prévision ⓕ pray·vee·zyon *forecast*

prévoir pray·vwar *forecast*

prière ⓕ pree·yair *prayer*

principal(e) ⓜ/ⓕ prun·see·pal *main*

printemps ⓜ prun·tom *spring (season)*

prise ⓕ preez *plug (electricity)*

prison ⓕ pree·zon *jail • prison*

prisonnier/prisonnière ⓜ/ⓕ pree·zo·nyay/pree·zo·nyair *prisoner*

privé(e) ⓜ/ⓕ pree·vay *private*

prix ⓜ pree *price*

prix ⓜ **d'entrée** pree don·tray *admission (price)*

probable pro·ba·bler *probable*

problème ⓜ pro·blem *problem*

prochain(e) ⓜ/ⓕ pro·shun/pro·shen *next (month)*

proche prosh *close*

produire pro·dweer *produce*

professeur ⓜ pro·fay·ser *teacher*

professeur ⓜ **(à l'université)** pro·fay·ser (a lew·nee·vair·see·tay) *lecturer*

professionnel(le) ⓜ/ⓕ pro·fay·syo·nel *professional*

profond(e) ⓜ/ⓕ pro·fon(d) *deep*

programme ⓜ pro·gram *programme*

programme ⓜ **des spectacles** pro·gram day spek·tak·ler *entertainment guide*

projecteur ⓜ pro·zhek·ter *projector*

prolongation ⓕ pro·long·ga·syon *extension (visa)*

promenade ⓕ prom·nad *ride*

promesse ⓕ pro·mes *promise*

promettre pro·may·trer *promise*

promouvoir pro·moo·vwar *promote*

propre pro·prer *clean*

propriétaire ⓜ/ⓕ pro·pree·ay·tair *landlady • landlord • owner*

prostituée ⓕ pro·stee·tway *prostitute*

protection ⓕ pro·tek·syon *protection*

protégé(e) ⓜ/ⓕ pro·tay·zhay *protected (species)*

protéger pro·tay·zhay *protect*

protège-slips ⓜ pl pro·tezh·sleep *panty liners*

provisions ⓕ pl pro·vee·zyon *food supplies • provisions*

prudence ⓕ prew·dons *caution*

psychothérapie ⓕ psee·ko·tay·ra·pee *psychotherapy*

public ⓜ pewb·leek *public*

publicité ⓕ pewb·lee·see·tay *advertisement*

puce ⓕ pews *flea*

puis pwee *then (next)*

puissance ⓕ **nucléaire** pwee·sons new·klay·air *nuclear power*

pull ⓜ pewl *jumper • sweater*

punir pew·neer *punish*

pur(e) ⓜ/ⓕ pewr *pure*

Q

quai ⓜ kay *platform*

qualification ⓕ ka·lee·fee·ka·syon *qualification*

qualité ⓕ ka·lee·tay *quality*

quand kon *when*
quantité ① kon·tee·tay *quantity*
quarantaine ① ka·ron·ten *quarantine*
quart ⓜ kar *quarter*
quatre ka·trer *four*
quel(le) ⓜ/① kel
quel/quelle ⓜ/① kel *what • which*
quelqu'un kel·kun *someone*
quelque chose kel·ker shoz *something*
quelquefois kel·ker·fwa *sometimes*
quelques kel·ker *some*
question ① kay·styon *question*
queue ① ker *queue • tail*
qui kee *which • who*
quincaillerie ① kung·kay·ree
  hardware store
quitter kee·tay *quit*
quotidien(ne) ⓜ/① ko·tee·dyun/
  ko·tee·dyen *daily*

R

race ① ras *race*
racisme ⓜ ra·sees·mer *racism*
raconter ra·kon·tay *tell (a story)*
radiateur ⓜ ra·dya·ter *radiator*
radical(e) ⓜ/① ra·dee·kal *radical*
radio ① ra·dyo *radio*
raide red *steep*
raison ① ray·zon *reason*
raisonnable ray·zo·na·bler *sensible*
ramasser ra·ma·say *pick up(something)*
randonnée ① ron·do·nay *hiking*
randonnée ① ran·do·nay *trek*
rapide ra·peed *fast • quick*
rapport ⓜ ra·por *connection*
rapports ⓜ pl sexuels protégés ra·por
  seks·wel pro·tay·zhay *safe sex*
raquette ① ra·ket *racquet*
rare rar *rare*
rasoir ⓜ ra·zwar *razor*
rassis(e) ⓜ/① ra·see(z) *stale (bread)*
rat ⓜ ra *rat*
rave ① raiv *rave*
réalisateur/réalisatrice ⓜ/①
  ray·a·lee·za·ter/ray·a·lee·za·trees
  director (film)

réaliser ray·a·lee·zay *direct (a film)*
réaliste ray·a·leest *realistic*
réalité ① ray·a·lee·tay *reality*
rebord ⓜ rer·bor *ledge*
récemment ray·sa·mon *recently*
receveur ⓜ rer·ser·ver *conductor (bus)*
recevoir rer·ser·vwar *receive*
réchaud ⓜ ray·sho *stove*
recherches ① pl rer·shairsh *research*
récolte ① ray·kolt *crop (gathered)*
recommander rer·ko·mon·day
  recommend
reconnaissant(e) ⓜ/①
  rer·ko·nay·son(t) *grateful*
reconnaître rer·ko·nay·trer *recognise*
reçu ⓜ rer·sew *receipt*
recueil ⓜ d'expressions rer·ker·yer
  dek·spray·syon *phrasebook*
recyclable rer·see·kla·bler *recyclable*
recyclage ⓜ rer·see·klazh *recycling*
recycler rer·see·klay *recycle*
rédacteur/rédactrice ⓜ/① ray·dak·ter/
  ray·dak·trees *editor*
réduire ray·dweer *reduce*
référence ① ray·fay·rons *reference*
réfrigérateur ⓜ ray·free·zhay·ra·ter
  refrigerator
réfugié(e) ⓜ/① ray·few·zhyay *refugee*
refuser rer·few·zay *refuse*
regarder rer·gar·day
  look • look at • watch
régime ⓜ ray·zheem *diet*
région ① ray·zhyon *region*
règles ① ray·gler *rules*
règles ① pl douloureuses ray·gler
  doo·loo·rerz *period pain*
reine ① ren *queen*
relation ① rer·la·syon *relationship*
religieuse ① rer·lee·zhyerz *nun*
religieux/religieuse ⓜ/① rer·lee·zhyer/
  rer·lee·zhyerz *religious*
religion ① rer·lee·zhyon *religion*
remboursement ⓜ rom·boor·ser·mon
  refund
remercier rer·mair·syay *thank*
remise ① rer·meez *discount*
remplir rom·pleer *fill*
rencontrer ron·kon·tray *meet*

rendez-vous ⓜ ron·day·voo
appointment • date
renseignements ⓜ pl ron·sen·yer·mon
information
réparer ray·pa·ray *repair*
repas ⓜ rer·pa *meal*
repasser rer·pa·say *iron (clothes)*
répondre ray·pon·drer *answer • reply*
réponse ① ray·pons *answer • response*
repos ⓜ rer·po *rest*
représenter rer·pray·zon·tay *represent*
république ① ray·pewb·leek *republic*
réseau ⓜ ray·zo *network*
réservation ① ray·zair·va·syon
reservation
réserver ray·zair·vay
book (make a booking)
respirer res·pee·ray *breathe*
ressort ⓜ rer·sor *spring (coil)*
restaurant ⓜ res·to·ron *restaurant*
rester res·tay *stay*
retard ⓜ rer·tard *delay*
retrait ⓜ rer·tray *withdrawal*
retrait ⓜ **des bagages** rer·tray day
ba·gazh *baggage claim*
retraité(e) ⓜ/① rer·tray·tay
pensioner • retired
réussite ① ray·ew·seet *achievement*
réveil ⓜ ray·vay *alarm clock*
réveiller ray·vay·yay *wake (someone) up*
revenir rerv·neer *return*
revenus ⓜ pl rerv·new *income*
rêver ray·vay *dream*
révolution ① ray·vo·lew·syon
revolution
rhume ⓜ **des foins** rewm day fwun
hay fever
riche reesh *rich • wealthy*
rien ryun *nothing*
rire reer *laugh*
risque ⓜ reesk *risk*
rivière ① ree·vyair *river*
riz ⓜ ree *rice*
robe ① rob *dress*
robinet ⓜ ro·bee·nay *faucet*
robinet ⓜ ro·bee·nay *tap*
rocher ⓜ ro·shay *rock*
rock ⓜ rok *rock (music)*

roi ⓜ rwa *king*
roller ⓜ ro·lair *rollerblading*
roman ⓜ ro·mon *novel*
romantique ro·mon·teek *romantic*
rond(e) ⓜ/① ron(d) *round*
rond-point ⓜ rom·pwun
roundabout (traffic)
rose roz *pink*
roue ① roo *wheel*
rouge roozh *red*
rouge ⓜ **à lèvres** roozh a lay·vrer *lipstick*
rougeole ① roo·zhol *measles*
rougeur ① roo·zher *rash*
route ① root *road*
royaume ⓜ rwa·yom *kingdom*
rue ① rew *street*
ruelle ① rwel *lane (city)*
rugby ⓜ rewg·bee *rugby*
ruines ① pl rween *ruins*
ruisseau ⓜ rwee·so *stream*
ruse ① rewz *trick*
rythme ⓜ reet·mer *rhythm*

S

s'allonger sa·lon·zhay *lie (not stand)*
s'amuser sa·mew·zay *enjoy (oneself)*
s'amuser sa·mew·zay *fun (have fun)*
s'amuser sa·mew·zay *have fun*
s'arrêter sa·ray·tay *stop (doing)*
s'asseoir sa·swar *sit*
s'ennuyer son·nwee·yay *bored (be)*
s'habiller sa·bee·yay *dress (oneself)*
s'inquiéter sung·kyay·tay *worry*
s'occuper de so·kew·pay der *look after*
sa ① sa *her • his*
sabbat ⓜ sa·ba *Sabbath*
sable ⓜ sa·bler *sand*
sac ⓜ sak *bag*
— **à dos** a do *backpack*
— **de couchage** der koo·shazh
sleeping bag
— **à main** a mun *handbag*
saint(e) ⓜ/① sun(t) *saint*
Saint-Sylvestre ① sun·seel·ves·trer
New Year's Eve
saison ① say·zon *season*
salaire ⓜ sa·lair *salary • wage*

salaud ⓜ sa·lo *bastard*

sale sal *dirty*

salle ⓕ sal *room*
— **d'attente** sal da·tont *waiting room*
— **de bain** sal der bun *bathroom*
— **de transit** sal der tron·zeet
transit lounge

salon ⓜ **de beauté** sa·lon der bo·tay
beauty salon

salope ⓕ sa·lop *bitch*

samedi ⓜ sam·dee *Saturday*

sandales ⓕ son·dal *sandals*

sang ⓜ son *blood*

sans son *without*

sans plomb son plom *unleaded*

sans-abri son·za·bree *homeless*

santé ⓕ son·tay *health*

satisfait(e) ⓜ/ⓕ sa·tees·fay/sa·tees·fet
satisfied

sauf sof *except*

sauna ⓜ so·na *sauna*

sauter so·tay *jump*

sauvage so·vazh *wild*

sauver so·vay *save*

savoir sa·vwar *know*

savon ⓜ sa·von *soap*

scénario ⓜ say·na·ryo *script*

scénariste ⓜ/ⓕ say·na·reest *scriptwriter*

scène ⓕ sen *stage*

science ⓕ syons *science*

science-fiction ⓕ syons·feek·syon
science fiction

scientifique ⓜ/ⓕ syon·tee·feek *scientist*

score ⓜ skor *score*

sculpture ⓕ skewl·tewr *sculpture*

se coucher ser koo·shay *go to bed*

se décider ser day·see·day *decide*

se disputer ser dees·pew·tay *argue*

se laver ser la·vay *wash (oneself)*

se mettre à genoux ser may·trer a
zher·noo *kneel*

se mettre en grève ser may·trer ong
grev *strike (go on strike)*

se plaindre ser plun·drer *complain*

se raser ser ra·zay *shave*

se rendre compte de ser ron·drer kont
der *realise*

se reposer ser rer·po·zay *relax (rest)*

se réveiller ser ray·vay·yay *wake up*

se souvenir ser soo·ver·neer *remember*

seau ⓜ so *bucket*

sec/sèche ⓜ/ⓕ sek/sesh *dry*

sécher say·shay *dry (clothes)*

second(e) ⓜ/ⓕ skon/skond *second*

seconde ⓕ skond *second (clock)*

secret ⓜ ser·kray *secret*

secrétaire ⓜ/ⓕ ser·kray·tair *secretary*

sécurité ⓕ say·kew·ree·tay
safety • security

sécurité ⓕ **sociale** say·kew·ree·tay
so·syal *social welfare*

sein ⓜ sun *breast*

sel ⓜ sel *salt*

selle ⓕ sel *saddle*

semaine ⓕ ser·men *week*

semblable som·bla·bler *similar*

séminaire ⓜ say·mee·nair *seminar*

sensation ⓕ son·sa·syon
feeling (physical)

sensibilité ⓕ **de la pellicule**
son·see·bee·lee·tay der la pay·lee·kewl
film speed

sensuel(le) ⓜ/ⓕ son·swel *sensual*

sentier ⓜ son·tyay *footpath*

sentiment ⓜ son·tee·mon
feeling (emotion)

sentir son·teer *smell*

séparé(e) ⓜ/ⓕ say·pa·ray *separate*

sept set *seven*

septembre ⓜ sep·tom·brer *September*

série ⓕ say·ree *series*

sérieux/sérieuse ⓜ/ⓕ say·ree·yer/
say·ree·yerz *serious*

seringue ⓕ ser·rung *syringe*

séropositif/séropositive ⓜ/ⓕ
say·ro·po·zee·teef/ say·ro·po·zee·teev
HIV positive

serpent ⓜ sair·pon *snake*

serrer dans ses bras say·ray don say
bra *hug*

serrure ⓕ say·rewr *lock*

serveur/serveuse ⓜ/ⓕ sair·ver/
sair·verz *waiter*

service ⓜ sair·vees
service • service charge

service ⓜ **militaire** sair·vees
mee·lee·tair *military service*

serviette ① sair·vyet
  briefcase • *napkin* • *towel*
serviette ① **hygiénique** sair·vyet
  ee·zhyay·neek *sanitary napkin*
ses pl say *her* • *his*
seule(e) ⓜ/① serl *only*
sexe ⓜ seks *sex*
sexisme ⓜ sek·see·smer *sexism*
sexiste sek·seest *sexist*
sexy sek·see *sexy*
shampooing ⓜ shom·pwung *shampoo*
short ⓜ short *shorts*
si see *if*
SIDA ⓜ see·da *AIDS*
siège ⓜ **pour enfant** syezh poor on·fon
  child seat
siffler see·flay *whistle*
signature ① see·nya·tewr *signature*
signe ⓜ see·nyer *sign*
simple sum·pler *simple*
Singapour sung·ga·poor *Singapore*
singe ⓜ sunzh *monkey*
situation ① see·twa·syon *situation*
situation ① **familiale** see·twa·syon
  fa·mee·lyal *marital status*
six sees *six*
skateboard ⓜ sket·bord *skateboarding*
ski ⓜ skee *skiing*
ski ⓜ **nautique** skee no·teek *waterskiing*
skier skee·yay *ski*
skis ⓜ skee *skis*
slip ⓜ sleep *panties* • *underpants*
socialisme ⓜ so·sya·lees·mer *socialism*
socialiste so·sya·leest *socialist*
société ① so·syay·tay *society*
sœur ① ser *sister*
soie ① swa *silk*
soigner swa·nyay *care for (someone)*
soigneux/soigneuse ⓜ/① swa·nyer/
  swa·nyerz *careful*
soir ⓜ swar *evening*
soirée ① swa·ray *night out* • *party*
soldat ⓜ sol·da *soldier*
solde ⓜ sold *balance (account)*
soleil ⓜ so·lay *sun*
solide so·leed *solid*
somme ① som *amount (money)*
sommeil ⓜ so·may *sleep*
somnifère ⓜ som·nee·fair *sleeping pill*

son ⓜ son *her* • *his*
sonner so·nay *ring (of phone)*
sortie ① sor·tee *exit*
sortir sor·teer *go out*
sortir avec sor·teer a·vek
  date (go out with)
souffrir soo·freer *suffer*
souhaiter sway·tay *wish*
soulever sool·vay *lift* • *raise*
sourd(e) ⓜ/① soor(d) *deaf*
sourire soo·reer *smile*
sourire ⓜ soo·reer *smile*
souris ① soo·ree *mouse*
sous soo *below* • *under*
sous-titres ⓜ soo·tee·trer *subtitles*
sous-vêtements ⓜ soo·vet·mon
  underwear
soutien-gorge ⓜ soo·tyung·gorzh *bra*
souvenir ⓜ soov·neer
  memory (recollection) • *souvenir*
souvent soo·von *often*
sparadrap ⓜ spa·ra·dra *Band-Aid*
spécial(e) ⓜ/① spay·syal *special*
spécialiste ⓜ/① spay·sya·leest *specialist*
spectacle ⓜ spek·ta·kler
  performance • *show*
sport ⓜ spor *sport*
sportif/sportive ⓜ/① spor·teef/
  spor·teev *sportsperson*
stade ⓜ stad *stadium*
stage ⓜ **en entreprise** stazh on
  on·trer·preez *work experience*
station ① **de métro** sta·syon der
  may·tro *metro station*
station ① **de taxi** sta·syon der tak·see
  taxi stand
station-service ① sta·syon·sair·vees
  petrol station
stérilet ⓜ stay·ree·lay *IUD*
stupéfiant ⓜ stew·pay·fyon *narcotic*
stupéfiant(e) ⓜ/① stew·pay·fyon(t)
  amazing
stupide stew·peed *stupid*
style ⓜ steel *style*
stylo ⓜ stee·lo *pen (ballpoint)*
suborner sew·bor·nay *bribe*
sucré(e) ⓜ/① sew·kray *sweet*
sud ⓜ sewd *south*
suivre swee·vrer *follow*

supérette ① **de quartier** sew·pay·ret der kar·tyay *convenience store*

supermarché ⓜ sew·pair·mar·shay *supermarket*

superstition ① sew·pair·stee·syon *superstition*

supplémentaire sew·play·mon·tair *additional • extra*

supporter sew·por·tay *support*

sur sewr *on*

sûr(e) ⓜ/① sewr *sure*

surf (des neiges) ⓜ serf (day nezh) *snowboarding*

surfer ser·fay *surf*

surnom ⓜ sewr·nom *nickname*

surprise ① sewr·preez *surprise*

survivre sewr·vee·vrer *survive*

synagogue ① see·na·gog *synagogue*

syndicat ⓜ sun·dee·ka *union (trade)*

syndrome ⓜ **prémenstruel** sun·drom pray·mon·strwel *premenstrual tension*

synthétique sun·tay·teek *synthetic*

syrop ⓜ **contre la toux** see·ro kon·trer la too *cough medicine*

T

ta sg inf ① ta *your*

tabac ⓜ ta·ba *tobacco*

table ① ta·bler *table*

tableau ⓜ ta·blo *painting (a work)*

tableau ⓜ **d'affichage** ta·blo da·fee·shazh *scoreboard*

taie ① **d'oreiller** tay do·ray·yay *pillowcase*

taille ① tai *size (general)*

tailleur ⓜ ta·yer *tailor*

talc ⓜ talk *baby powder*

tambour ⓜ tom·boor *drum*

tampon ⓜ **hygiénique** tom·pon ee·zhyay·neek *tampon*

tante ① tont *aunt*

tapis ⓜ ta·pee *rug*

tarif ⓜ ta·reef *fare*

tarifs ⓜ pl **postaux** ta·reef pos·to *postage*

tasse ① tas *cup*

taux ⓜ **de change** to der shonzh *currency exchange*

taux ⓜ **de change** to der shonzh *exchange rate*

taxe ① taks *tax*

— **à la vente** a la vont *sales tax*

— **d'aéroport** da·ay·ro·por *airport tax*

taxi ⓜ tak·see *taxi*

technique ① tek·neek *technique*

télé ① tay·lay *TV*

télécarte ① tay·lay·kart *phone card*

télécommande ① tay·lay·ko·mond *remote control*

télégramme ⓜ tay·lay·gram *telegram*

téléphérique ⓜ tay·lay·fay·reek *cable car*

téléphone ⓜ tay·lay·fon *telephone*

téléphone ⓜ **portable** tay·lay·fon por·ta·bler *mobile phone*

téléphone ⓜ **public** tay·lay·fon pewb·leek *public telephone*

téléphoner tay·lay·fo·nay *telephone*

télescope ⓜ tay·lay·skop *telescope*

télésiège ⓜ tay·lay·syezh *chairlift (skiing)*

télévision ① tay·la·vee·zyon *television*

témoin ⓜ tay·mwun *witness*

température ① tom·pay·ra·tewr *temperature*

temple ⓜ tom·pler *temple*

temps ⓜ tom *time (general)* • *weather*

tennis ⓜ tay·nees *tennis*

tennis ⓜ **de table** tay·nees der ta·bler *table tennis*

tension ① **artérielle** ton·syon ar·tay·ryel *blood pressure*

tente ① tont *tent*

terrain ⓜ tay·rung *ground*

— **de camping** der kom·peeng *campsite*

— **de golf** der golf *golf course*

— **de jeux** der zher *playground*

— **de sport** der spor *sports ground*

Terre ① tair *Earth*

terre ① tair *earth* • *land*

terrorisme ⓜ tay·ro·rees·mer *terrorism*

tes pl inf tay *your*

test ⓜ **de grossesse** test der gro·ses *pregnancy test kit*

tête ① tet *head*
tétine ① tay·teen *pacifier • dummy*
teush tersh *hash*
théâtre ⓜ tay·a·trer *drama (theatre)*
théâtre ⓜ tay·a·trer *theatre*
timbre ⓜ tum·brer *stamp*
timide tee·meed *shy*
tire-bouchon ⓜ teer·boo·shon *corkscrew*
tirer tee·ray *pull • shoot*
tissu ⓜ tee·sew *fabric*
toilettes ① pl twa·let *public toilet*
toit ⓜ twa *roof*
tombe ① tomb *grave*
tomber tom·bay *fall*
ton ⓜ sg inf ton *your*
tonalité ① to·na·lee·tay *dial tone*
tôt to *early*
toucher too·shay *feel • touch*
toujours too·zhoor *always*
tour ① toor *tower*
touriste ⓜ/① too·reest *tourist*
tourner toor·nay *turn*
tournoi ⓜ toor·nwa *tournament*
tous les deux too lay der *both*
tous les jours too lay zhoor *every day*
tout too *all • everything*
— **droit** drwa *straight ahead*
— **le monde** ler mawnd *everyone*
— **près** pray *nearby*
tout(e) seul(e) ⓜ/① too(t) serl *alone*
toux ① too *cough*
toxicomanie ① tok·see·ko·ma·nee *drug addiction*
traduire tra·dweer *translate*
trafiquant ⓜ **de drogue** tra·fee·kon der drog *drug dealer*
train ⓜ trun *train*
traite ① **bancaire** tret bong·kair *bank draft*
traitement ⓜ tret·mon *treatment*
tranchant(e) ⓜ/① tron·shon(t) *sharp (blade, etc)*
tranche ① tronsh *slice*
tranquille trong·keel *quiet*
transfert ⓜ trons·fair *transfer*
transport ⓜ trons·por *transport*

travail ⓜ tra·vai *job • work*
— **dans un bar** don zun bar *bar work*
— **intermittent** un·tair·mee·ton *casual work*
travailler tra·va·yay *work*
traverser tra·vair·say *cross*
tremblement ⓜ **de terre** trom·bler·mon der tair *earthquake*
très tray *very*
tribunal ⓜ tree·bew·nal *court (legal)*
tricheur/tricheuse ⓜ/① tree·sher/ tree·sherz *cheat*
tricot ⓜ tree·ko *knitting*
triste treest *sad*
trois trwa *three*
troisième trwa·zyem *third*
tromper trom·pay *trick*
trop tro *too (expensive etc)*
trop de tro der *too much (rain etc) • too many (people etc)*
trou ⓜ troo *hole*
trousse ① **à pharmacie** troos a far·ma·see *first-aid kit*
trouver troo·vay *find*
T-shirt ⓜ tee·shert *T-shirt*
tu tew *you (inf)*
tuer tew·way *kill*
tuer (d'un coup de pistolet) tew·way (dung koo der pee·sto·lay) *shoot (and kill someone)*
type ⓜ teep *type*
typique tee·peek *typical*

U

ultrason ⓜ ewl·tra·son *ultrasound*
un peu ⓜ um per *a little*
un(e) ⓜ/① un/wen *a/an • one*
une fois ewn fwa *once*
uniforme ⓜ ew·nee·form *uniform*
union ① ew·nyon *union*
université ① ew·nee·vair·see·tay *university*
univers ⓜ ew·nee·vair *universe*
urgent(e) ⓜ/① ewr·zhon(t) *urgent*
usine ① ew·zeen *factory*
utile ew·teel *useful*
utiliser ew·tee·lee·zay *use*

V

vacances ① pl va·kons
holidays • vacation
vaccination ① vak·see·na·syon
vaccination
vache ① vash *cow*
vagin ⓜ va·zhun *vagina*
vague ① vag *wave*
valeur ① va·ler *value (price)*
valider va·lee·day *validate*
valise ① va·leez *suitcase*
vallée ① va·lay *valley*
varappe ① va·rap *rock climbing*
végétarien/végétarienne ⓜ/①
vay·zhay·ta·ryun/vay·zhay·ta·ryen
vegetarian
véhicule ⓜ vay·ee·kewl *vehicle*
veine ① ven *vein*
vélo ⓜ vay·lo *bicycle*
vélo ⓜ **tout terrain (VTT)** vay·lo too
tay·run (vay·tay·tay) *mountain bike*
vendre von·drer *sell*
vendredi von·drer·dee *Friday*
venimeux/venimeuse ⓜ/①
ver·nee·mer/ver·nee·merz *poisonous*
venir ver·neer *come*
vent ⓜ von *wind*
vente ① vont *sale*
vente ① **aux enchères** vont o zon·shair
auction
ventilateur ⓜ von·tee·la·ter
fan (machine)
vérifier vay·ree·fyay *check*
vérité ① vay·ree·tay *truth*
verre ⓜ vair *drink (alcoholic) • glass*
verre ⓜ vair
verres de contact ⓜ vair der kon·takt
contact lenses
vers vair *toward (direction)*
vers ⓜ vair *worms*
vert(e) ⓜ/① vair(t) *green*
veste ① vest *jacket*
vestiaire ⓜ vays·tyair *cloakroom*
vêtements ⓜ vet·mon *clothing*
veuf ⓜ verf *widower*
veuve ① verv *widow*
via vee·a *via*

viande ① vyond *meat*
vide veed *empty*
vie ① vee *life*
vieux/vieille ⓜ/① vyer/vyay *old*
vigne ① vee·nyer *vine*
vignoble ⓜ vee·nyo·bler *vineyard*
VIH (virus immunodéficitaire humain)
ⓜ vay·ee·ash (vee·rews ee·mew·no·d
ay·fee·see·tair ew·mun) *HIV*
village ⓜ vee·lazh *village*
ville ① veel *city • town*
vin ⓜ vun *wine*
violer vyo·lay *rape*
violet(te) ⓜ/① vyo·lay(·let) *purple*
virus ⓜ vee·rews *virus*
visa ⓜ vee·za *visa*
visage ⓜ vee·zazh *face*
visite ① **guidée** vee·zeet gee·day
guided tour
visiter vee·zee·tay *visit (museum etc)*
visiteur/visiteuse ⓜ/① vee·zee·ter/
vee·zee·terz *visitor*
vitamine ① vee·ta·meen *vitamin*
vitesse ① vee·tes *speed*
vivant(e) ⓜ/① vee·von(t) *alive*
vivre vee·vrer *live*
voile ① vwal *sail • sailing*
voir vwar *see*
voiture ① vwa·tewr *car*
voiture ① **de police** vwa·tewr der
po·lees *police car*
vol ⓜ vol *flight • robbery*
volé(e) ⓜ/① vo·lay *stolen*
voler vo·lay *fly • rob • steal*
voleur/voleuse ⓜ/① vo·ler/vo·lerz *thief*
volume ⓜ vo·lewm *volume*
vomir vo·meer *vomit*
vos pl pol vo *your*
voter vo·tay *vote*
votre pol sg vo·trer/vo *your*
vouloir voo·lwar *want*
vous pl pol voo *you*
voyage ⓜ vwa·yazh
journey • tour • trip
voyage ⓜ **d'affaires** vwa·yazh da·fair
business trip
voyager vwa·ya·zhay *travel*
voyageur/voyageuse ⓜ/①
vwa·ya·zher/vwa·ya·zherz *passenger*
vrai(e) ⓜ/① vray *real*

V

french-english

253

vrai(e) ⓜ/ⓕ vray *true*
vraiment vray·mon *really*
vue ⓕ vew *view*

W

wagon-lit ⓜ va·gon·lee *sleeping car*
wagon-restaurant ⓜ va·gon·res·to·ron
  dining car
week-end ⓜ week·end *weekend*

Y

yeux ⓜ yer *eyes*
yoga ⓜ yo·ga *yoga*

Z

zéro zay·ro *zero*
zoo ⓜ zo *zoo*

R

S

T

V

W

What kind of traveller are you?

A You're eating chicken for dinner *again* because it's the only word you know.

B When no one understands what you say, you step closer and shout louder.

C When the barman doesn't understand your order, you point frantically at the beer.

D You're surrounded by locals, swapping jokes, email addresses and experiences; other travellers want to borrow your phrasebook or audio guide.

If you answered A, B or C, you NEED Lonely Planet's language products...

- **Lonely Planet Phrasebooks** – every phrase you need in every language you want
- **Lonely Planet Language & Culture** – laugh and learn as you explore the richness of English idiom as it's spoken around the world
- **Lonely Planet Fast Talk** – enjoy hassle-free sightseeing, shopping and dining using our essential phrases for short trips and weekends away
- **Lonely Planet Small Talk** – pack light with our quick-hit language guide featuring 10 languages per book
- **Lonely Planet Phrasebook & Audio CD** – read, listen and talk like a local with our complete phrasebook plus a bonus CD of 400 key phrases
- **Lonely Planet Phrasebooks for iPhone and iPod touch** – download more than 600 phrases with corresponding audio, available on the App Store

...and this is why

- **Talk to everyone everywhere**
  Over 120 languages, more than any other publisher
- **The right words at the right time**
  Quick-reference colour sections, two-way dictionary, easy pronunciation, every possible subject – and audio to support it

Lonely Planet Offices

Australia
90 Maribyrnong St, Footscray,
Victoria 3011
☎ 03 8379 8000
fax 03 8379 8111
✉ talk2us@lonelyplanet.com

USA
150 Linden St, Oakland,
CA 94607
☎ 510 250 6400
Toll free 800 275 8555
fax 510 893 8572

UK
2nd fl, 186 City Rd,
London EC1V 2NT
☎ 020 7106 2100
fax 020 7106 2101

lonelyplanet.com

The topics covered in this book are listed below in French. If you're having trouble understanding French, show this page to the person you're talking to so they can look up the relevant section.